Hawthorne's Son

HAWTHORNE'S SON

The Life and Literary Career
of Julian Hawthorne

by Maurice Bassan

Ohio State University Press, Columbus, Ohio

COPYRIGHT © 1970

BY THE OHIO STATE UNIVERSITY PRESS

All Rights Reserved.

Library of Congress Catalogue Card Number 70–83142

Standard Book Number 8142–0003–6

Printed in the United States of America

To
Ellanore

Table of Contents

Illustrations

Preface

The literary reputation of Nathaniel Hawthorne's only son, Julian, led some critics in his own day to compare him favorably with George Eliot, Henry James, and William Dean Howells, as well as his father. This was a mistake, but time has repaired it—indeed, has savagely reversed the scales.

Julian, the young pretender to the glorious family name, certainly outwrote his somewhat sluggish father quantitatively: he was the author of no less than twenty-six long and short novels, over sixty short stories, almost a hundred essays, and several lengthy works of biography and autobiography. Yet who today remembers a single one of his books—unless it be the still well-regarded *Nathaniel Hawthorne and His Wife,* the reverential biography? The primary reason for Julian Hawthorne's decline ought to be stated frankly at the outset: in an age of giants like Clemens and James—to speak only of his American contemporaries—Hawthorne was a pygmy. He was a fascinating but shallow man, and his works reflect more of the shallowness than of the fascination. "No good novel," James wisely remarks, "will ever proceed from a superficial mind." Yet, surprisingly, there are quite genuine if rare treasures scattered here and there in the works of the younger Hawthorne, treasures that ought to be recovered unapologetically.

There are many other reasons for the dusty shroud on Hawthorne's reputation, some of them instructive as examples of critical illogic and of shifting fashions in literary taste. First, certain extraliterary features had entered into the criticism of his fiction before the publication of his last novels in 1896. It is almost impossible to find an account of Hawthorne's work that does not seek to draw an essentially irrelevant evaluative comparison between the creations of father and son. In this form, perhaps, did the old Hathorne curse descend yet another generation. According to Lionel Stevenson, the son "was either condemned out of hand, on the assumption that he was trying to capitalize his relationship, or else he was measured solely by the criterion of his father's work. Good qualities were praised as survivals of the paternal genius, and anything which the critics disliked was branded as a pathetic lapse from the Hawthorne tradition." [1] As Julian Hawthorne said ironically of this extrinsic criticism: "A disquisition upon the mantle of Nathaniel Hawthorne, and an analysis of the differences and similarities between him and his successor, generally fill so much of a notice as to enable the reviewer to dismiss the book itself very briefly." [2]

There were other reasons for the hostile reactions of some critics. Hawthorne engaged in several noisy literary quarrels: with the New York *Sunday Times,* with fellow members of the Authors Club, with his brother-in-law George Parsons Lathrop, and with James Russell Lowell—among others. These quarrels, considered together with Hawthorne's openly professed commercialism and his exploitation of sensual themes, alienated him from the affections of the genteel critics. They were further disaffected by his antididactic approach to literature, for he believed that art, far from embodying a conscious moral purpose, should be itself the "test of morality." [3] He made some enemies by attacking the position of Howells and such local-color writers as Bret Harte with respect to a national literature; he urged writers to seek an American point of view, not necessarily American materials. [4] Finally, his spirited defense of imagination and ideality in fiction, extending to the use of supernatural phenomena, allied him with an outdated school.

After 1896, when Julian Hawthorne turned from the writing of fiction to an exclusively journalistic career, he was rarely again treated seriously as an imaginative writer. In 1901, for example, he was labeled by Oscar Adams as "a novelist who has inherited his father's originality, but whose work is often careless and hasty in construction and of ephemeral interest only." [5] Fred L. Pattee, the last literary historian to discuss Hawthorne's work, wrote his comment in 1917, four years after the former novelist had been sent to Atlanta Penitentiary for engaging in a Canadian mining-stock fraud, and perhaps some features of his judgment, like those of earlier critics, are extraliterary. "In his earlier days," said Pattee, "he devoted himself to themes worthy of the Hawthorne name and treated them in what fairly may be called the Hawthorne manner. . . . But the man lacked seriousness, conscience, depth of life, knowledge of the human heart. After a short period of worthy endeavor he turned to the sensational and the trivial, and became a yellow journalist." [6] The trite comparison with the elder Hawthorne (like Oscar Adams's), the absence of literary analysis of the writer's admittedly "worthy endeavor," the low blow aimed at the lack of "conscience," all mark Pattee's statement as critically valueless.

The year of Hawthorne's eighty-fifth birthday celebration, 1931, saw a very minor resurgence of interest in his work, which had been passed over in silence by every American literary chronicler. Professor Stevenson, in a brief article rather extravagantly naming Julian Hawthorne "Dean of American Letters," sought to revive his reputation as a writer of fiction. He placed Hawthorne outside the two main camps of the late nineteenth century—Clemens and Harte on the one hand, and Howells and James on the other. "His literary ability," Stevenson declared, "was obviously far in advance of Fawcett and Roe and their tribe, and yet he used melodramatic episodes which appealed to their following. He seemed to know both England and the United States thoroughly, and much of continental Europe as well, and yet he showed none of the superiority of the expatriate. He avoided the current literary prejudices with bland tolerance." [7] Stevenson believed that Hawthorne's literary squabbles, his forcible opinions, the supposed immorality of his novels, his commercialism, and his very versatility, all combined to obscure the excellence of his fiction. The critic emphasized the pervasive strain of Gothic romanticism in his work, but stressed that the Gothic elements were introduced with a new scientific vocabulary. He found a "primitive vigor" in Hawthorne's novels, positive ideas, and an "indefinable guilelessness." [8]

Thirteen years later, Professor Harold P. Miller assessed Julian Hawthorne's life and career for the *Dictionary of American Biography*. His early stories, Miller wrote, showed the unmistakable influence of the elder Hawthorne, extending even to the duplication of scenes and proper names. "Hawthorne's attitude toward his own writing was frankly commercial," declared the biographer. "He wrote rapidly, revised little, lost interest in his novels before he completed them, and had few illusions regarding their worth. . . . Partial to stories of the occult and of psychological abnormality, he lacked his father's ability to establish and sustain the tone or atmosphere which they demanded." [9] Miller echoes Stevenson's view that Julian Hawthorne's fiction blended supernatural and realistic elements, and it is on this basis that he believes it to have little more than historical value. The biographer's encomiums are reserved for the son's treatments of his father's life and work. Citing Charles F. Richardson's judgment (in 1888) of *Nathaniel Hawthorne and His Wife* as "the best biography written in America," Miller declares that Julian Hawthorne, in analyzing the contributions of the notebooks to the fiction of Nathaniel Hawthorne, in relating this fiction to the environment in which it took shape, and in insisting upon the cheerfulness and sanity of a temperament often regarded as morbid, has appreciably influenced modern interpretations of the father.

The last important critical essay on Julian Hawthorne appeared in 1957, when Professor George Knox traced the novelist's career sympathetically, reviewed his critical opinions, and noted, as had Stevenson, that "trying scientifically to explain the fantastic and the bizarre, he constructed gargoyles." [10] Basing his article largely on Hawthorne's contributions to the

Pasadena *Star-News* in the years 1923–34, Knox found Hawthorne to be under the guidance of an "inspirational esthetic," and stressed that his main trouble as an artist was that he felt insincere when he had to contrive what at the moment of writing he did not deeply feel. Knox notes that in his later days, Hawthorne was able to extend his aesthetic into a political dimension, seeing art as one of the great social functions of mankind and the binding force in socialist brotherhood. In his last years in California, Knox concludes, "he carried on steadily the fight for high standards in American literature, acidly attacking the easy biographers, translators who posed as original artists, and the hucksters who he felt were producing most twentieth century literature." [11]

Other commentators on Julian Hawthorne have been about as scarce as readers. Charles E. Honce's *A Julian Hawthorne Collection* (1939) expands the bibliography in P. K. Foley's *American Authors* on the basis of his own collection and correspondence with the author before 1934. Vernon Loggins's occasionally inaccurate *The Hawthornes* (1951) traces Hawthorne's life briefly and scathingly, on the whole dismissing him in favor of glorifying his sister Rose Hawthorne Lathrop, Mother Alphonsa, the most saintly descendant of Nathaniel; and the same may be said of the major biography of Rose, *A Fire Was Lighted* (1948), by Theodore Maynard. Carl J. Weber and George Knox have written separate, entertaining accounts of the Lowell-Hawthorne feud of 1886, and Professor Knox has added an analysis of the Hawthorne-James relationship and a study of the reception in Germany of Hawthorne's *Saxon Studies*. The present writer has published studies on the Julian Hawthorne Collection at Yale University, on Hawthorne's use of his Aunt Ebe's recollections for his major biography, and on a literary quarrel of the 1880's centering upon the admission of Will Carleton to the Authors Club. As Professor Stevenson noted over thirty years ago, despite Julian Hawthorne's considerable and partly merited success in his own day, a powerful battery of forces, not the least of which was the sway of literary fashion, has unconsciously conspired to efface his contribution to American letters.

Julian Hawthorne's long literary career was marked by an extraordinary fecundity and versatility that served, in his lifetime, to obscure his attempts to embody an integrated interpretation of the Concord tradition in his fiction, biography, and criticism. Chief among the great figures of this tradition, and the one by whose standards Julian Hawthorne continuously measured himself, was the writer's father, Nathaniel Hawthorne. During his early career Julian Hawthorne learned to live under the shadow of his father and developed those curiously mixed ideas of veneration for the paternal name and occasional exploitation of it for venal reasons that were to mark his life to the end. It is in the context of the parental accomplishments that one must understand what Julian Hawthorne did and what he was, and not—at least, not primarily—in the context of contemporaneous literary fashion, for Hawthorne was always relatively uninvolved as an artist (though not as a critic or as a man) in the literary crosscurrents of his day.

This critical biography does not seek to resurrect Julian Hawthorne's reputation to that equality with his "rivals" Henry James and William Dean Howells that the critic John Nichol advocated over eighty years ago, nor to shut its eyes to the hackwork and commercialism that sapped the vitality of Hawthorne's imagination. Nor does it attempt to evaluate the younger Hawthorne's work by the touchstone of the elder Hawthorne's literary accomplishment. It does not, again, yield to the temptation (common to many biographies) to trace dubious hereditary characteristics from the parents to the child. Nor does it presume to be able to show that perfectly neat but almost always fallacious correspondence between the events of a writer's life and the themes of his writings that is so attractive to innocent readers.

So much for negative considerations. On the other hand, I hope to be able to demonstrate that the life and career of Julian

Hawthorne can best be understood in the context of the parental image, by which I mean Nathaniel Hawthorne as man, as father, as writer, as social critic, and as literary theoretician. The image—which persisted from young Hawthorne's boyhood in Concord to his senescence in Pasadena, and which, indeed, no one allowed him for a moment to forget—did not daunt Julian Hawthorne. He did not deliberately court the obscurity into which he has fallen. On the whole the parental image strengthened rather than demoralized his life and his art. Julian Hawthorne faced up to his heritage with a muscular intellectual vigor perhaps uncommon in those born to a famous name.

Three complementary directions are followed in this book. I have told—for the first time and in some detail—the story of Julian Hawthorne's often colorful life, demonstrating how that life was shaped by the formative years in Nathaniel Hawthorne's household, by public reaction to the younger Hawthorne's prosecution of an active literary career, and by Julian's own peculiar temperament. Second, I have analyzed—selectively—the writings of Julian Hawthorne, from his earliest short stories to his last volumes of reminiscences, and traced his literary techniques, his critical viewpoints, his thematic preoccupations, and his social philosophy to his interpretation of the craftsmanship and theories of Nathaniel Hawthorne. Lest it be inferred that the younger Hawthorne's life and career have been viewed mechanically as a simple reflex to the parental image, I hasten to add that the life had of necessity to be considered as shaped by such forces as the economic demands of Hawthorne's large family and the thought as also nurtured by such secondary influences as Emerson and Swedenborg. Finally, I have sought to identify those writings from Julian Hawthorne's enormous output (chronicled in the Bibliography) that remain worthy of serious attention.

Although the whole of this study will perform these tasks, it may be useful at this point to sketch the main outlines of my argument; the text itself will offer ample documentation. In his famous preface to *The House of the Seven Gables,* Nathaniel

Hawthorne had distinguished carefully between the Novel and
the Romance: the former, he declared, aims "at a very minute
fidelity, not merely to the possible, but to the probable and
ordinary course of man's experience," whereas the latter,
though it "sins unpardonably so far as it may swerve aside
from the truth of the human heart, has fairly a right to present
that truth under circumstances, to a great extent, of the writer's
own choosing or creation." [12] This distinction forms one of the
bases for Julian Hawthorne's own theory of fiction, and his
imaginative work evidences a split, at first clear but later less
distinct, between these two modes. Hawthorne's realistic novels
are the progeny of his first major work, *Bressant* (1873), and
his romances descend from the earliest tales and from *Idolatry*
(1874); this distinction has been adopted as a useful organiz-
ing principle. In writing his romances, Julian Hawthorne
adopted from his father's stories not only particular settings,
themes, and even characters, but also the elder Hawthorne's
predilection for the more sensational elements of an already
moribund Gothic romanticism. Indeed, the younger Hawthorne
went beyond his father in asserting not merely the necessity of
mingling "the Marvellous" as a "slight, delicate, and evanes-
cent flavor" in his romances but the salutary effects upon literary technique of overtly fanciful and supernatural materials.
Julian Hawthorne's often asserted belief in spiritual reality,
which undoubtedly sprang, at least in part, from his reading of
Emerson, informs not only the sincerity of his use of the
marvelous but the power of his critical theories on imagination
and the nature of art. The aim of fiction, he believed, was to
achieve the "loftier reality" through "spiritual intuition"; he
thus deplored such contemporaneous tendencies as the ascendancy of impersonal science, the rise of agnosticism, and "the
photographic method of novel-writing." In defending the principles of ideality in fiction and poetry, Hawthorne was defending not only his own practice but the Hawthorne tradition in
literature, as he understood it.

From the romances and tales of his father, Julian Hawthorne adopted also several important thematic concerns. The first, and more obvious, of these themes was the hereditary transmission of sin through several generations and a final expiation by the last descendant of the line. In the novel *Garth,* for example, this theme and its setting in an ancestral home bear marked resemblances to the elder Hawthorne's treatment in *The House of the Seven Gables.* A second adopted theme is the primacy of love over selfish intellect. Dominated by their towering ambition and their pride and alienated from the communion of their fellow human beings, such heroes as Bressant, Balder Helwyse, Sebastian Strome, and Warren Bell painfully achieve a state of grace through the growth of their capacity to love. However, their destinies, it should be noted, are not so tragic as those of Nathaniel Hawthorne's Ethan Brand, Aylmer, and Hollingsworth. Julian utilized other themes for which he is scarcely or not at all indebted to his father. He developed a series of contrasts, for example, between spiritual and carnal love; and he painted glowingly the virtues of innocent country life as opposed to the evils of the metropolis. A projection of his personal dilemma may be discerned in the recurring theme of the disparity in ideals and accomplishments between a father and his son. Further, Hawthorne's psychological doubts concerning his own pretensions to the Hawthorne name and eminence seem to be projected into at least five of his novels— ranging from his earliest to his last—in which we detect the "changeling" motif of a child living out his life under false pretenses and finding a measure of happiness only as he discovers and secures his identity.

Nathaniel Hawthorne's haphazard involvement in socialism was also to strike a dominant chord fifty years later in the life and writings of his son. The influence of his father's example and an honest application of the doctrine of love and brotherhood that he promulgated in his fiction were among the forces that led Julian to embrace the socialist ideal of government and economy. He was led in this direction also by his devotion to personal and aesthetic liberty, ideals that he felt could best be served in a socialistic community.

The devotion to his father's life and literary achievement that he had manifested in his fiction, criticism, and social views by the flattery of imitation and adaptation received its most obvious public embodiment in the long series of books and articles that Julian Hawthorne wrote about his father. These included not only an edition of Nathaniel Hawthorne's works, the editing of two of his unfinished romances, and various critical sketches but an imposing biographical work, *Nathaniel Hawthorne and His Wife* (1884), which critics at the time compared favorably with Boswell's *Life of Johnson* and which is still regarded as indispensable for a full understanding of the elder Hawthorne's career. Although the later biographical works, which gradually came to adopt autobiographical elements, are more frivolous and gossipy, the total impression gathered from Julian Hawthorne's studies of his father is of a student who, through his love and his intelligence, has understood the life and art of a great man.

It is a pleasure to record my indebtedness to Professor James D. Hart, of Berkeley, under whose direction this work was originally undertaken and with whose friendly counsel it was completed. Kenneth J. Carpenter, Leslie Clarke, Eliza Chugg, and Virginia Roecker have been of inestimable aid in my research in the Rare Books Department of the General Library, University of California, Berkeley. George Knox offered me both friendship and seminal advice, and I am grateful also for the comments and encouragement afforded me by John Gordan, Charles E. Honce, Norman Holmes Pearson, Howard H. Quint, Henry Nash Smith, Lionel Stevenson, and Randall Stewart.

The novelist's son and grandson, John F. B. Hawthorne and Manning Hawthorne, supplied me with valuable biographical material. I am especially indebted to Manning Hawthorne for permission to quote from his grandfather's published and unpublished writings.

For permission to print letters and manuscript materials from their holdings, I wish to thank the Duke University Library; the Huntington Library, San Marino, California; the New Hampshire Historical Society; the Henry W. and Albert A. Berg Collection of the New York Public Library, Astor, Lenox, and Tilden Foundations; the Stauffer Collection of the New York Public Library; the Pierpont Morgan Library, New York City; the Rosenberg Public Library, Galveston, Texas; the General Library of the University of California, Berkeley; the University of Southern California Library; the Washington State University Library; and the Collection of American Literature, Yale University Library. I should like to add a word of appreciation to the curators and directors of these repositories for their gracious assistance.

For other permissions I am indebted to the Trustees of the Estate of Clara Clemens Samossoud (Mark Twain's daughter); the Bruce Publishing Company; Mrs. Constance Garland Doyle and Mrs. Isabel Garland Lord; George Knox; and Lionel Stevenson.

Prudence Gallup faithfully typed the largest portion of the manuscript.

I also offer an inadequate word of thanks for the day-to-day encouragement of my wife, Ellanore.

M. B.

September, 1969

Hawthorne's Son

1

Nathaniel Hawthorne and His Son

1. An Initiation

At two o'clock in the morning of May 19, 1864, the secret initiation rites of the Harvard fraternity Delta Kappa Epsilon were reaching their grotesque conclusion. Julian Hawthorne, a sturdy, well-muscled freshman of seventeen, was led blindfolded into a silent crypt and helped into a coffin. There he was to lie until the resurrection. But he had for a while the companionship of a friendly demon; and finally, he was snatched out of the coffin and pulled upstairs into a brightly lighted room where, his bandages removed, he joined the other members of the secret society in drinking some claret punch.[1]

At that very hour, in the Pemigewasset House in Plymouth, New Hampshire, General Franklin Pierce, awakened by the persistent howling of a dog in the courtyard, rose and went to the bedside of his friend Nathaniel Hawthorne. The author lay very still. Pierce "laid his hand on the sleeper's heart, and found that it had stopped beating." [2]

As Nathaniel Hawthorne's son rode back to Concord with

his father's friend and publisher James T. Fields, in order to join the bereaved family for the funeral, he must have thought of the weird parody of death that had been enacted during the rites of initiation. In the Hawthorne household, as in the elder Hawthorne's fiction, what began as masquerade frequently ended as reality. For young Julian Hawthorne, fresh from the rites of the "Deeks," the news of his father's death gave him very nearly his darkest hour. "My life," he declared long after, "had been so wholly one with my father and mother that I couldn't comprehend being severed from either of them." [3] It was appropriate that when the severing came, it should come associated in his mind with a ritual of initiation, with the idea, perhaps, of a rebirth; the same phenomenon of initiation into life was also closely interwoven in the young man's mind with the death of his mother seven years later. To be sure, he wrote in his *Memoirs,* though he knew it was his duty to be manly and comforting to his family, he felt his incompetence as if he had lost his arms and legs; [4] but his mother remarked sagely, "It has made a man of him." [5]

The death strengthened the ideal vision of Nathaniel Hawthorne as father and as writer that young Julian Hawthorne carried with him untarnished to his own grave. This vision, and the concurrent initiation into manhood and responsibility, led ultimately to a career of literary achievement, though of a different order from that of the father. The younger Hawthorne's manhood was to be continuously inspired by the remembrance of what the father had done and what he had been. In tracing the early years of Julian Hawthorne from his birth in Boston in 1846 to his initiation into manhood almost eighteen years later, one must keep in mind the profound influence that the author of *The Scarlet Letter* was to exert on his son. Although much of what follows must necessarily be told from the point of view of Nathaniel Hawthorne, we can clearly detect the influence of the elder Hawthorne's attitudes upon young Julian.

2. The Black Prince

In a letter to his friend Horatio Bridge written when his first child, Una, was less than a month old, Nathaniel Hawthorne said, "I am happy to tell you that our little girl is remarkably healthy and vigorous, and promises, in the opinion of those better experienced in babies than myself, to be very pretty"; and he added, significantly, "I think I prefer a daughter to a son." [6] Hawthorne's tentatively expressed opinion here would seem to be confirmed by what we know of his reactions to the birth of his second child and only son, Julian, on June 22, 1846, two years later.[7] Hawthorne's wife Sophia wrote to Bridge rather jestingly when Julian was six months old that Una's "little brother is an entire contrast to her ladyship. His father called him the Black Prince during the first weeks of his life, because he was so dark in comparison with her. . . . His father declares he does not care anything about him because he is a boy, and so I am obliged to love him twice as much as I otherwise should." [8] The Black Prince could scarcely have felt unwanted in the affectionate and sometimes even cloying atmosphere of the Hawthorne household. And when he was born, the family was better off financially than it had been at any time since the marriage in 1842, for Hawthorne had just been appointed by President Polk as Surveyor for the District of Salem and Beverly and Inspector of the Revenue for the Port of Salem. There remains, then, merely a suggestion that a boy, as such, was not especially desirable. If this initial trepidation is indeed a fact and can be psychologically traced at all, it may possibly be connected to the father's concern about the trans-mission of the hereditary shames of the family to still another generation. Mistakenly projecting his own anxieties and sense of guilt into a baby, Hawthorne also extended his sympathy: he did not wish his son to suffer as he had suffered. Julian Haw-thorne, it may be remarked here, did not suffer. The thematic concern in his own fiction with the hereditary transmission of the guilts of past generations was largely a literary posture derived from the elder Hawthorne's writings, and not, as in Nathaniel Hawthorne, a psychological obsession that could be transmuted into artistic form.[9]

Whatever his attitude toward the birth of a son who would bear upon his shoulders the contumely associated with the family name after Puritan times, Nathaniel Hawthorne grew to love the boy Julian deeply, and the child wrought significant changes in his own view of human nature. "He is truly a happy little soul," he wrote in his journal when his subject was almost three, "if ever one there were on earth; and, for his sake, I am the more inclined to think that the race of man was not created in bitterness, and for their misery, but in infinite benevolence, and for eternal blessedness." [10]

It was at approximately this period that Julian's own recollections of his father began. He was able in his later years to describe with great fidelity the study in the Mall Street house in which *The Scarlet Letter* was written. Of his father he wrote with gentle touches of unobtrusive symbolism:

> I see a tall, strong man, whose wide-domed head was covered with wavy black hair, bushing out at the sides. It thinned somewhat over the lofty crown and brow; the forehead was hollowed at the temple and rounded out above, after the Moorish style of architecture. Under heavy dark eyebrows were eyes deepset and full of light, marvellous in range of expression, with black eyelashes. All seemed well with me when I met their look. The straight, rather salient nose had a perceptible cleft at the tip, which, I was told, was a sign of good lineage . . . so that I was much distressed by the smooth plebeian bluntness, at that time, of my own little snub.[11]

Physically—despite his nose—the young son was very impressive. Sophia wrote the following description of her second child in November of 1846:

> As to Baby, his cheeks, eyes, and limbs affirm enormous well-being. He weighs twenty-three pounds, which is within two

pounds of Una's weight when she was eighteen months old,— and he is not quite five months old. His mighty physique is not all fat, but he is modelled on a great plan in respect to his frame. Una looks like a fairy golden-hair beside him; she is opaline in lustre and delicacy.[12]

A month later she called him "decidedly, I think, a *brun;* but his complexion is brilliant and his eyes dark gray, with long black lashes, like Mr. Hawthorne's. . . . He is a Titan in strength and size, and though but six months old, is as large as some children of two years." [13] Horatio Bridge pictured him as "a good-natured, laughing young giant" at Lenox in 1850, when Julian was just four years old.[14] The father thought to describe his "chunky little figure" as "looking like an alderman in miniature." In another journal entry he noted: "Julian's are very good legs . . .—stout, sturdy, energetic little legs, and possessed of much character, especially when seen from behind, while he is shoving a chair before him, or otherwise bringing their muscles into play. . . . There never was a gait more expressive of childish force and physical well-being than his; no faintness, weakness, weariness about it." [15] In the opinion of more than one observer, physically the child was "superb." [16]

Julian Hawthorne's physique was joined to a temperament at once imaginative and sanguine; indeed, the youth's lively imagination was continually encouraged and nurtured by his parents. And despite the frequent wanderings of the Hawthorne clan throughout his youth, his life at home was characterized by an enveloping warmth and sense of security. The following description in Hawthorne's journal of an evening at Lenox is characteristically expressive of the mutual tenderness in the family.

> Mamma has gone up stairs to get him, and I hear his voice, and now his downright little footsteps, his laugh—and here he comes gladsomely in, with the illustrated almanac, which he has capitulated to be allowed to look at—else he would not come down. Mamma begins to undress him; he remonstrates, and demands to be allowed to 'see when I'm bareness'—that is, to look at the

book after he is undressed. There he is, in his bareness, his face brimming over with good-humor and fun, so that it throws a light down upon the pictures he is looking at. Now, mamma is putting on his night-gown; and as his head comes through the opening, still he looks at the pictures. Now he prattles—"I'm little angel, and I have wings coming out of my shoulders. No, I'm a bird—I'm a bird of Paradise—I'm a parrot." . . . His mother asks, 'Julian, what have you to say to Papa?'—He sits repeating Mother Goose's melodies, "Dimery-dimery Dock' &c&c. He will not give the watchword, but talks all sorts of nonsense. "Good night, my little son!" 'Good night, my daughter,' answers he. At last, "Papa, I'm quite ready";—so his day closes, and I lug him up to bed—he giving his mother sweetest kisses and embraces, till the very last moment.[17]

The attitudes of Nathaniel and Sophia Hawthorne toward their children were sharply distinct. As the son was to note in his biography of his parents, "The mother sees goodness and divinity shining through everywhere; the father's attitude is deductive and moralizing." [18] One of Hawthorne's biographers puts the matter somewhat differently. In writing about the children, he declares, "Sophia was ecstatic: the children were unfallen angels to her. While loving and admiring them not a bit less, Hawthorne had a strong sense of fact and a strong sense of humor." [19] Sophia wrote her mother that "the graces of heaven fill the hearts of my children," [20] and no doubt she was attempting to be literal. Hawthorne was not unaware of the mother's habit of mind; he notes in his journal, "Mamma says he [Julian] likes the best book in the house—I say, he likes the book that is kept from him." [21] To the same end the following brief dialogue is entered:

"Are you a good little boy?" quoth I to Julian. "Yes," said he.—"What are you good for?" asked I.—"Because I love all people," answered he. His mother will be in raptures with this response—a heavenly infant, powerless to do anything but diffusing the richness of his pure love throughout the moral atmosphere, to make all mankind happier and better!!!!! [22]

The number of exclamation points here measures the divergence in attitude between Hawthorne and his "ecstatic" wife. But Julian Hawthorne was quite correct in pointing out his father's own tendency toward "moralizing." In such early passages as the following, the banal moral reflection seems to bear little resemblance to its ostensible source:

> I have just been for a walk round Buffum's corner, and returning, after some half hour's absence, find Una and Julian gone to bed. Thus ends the day of these two children,—one of them [Una] four years old, the other some months less than two. But the days and the years melt away so rapidly that I hardly know whether they are still little children at their parents' knees, or already a maiden and a youth, a woman and a man. This present life has hardly substance and tangibility enough to be the image of eternity. The future too soon becomes the present, which before we can grasp it, looks back upon us as the past. It must, I think, be only the image of an image.[23]

Another, more typical, comment was the following, which blends the reportorial with the moral approach, without losing sight of the original object described:

> Julian was greatly fascinated by a rocking-horse, and wished to buy it; and for that purpose, took from his pocket a little toy-cup of pewter, which he greatly valued, and offered it in exchange. The bargain being declined, he was vastly grieved, and came home roaring. There is something queerly pathetic in this; the poor little boy offering all he had—what he deemed one of the treasures of the world—and meeting a refusal. I suppose it surprised him as much as it might hereafter, were he to proffer his heart, and have it rejected with scorn.[24]

Objective descriptions of his son in these early years are balanced occasionally by Hawthorne's introspective appraisals, which may often be taken as projections of his own view of the world that the child was to enter. The father explicitly compares himself with his son, for example, in commenting on the boy's constant stream of talk: "It is his desire of sympathy that

9

lies at the bottom of the great heap of his babblement. He wants
to enrich all his enjoyments by steeping them in the heart of
some friend. I do not think him in danger of living so solitary a
life as much of mine has been." [25] A more characteristic entry
appears on July 29, 1849, when the son was just three years
old; here Hawthorne strikes a theme that is to be dominant
whenever he speaks of the education of a child:

> Julian has too much tenderness, love, and sensibility in his
> nature; he needs to be hardened and tempered. I would not take
> a particle of the love out of him; but methinks it is highly
> desirable that some sterner quality should be interfused through-
> out the softness of his heart; else, in course of time, the hard
> intercourse of the world, and the many knocks and bruises he
> will receive, will cause a morbid crust of callousness to grow
> over his heart; so that, for at least a portion of his life, he will
> have less sympathy and love for his fellow-beings than those
> who began life with a much smaller portion. After a lapse of
> years, indeed, if he have native vigor enough, there may be a
> second growth of love and benevolence; but the first crop, with
> its wild luxuriance, stands a good chance of being blighted.[26]

Surely this is a remarkably severe moral forecast for a child of
three! The view of the "hard intercourse of the world" seems
almost transparently Hawthorne's own, and it is echoed in the
account of the visit to the Brownings at the Casa Guidi in
Florence nine years later. Hawthorne was struck by the appearance of the Brownings' little son Robert, whom they called
"Pennini." The image of his own brawny young son must have
been called forth by this frail child, and in Hawthorne's description the comparison of the two boys is implicit:

> I never saw such a boy as this before; so slender, fragile, and
> spirit-like,—not as if he were actually in ill-health, but as if he
> had little or nothing to do with human flesh and blood. His face
> is very pretty and most intelligent, and exceedingly like his
> mother's. He is nine years old, and seems at once less childlike
> and less manly than would befit that age. I should not quite like
> to be the father of such a boy, and should fear to stake so much
> interest and affection on him as he cannot fail to inspire. I

wonder what is to become of him,—whether he will ever grow to be a man,—whether it is desirable that he should. His parents ought to turn their whole attention to making him robust and earthly, and to giving him a thicker scabbard to sheathe his spirit in.[27]

Hawthorne's ideal, then, may be summarized as not merely physical strength, though that is desirable, but a coupling of physical and emotional resiliency. This dual resiliency his own son was fortunate enough to develop, though whether he achieved it with his father's aid seems doubtful. At any rate, the childish "Titan" grew into the best gymnast in his class at Harvard, and indeed survived to the age of eighty-eight, while emotionally, his thick-scabbarded spirit, with remarkable powers of readjustment, survived several savage onslaughts, most notably the dismal shame of a year in Atlanta Penitentiary.

An accurate picture of Hawthorne's view of the parental compensations may be seen in the section of his Lenox journal that he called "Twenty Days with Julian and Little Bunny." [28] These were some of the happiest days that the five-year-old Julian Hawthorne spent at the "Red Shanty" in the Berkshires, for his mother had gone off with Una, his new baby sister Rose (born in May, 1851), and Elizabeth Palmer Peabody ("E.P.P."), leaving Julian in full possession of his father. During these rainy, joyful weeks of July and August, 1851, Hawthorne began his reading of Fourier in preparation for the writing of *The Blithedale Romance,* received calls from the G. P. R. James family, the Duyckincks, and Herman Melville (whom Julian liked "as well as me," his father wrote), and supervised the boy's fishing in the nearby lake and his care of the rabbit, Bunny. The following entries give a delightful picture of the daily activities at the Red Shanty:

[July 28, 1851]
At seven o'clock, A.M. Wife, E. P. P., Una, and Rosebud, took their departure, leaving Julian and me in possession of the Red

Shanty. The first observation which the old gentleman made thereupon, was—"Papa, isn't it nice to have baby gone?" His perfect confidence of my sympathy in this feeling was very queer. "Why is it nice?" I inquired. "Because now I can shout and squeal just as loud as I please!" answered he. And for the next half hour he exercised his lungs to his heart's content, and almost split the welkin thereby. Then he hammered on an empty box, and appeared to have high enjoyment of the racket which he created. In the course of the forenoon, however, he fell into a deep reverie, and looked very pensive. I asked what he was thinking of and he said, "Oh, about mamma's going away. I do not like to be away from her;"—and then he romanticized about getting horses and galloping after her. He declared, likewise, that he likes Una, and that she never troubled him.

I hardly know how we got through the forenoon. It is impossible to write, read, think, or even to sleep (in the daytime) so constant are his appeals to me in one way or another; still he is such a genial and good-humored little man that there is certainly an enjoyment intermixed with all the annoyance.

[July 29, 1851]

Next we went out and gathered some currants. He babbles constantly, throughout all these various doings, and often says odd things, which I either forget, or cannot possibly grasp them so as to write them down. Among other things, . . . he speculated about rainbows, and asked why they were not called sun-bows, or sun-rain-bows; and said that he supposed their bow-strings were made of cobwebs; which was the reason why they could not be seen. Some of the time, I hear him repeating poetry, with good emphasis and intonation. He is never out of temper or out of spirits, and he is certainly as happy as the day is long. He is happy enough by himself; and when I sympathize or partake in his play, it is almost too much; and he nearly explodes with laughter and delight.

[August 11, 1851]

He proposed to go to "Mamma's Rock," as he has named a certain large rock, beneath some walnut-trees, where the children went with Phoebe [Sophia] to gather nuts, last autumn. He informed me that, when he was grown up, he should build a house for his mother, at this rock, and that I might live there too. "When I am grown up," he said, "everybody must mind me!" . . . We spent some time here, and then came home through the pasture; and the little man kept jumping over the high weeds and the tufts of everlasting flowers;—while I compared his overflowing sprightliness with my own reluctant footsteps, and was content that he should be young instead of I.

In this period of secure childhood in the Hawthorne household we may place the earliest known of Julian Hawthorne's letters. It was written by the five-year-old boy to his aunt, Maria Louisa Hawthorne:

Dear Aunty;

I have found the blocks of the French puzzle-brain. They were in Una's pocket. Una is a kind of magpie.

I have found a place to coast near the house. Baby has pulled all the yarn out of mamma's basket. She can get up herself by a chair and stand a great while.

Papa, mamma and I went to Concord on Monday to see the house in a sleigh. I liked one room very much. The sleigh squeaked on the ground sometimes.

Julian Hawthorne.[29]

3. England and the Continent

"The two older children are filled with wonder and hope," [30] Sophia Hawthorne wrote to her father six weeks before the family of five sailed for Liverpool on board the Cunard paddle-wheel steamer *Niagara* in June, 1853. After a short stay at Mrs. Blodgett's boardinghouse in Liverpool, where the father and son were later to spend the better part of a year together, the family moved on to a stone villa in the nearby suburb of Rock Ferry.

Life in the tiny private community called "Rock Park" was very pleasant. During the first winter Hawthorne read to his family *Robinson Crusoe, Don Quixote,* and the poetry of Scott. He played games with the children, improvised such stories as that of the marvelous General Quattlebum, with whom he was engaged in constant mortal combat, and taught them to make paper boats. Favorite pastimes were battledore and shuttlecock, and fencing. " 'Papa plays with the foil in a very funny way,' Julian told his elder sister; 'he whirls it round and round and then pokes away so fast that I have to laugh so that he generally hits me.' " [31]

The eternal childish questions that had so perplexed Hawthorne at Lenox were continuing to pour forth from his seven-year-old son as he spent long afternoons with his father in the latter's office at the consulate. Young Hawthorne would sit atop several volumes of Congressional Proceedings across the desk from his father, scrawl long letters back home, stare out the window at the cotton bales going up the sides of the warehouse opposite on long ropes, and pester his father unmercifully. When the son was visiting, the two would go out for lunch to a baker's shop and stand eating their bread and butter and cheese; or perhaps they would wander to the local museum, or to the zoological gardens. At the end of the day they would go down to the steamboat landing and take the boat two miles up the muddy river to Rock Ferry and home. On Sundays, "Mrs. Hawthorne, with the two elder children, would go to the Unitarian Chapel in Renshaw Street, and listen to eloquent sermons from the Rev. W. H. Channing, the American; but Hawthorne himself never attended church." [32]

Julian Hawthorne's religious training, we may gather, was almost exclusively his mother's responsibility. "Our mother," he wrote, "was a spontaneous incarnation of religious faith"; as to his father, "there was little touching religion in such conversation as we overheard, or in his writings." [33] A most revealing insight into the religious affairs of the family is the following reminiscence of Julian Hawthorne:

> In England, in the 1850's, it was the custom to open the day with prayer, in which the whole household joined. It was deemed incumbent upon us, therefore, as the family of the American Consul, when we were in Liverpool, to maintain a religious attitude; so our father bought the Book of Common Prayer, and

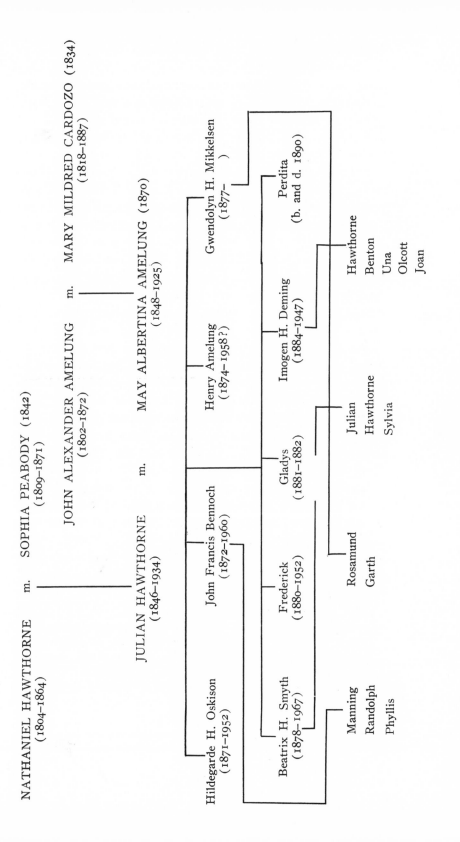

read aloud each morning to the assembled family and servants. . . . He would tackle whatever job came to him, as a matter of course.[34]

In Italy the father and son expressed their boredom with religious touring. On an Easter Sunday in 1858, for example, while in Rome, Hawthorne noted that he "went with Julian to St. Peter's . . . but Julian grew weary (to say the truth, so did I), and we went on a long walk." [35] And again, in Perugia, the mother and daughters "streamed forth immediately, and saw a church; but Julian, who hates them, and I, remained behind." [36] The children, Julian Hawthorne asserted, grew up in reverence; but his own view was perhaps very close to his father's, who, he says, " 'believed' in God, but never sought to define him." [37] Throughout his long life the question of God seems to have concerned Julian Hawthorne only theoretically, never personally. He was to wander happily through the fairyland of Swedenborgian mysticism, but his temperament can scarcely be described at any point in his life as religious. This is a fact perhaps all the more remarkable since his sister Una became attached to an Anglican order, and Rose, who at first joined the Catholic church with her husband, later, after her separation from him, became a lay sister and ended her saintly life as Mother Alphonsa.

Hawthorne, during the years in England, was often led to think seriously of his children's future. He worried lest they become "exiles and outcasts through life" because of the long separation from things American.[38] In his journal he wondered: "What sort of character will it form in the children, this unsettled, shifting, vagrant life, with no central home to turn to, except what we carry in ourselves?" [39] Once, after Mrs. Hawthorne and the girls had departed for Lisbon to visit their friends the O'Sullivans, Hawthorne and his son wandered out in the streets to witness the celebration that marked the end of the Crimean War. Noting that they stayed out beyond the lad's

regular bedtime, Hawthorne wrote in his notebook: "I wonder
what his mother would have said. But the old boy must now
begin to see life, and to feel it." [40]

Nathaniel Hawthorne wrote quite fully to his wife about
their son during this period of father-and-son domesticity in
Mrs. Blodgett's boardinghouse. Nine-year-old Julian Hawthorne springs vividly to life in these letters:

> The other day, speaking of his first advent into this world,
> Julian said, "I don't remember how I came down from Heaven,
> but I'm very glad I happened to tumble into so good a family!"
> He was serious in this; and it is certainly very queer, that, at
> nearly ten years old, he should still accept literally our first
> explanation of how he came to be among us. . . .
>
> Julian looks like a real boy now; for Mrs. Blodgett has his
> hair cut at intervals of a month or so, and though I thought his
> aspect very absurd, at first, yet I have come to approve it rather
> than otherwise. The good lady does what she can to keep his
> hands clean, and his nails in proper condition—for which he is
> not so grateful as he should be. There is to be a ball at his
> dancing school, next week, at which the boys are to wear jackets
> and white pantaloons; and I have [commissioned] Miss Maria
> to get our old gentleman equipped in a proper manner. It is
> funny how he gives his mighty mind to this business of dancing,
> and even dreams, as he assures me, about quadrilles. His master
> has praised him a good deal, and advanced him to a place among
> the elder scholars. When the time comes for Julian to study in
> good earnest, I perceive that this feeling of emulation will
> [rouse] his steam to a prodigious height. In drawing (having no
> competitors) he does not apply himself so earnestly as to the
> Terpsichorean science; yet he succeeds so well that, last night, I
> mistook a sketch of his for one of the master's. Mrs. Blodgett
> and the ladies think his progress quite wonderful; the master
> says, rather coolly, that he has a very tolerable eye for form.

> [December 11, 1855]
> Julian is outgrowing all the clothes he has, . . . and absolutely
> bursting through his trousers. No doubt thou wouldst blaspheme
> of his appearance; but all boys are the awkwardest and unbeau-
> tifullest creatures whom God has made. I don't know that he
> looks any worse than the rest. I have given Mrs. Blodgett the

fullest liberty to get him whatever she thinks best. He ought to look like a gentleman's son, for the ladies of our family like to have him with them as their cavalier and protector, when they go a-shopping. It amazes me to see the unabashed [front] with which he goes into society.[41]

The Hawthornes were inveterate letter-writers and journal-keepers, and the son's propensity for keeping detailed records of his adventures and travels may be seen as early as the age of ten. This first literary imitation of his father is worth noting. On May 23, 1857, Julian Hawthorne is writing a diary from Lincoln, a diary that was continued intermittently through the family's trip to Scotland, abroad to France and Italy, and back to Redcar, England, in 1859. The diary entries parallel in a childish and often amusing way the extensive, brilliant observations of the elder Hawthorne in his English and Continental journals. Several extracts will suffice to give an impression of young Hawthorne's journal-keeping:

[Lincoln, May 23, 1857]
We started from Southport May 22, 1857 for Lincoln. It was a very fine day and the sun was very hot, indeed it was a great deal too hot for papa and mamma, but I did not feel too hot at all. I had a veal pie which mamma made me stuff down in an awful hurry. In the cars I had some raisins and a Maccaroon which kept me from starving while we were on our journey. . . . When we got to Lincoln we found that there were no cabs. So we took the Saracen's Head Omnibus, and came to the Saracen's Head Hotel. Papa thinks that it is a very old one, and that it was in the time of the Crusades when Saracens' Heads used to be cut off. There is a great big picture of the Saracen's Head in the yard and in the bottoms of the bowls and sides of pitchers and all those sorts of things. It is very handsome and Mamma thinks that it is the head of Saladin. . . . We went up a very steep hill to the cathedral which is a great deal better than York Minster, and as large round as Southport. . . . As we were walking round it I found a piece of stone that had dropped from the cathedral. I picked it up after first making myself sure that it was really a piece of it by looking at the place where it had dropped from. . . . It is very curious that it should be lying

there because mamma says that they are very careful to pick up all the pieces that drop down because they are very precious, so I think I was very lucky to get it. I mean to label it, so that nurse will not throw it away as she did my other ones without knowing what she is doing. . . .[42]

[Dumfries]
We went to a field where Burns ploughed up the daisy and the mouse, and papa got a good many of the daisies, to remember it by. They were all the children of the one that was ploughed up.[43]

Later that year, Julian sent one of his longest letters to his sister Una while his parents and he were in Manchester. It conveys the child's awareness of his father's growing physical infirmity:

After a little while we had our dinner, at least I had my dinner but Papa not being perfectly well could not eat any. There was very little, even Papa himself said so, so there must have been. Then after dinner I read the Faery Queen until my master came and papa lay down. After a while he came and I had my lesson which he said was very well done. . . . He set me up a mark to Lunge at, at least he marked the place where I was to set it up. . . . Then I went to bed after having had a warm bath. . . . Yesterday I drew papa and made a funny mess of him. I wish that I could send it but it is too big. Poor papa went to bed before I did last night, but for some time I unintentionally kept him awake with hammering until at last mamma came and told me to stop. I do not believe that papa ever went to bed so early before. . . . I wish papa was better so that he could fight me with the foils but he has got an ache in his arms, so he cannot.[44]

After winding up his affairs at the consulate and taking extended trips through England with his family, Hawthorne departed for the Continent in 1858. In preparation for the Italian sojourn the children were required to read Grote and Gibbon and to learn by heart Macaulay's *Lays of Ancient Rome*.[45] Soon joined by the lady astronomer Maria Mitchell, whom the boy was to remember with particular fondness for many years,[46] the party journeyed through France to Italy, with the children's governess, Miss Ada Shepard,[47] serving also as a very much needed interpreter. Julian Hawthorne's earliest recollection of Rome was of sliding on the ice surrounding a fountain near St. Peter's. The months in Italy were chronicled with great detail in Hawthorne's Italian journal; in one memorable scene his son is pictured at a Roman carnival wearing "a black mask, which made him look like an imp of Satan." [48] Considerable attention is paid to the boy's childish propensity for collecting lizards in Rome:

> These reptiles are very abundant, and Julian has already brought home several, which make their escape and appear occasionally, darting to and fro on the carpet. Since we have been here, Julian has taken up various pursuits in turn. First he devoted himself to gathering snail-shells, of which there are many sorts; afterwards he had a fever for marbles, pieces of which he found on the banks of the Tiber. . . . It would not be difficult, from the spoil of his boyish rambles, to furnish what would be looked upon as a curious and valuable museum in America.[49]

Indeed, from his tenth to his fourteenth year, young Julian Hawthorne was fascinated by natural history, and especially by shells, and one immediate result was the creation of his first book, as distinct from his extensive diaries. This was a ninety-nine page notebook detailing observations of fifteen shells, with illustrative drawings of each. In the typical description of *Helix Muralis,* the lad combines descriptive, aesthetic, geographical, and historical approaches to his subject, and one can see the genuine, if immature, scholarly inclinations he demonstrated this early in life. The entry begins:

> [Florence, 1858]
> This handsome shell, which certainly deserves the name of a wall snail, is found exclusively on walls. It is born there, it grows there, and it dies there. It is, to be sure, found on precipices and such places, but they are very much the same as walls. And if there were neither walls nor precipices in the world, one would hardly think that the shell would be in exist-

ence. In regard to what part of the wall it is mostly found on, it may be said that generally before a rain, it may be found under the ledges on the tops of walls, (when there are any), and also when very old walls are in question, if you look into the holes which perforate them in every direction you will be pretty sure to find some. With them are, very often, that elegant . . . shell Clausilia Rubigumia about which more will be said presently. In or after a shower they are generally found crawling out of their sleeping rooms, and this is the best time to catch them, for then they are most easily seen. In regard to other places, they are found in great numbers congregated on precipices, or places where rocks are broken leaving a flat surface. Unmarked varieties are often met with. Indeed very many banded and marked land shells seem to have varieties among [those] which are unmarked.

The color of the shell, its precise measurements, and the shape of its whorls are then described with minute fidelity. The writer concludes his discussion with a historical speculation:

The Romans eat these snails, not the whole of them, but only their feet. In ancient times the most wealthy people used to eat snails, and perhaps they eat the very ones the poorest people eat nowadays. It is most probable, for there are a great many different kinds of snails around Rome, and the Romans would probably select the best.[50]

This scholarly pursuit was joined with lively social intercourse. Notable among the children with whom the younger Hawthorne clan were familiar were Edmund and Hubert Thompson, sons of the artist C. G. Thompson, who had painted Hawthorne's portrait in America. The boys guided Julian around Rome, and he was able to say that he became more familiar with that city and its environs than he had ever been with his native Boston. But even this brief friendship was to be severed, and the "unsettled, shifting, vagrant life" continued. After traveling through Italy in 1859 and pausing in Rome until Una recovered from a severe attack of Roman fever, the family finally left for France and, subsequently, Redcar, Englànd, where Hawthorne wrote the final draught of *The Marble Faun* and attended to the details of its publication in both England and America in the early spring of 1860. The family left for America in June of that year. By 1859 the tone of young Hawthorne's diary entries had changed. After all, he was now thirteen. He writes, in Redcar, on July 24:

> This is intended to be a description of my experience on the shore . . . , a journal of the beach, leaving out all description of my other experiences. We, the Hawthorne family, arrived in . . . Redcar on Friday, June the twenty second 1859 after a sojourn in France and Italy. We came here principally for my father to finish a book which he had been composing in Italy. I believe he came in some measure on account of myself, as I am, as will hereafter be seen a great lover of the sea and the objects therein.

In a word, the tone of the Redcar diary is more pompous and self-conscious than that of the earlier European entries. Julian Hawthorne again collected shells and rocks, and even built a boat. He would walk out with his father almost every day after dinner. "We generally went northward along the sand," he recalled in later years, "and at a certain point of the coast, where there was a sort of inlet, Hawthorne would seat himself, and allow the boy to go in swimming." [51] In such scenes we can sense the intimacy between father and son that had first developed at the Red Shanty, been nurtured at Mrs. Blodgett's, and was to continue in fact until Hawthorne's death five years later, and in Julian's recollection ever thereafter.

4. The Sanborn School and Harvard

The decision to return to America after the long European sojourn of seven years was not an easy one for Nathaniel Hawthorne to make. "It sickens me to look back to America," he wrote Horatio Bridge as early as 1854, when he had been away from New England scarcely a year. "If it were not for my children I should probably never return, but—after quitting office—should go to Italy, and live and die there. . . . But it will never do to deprive them of their native land, which I hope will be a more comfortable and happy residence in their day than it has been in ours." [52] Hawthorne's reasoning on behalf of his children was at once hard-headed and a projection of personal feelings. In 1856 he wrote to Bridge that he planned to return to America "in about two years from this time. For my own part, I should be willing to stay abroad much longer . . . but the children must not be kept away so long as to lose their American characteristics, otherwise they would be exiles and outcasts through life." [53]

Dominant, too, in Hawthorne's thoughts, as always, were money worries, aggravated by the consciousness of his children's needs after the return to the United States. In 1855 he wrote to Bridge that he and Sophia were in "good spirits" about the Liverpool salary. "I shall have about as much money as will be good for me," he added. "Enough to educate Julian, and portion off the girls in a moderate way, that is, reckoning my pen as good for something. And, if I die, or am brain-stricken, my family will not be beggars, the dread of which has often troubled me in times past." [54] To his publisher William Ticknor he wrote, four years later, that if he were only rich enough, he would abandon publishing books; but, he added, "with a wing of a house to build, and my girls to educate, and Julian to send to Cambridge, I see little prospect of the 'dolce far niente,' as long as there shall be any faculty left in me." [55] This is the first indication we have that Hawthorne had decided to educate the lad at Harvard College. We can only guess why Julian was sent there rather than to Hawthorne's alma mater, Bowdoin; probably both the father and son wished the young man to remain as close as possible to the family because of the elder Hawthorne's failing health.

When the Hawthornes returned to their familiar quarters at the Wayside in Concord in June, 1860, Una, still frail from her long illness, was sixteen, Julian fourteen, and little Rosebud nine. The years between 1860 and 1864, when Nathaniel Hawthorne died, were to be singularly happy ones for his son, who participated in all the social activities of "genial Concord" (in his phrase) with zest and high spirits. The next-door neighbors at "Apple-Slump," the Alcotts, provided the youngster with companions in Abbie and Louisa May; at the Emerson household he was friendly with Edith and Edward; [56] and there were the innumerable companions at Sanborn's school: Sam Hoar, the two younger James brothers Wilkie and Bob, Ned Bartlett, and Frank Stearns. Julian later reported that he had been romantically linked by adolescent gossips to Abbie Alcott; but even though he declares that some of the maidens at the school were "distractingly lovely," he adds that "I was as bashful as an oyster, and shut my shell." [57]

Julian Hawthorne came to Frank Sanborn's famous coeducational school without any formal preparation. What he knew was a function of the people he had known—several of them, to be sure, like the learned Miss Shepard, hired partly for the purpose of educating the young lad. "My aesthetic culture," he recalled, "began with my mother in the nursery. . . . She had a great gift in the fine arts." [58] Indeed, Sophia seems to have done her best to encourage her son's not inconsiderable interest in drawing, a talent, if it was such, that he shared with his two sisters. While at the Castle of Chillon in Switzerland in 1859, Hawthorne had noted in his journal that his son sketched "everything he sees, from a wild flower or a carved chair to a castle or a range of mountains," [59] and verbally re-created the amusing picture of his two older children, their governess, and his wife, seated all in a row on a bench, sketching the mountains. [60] Young Hawthorne became particularly interested in the art of illumination, inspired, apparently, by seeing his mother's illuminated copy of the Book of Ruth that she had bought near the end of their stay in Europe. [61] He set to work with the manuals and recalled:

Some of my efforts were entrusted to book shops for exhibition, at the dignified price of one hundred dollars each. Several of them were bought, and they may turn up centuries hence at auctions of bibelots, for the paints were the best of Windsor and Newtons, and the gold was pure from the mine. I spared no expense, actually using my $100 checks for the purpose—an unusual dissipation, for a husky lad in his teens. It had its useful side; for afterward, when I came to make mechanical designs in General McClellan's New York office, I had the technique at my fingers' ends.[62]

Perhaps the largest share in the pre-Sanborn education of his son was taken by the father himself, who began by "tightening his belt" and teaching his son Latin at the age of twelve, and Greek also—"his own acquaintance with these languages being sound, if not critical." [63] Julian used to look up his Latin words in the huge Andrews and Stoddart lexicon, but sometimes tried to skip his work by guessing at cognates. "When the Latin author," he relates, "said that the messengers, traveling by relays, finished their journey 'continuo cursu,' and I considered the difficulties of the undertaking, I needed no dictionary to interpret the passage, and informed my father that the riders completed their journey with 'continual cursing.' Upon which he burst into shouts and roars of Homeric laughter, throwing himself back in his chair and kicking up his feet." [64] The son proudly preserved a copy of a letter he had written to "Care mea pater," entirely in Latin, on May 15, 1860.[65]

Among the more instructive as well as charming pastimes of the Hawthorne household were the family readings. The children were accustomed from their earliest years to hearing poetry and fiction read by their father and, less frequently, by their mother. Both parents, wrote their son years later, "seem to have been born good readers; there were music, variety, and expression in every tone, and the charm of feeling that the reader was in sympathy with the reading." [66] Among Julian Hawthorne's memorable experiences was his father's reading of his own *Wonder-Book* and *Tanglewood Tales,*[67] as well as one of the father's favorite books, *The Pilgrim's Progress,* to whose language and characters the son was continually to allude in later years.[68] At three he seems to have heard of *Gulliver's Travels*.[69] Sophia read Spenser to the children as early as 1851, and the father read *The Faerie Queene* while the family was in England. "I beheld the knights in their shining armor, their crested helmets, their lances and excaliburs, and pined to be one of them," the son remembered sentimentally:

> My mother, perceiving the moral advantage of knighthood, . . . promptly fitted me with a helmet, on the crest of which blazed the Dragon of the great Pendragon-ship with wings outspread; and a glorious tail streaming behind it was made of cardboard covered with silver paper. In the sunshine in our back garden my aspect, prancing to and fro, was glorious; and my father contributed a real sword of tempered steel with a gilded hilt and a scabbard of black leather. . . . No doubt Edmund Spenser would have been gratified.[70]

Books were perpetually welcome presents for the young lad in England, especially, it would seem, those from Hawthorne's publisher Ticknor.[71] Back in Concord in the early 1860's, Hawthorne read to the assembled family "the whole of Walter Scott's novels, taking up the volumes night after night, until all were completed."[72] There were readings, too, of other English classics: Milton and Shakespeare, Macaulay and DeQuincey, Wordsworth and Tennyson.[73]

Julian Hawthorne's bluestocking aunt, Elizabeth Peabody, also contributed to his education by teaching him "ancient history, dates and all, by colored diagrams, without my knowing that I was being taught";[74] and indeed, the general influence of his learned Aunt Lizzie was profound upon the boy. A devoted but ignorant English governess was succeeded by the brilliant Miss Shepard, a graduate of Antioch College, who guided the children through nineteenth-century poetry and the French and Italian languages; but though she knew everything, the boy remembered, she did not possess the teaching gift.[75] Hawthorne's English experiences in dancing school had been supplemented, finally, by instruction in the smallsword and the broadsword, in which he displayed his growing athletic prowess.[76]

When Nathaniel Hawthorne returned to Concord, Sanborn's school, which its master conceived of as successor to the Thoreaus' Concord Academy, was housed in a gray building with a big stove in the center. Three walls were paneled with blackboards, and the master's desk was on a low dais at the entrance end. The pupils sat at desks accommodating two each, the girls on one side of the central aisle, the boys on the other; and Julian remembered that "we were a very ladylike and gentlemanly lot." [77] Hawthorne was probably induced to send his son to the school (so, at least, Sanborn himself believed) by a letter from Ellery Channing, although indeed he would have found out about the virtues of the school from other friends. Channing wrote:

> In numbering over the things that had been added to the town, t'other day, I left out the first and best, which is, the school for girls and boys, under the charge of Mr. Sanborn. No words that I could use on this occasion could do justice to his happy influence on the characters of those confided to him, and more especially of the girls. . . . His scholars are from desirable families. . . . Nothing seems to me more unfortunate in this land of activity than to bring up children in seclusion without the invaluable discipline that a good school presents.[78]

This last sentence in particular must have struck home to Hawthorne, ever conscious of the evil effects of the "seclusion" of his own early years. Hawthorne wrote to Bridge on September 3, 1860: "Julian (poor little wretch) begins to go to school tomorrow, for the first time in his life—his education having hitherto been private." [79] The father failed, however, to take Channing's hint about sending the girls to the school.[80]

Frank Sanborn himself was, in Julian Hawthorne's recollection, a "tall, wiry, long-limbed young scholar with brilliant dark eyes looking keenly beneath a great shock of black hair, a quick, kindly, humorous smile brightening over his thin, fresh-hued face and finely moulded features, expressive at once of passion and self-control. He walked with long steps, and with a slight bending of the shoulders, as if in modest deprecation of his own unusual stature." [81] An ardent abolitionist and champion of John Brown, he had had to escape United States marshals sent to arrest him for complicity in the Brown plots. His personal manner belied the fieriness of his views, but young Hawthorne, "perplexed by his feminine gentleness," and perhaps angered at receiving next to the lowest mark in declamation, admitted to being "strongly prepossessed against him." As for his schoolmates, Julian expected treatment in accord with the more brutal revelations of *Tom Brown's School Days.* His father had advised, " 'If the boys attack you, always go for the biggest one!' And he smiled airily, as if bloodshed were his middle name." [82] However, Julian was surprised at finding a peaceable set of well-behaved youngsters, shy and rather curious about the new boy with his British phrases and his ignorance of Yankee school customs.

The very extensive social curriculum outweighed the academic; even the Hawthorne girls participated in the weekly school dances and picnics that were held several times a year. For the boys there were also baseball, rowing, and cricket, introduced into the school by Hawthorne's chum Frank Stearns. Picnics were held at Esterbrook Farm, five miles north in the woods, or at Flint Pond; there was bathing and skating at Walden Pond, and the regatta on the river below the old Red Bridge; there was the grand masquerade in the Town Hall, at which Julian Hawthorne once appeared in resplendent costume as the Duke of Buckingham; and there was occasionally a week's encampment on Monadnock Mountain, with an absence of chaperones for the boys and girls that must have shocked Sophia Hawthorne. In June, 1862, the Hawthornes invited forty young people of Concord to the Wayside for a dance. In his *Memoirs* Hawthorne recounts the gay and pleasant life of the social young scholars with considerable charm.

But two years after he entered Sanborn's school, his mother was prompted to send a long letter, which she rather appropriately termed a "Jeremiad," to the schoolmaster, complaining about the evil effects of excessive social activity upon her son, and children in general. And her letter contains remarks significant in showing her attitude toward her only son. She declared emotionally:

> I actually dread the coming term, because, instead of solemn study and serious, thoughtful mental effort, it is as if Julian, in this last important year, were again about to plunge into the dissipations of society—all sorts of sport, flirtations, trifling, weary sittings up of nights, reluctant risings in the morning; jaded spirits, plans for fun—everything except a brave and attentive grappling with knowledge, as a school should be. With all my might I must pray that you will see fit to forbid all committees for providing "good times," especially. . . . Julian, I saw, was quite wearied out mentally, (or rather, *in spirits*), by his share of idle work of this kind. For he always enters so conscientiously into what is assigned him, that, when one of a committee, he had no fresh powers to give to his important lessons, because he was wasted on nonsense. . . .
>
> When Julian left Concord for the sea, he expressed to me how thankful he was that he should be relieved for six or eight weeks from attending to young ladies. He said he was tired of the worry and excitement of it. Was not this a precious confession for a *preux chevalier?* . . .
>
> Julian was a sacredly folded bud when we brought him home to America, with a genuine reverence for woman; and now he is forcibly bloomed into a *cavaliere servente* before his wisdom teeth have had time to prick through,—and comments upon flirts and coquettes like an experienced man of the world. But as far as Julian is concerned, he is very good, and true and single-hearted, and cannot easily be spoiled; though his time can be and has been much wasted by inappropriate and unimportant claims and cares.[83]

A year or so later, after Julian Hawthorne had left Sanborn's "Academy" and entered Harvard, Sophia was able to continue writing of her son in the way that obviously satisfied her gentility and her sense of fit motherhood. She declared to Horatio Bridge:

> He is very strong and very gentle, and—you will forgive a mother for saying this—he is entirely of the aesthetic order, and his absence and unobservance of worldly considerations will probably not advance him in the dusty arena of life; but he will be unspoiled for the next world, I think, and I hope he will be able to make at least a living in this.[84]

It is almost inevitable for us in reading over these letters of Sophia to reach the conclusion that young Hawthorne presented one appearance at home and another, very different, with his Sanborn and Harvard friends. For surely, if anyone was calculated to succeed in the dusty arena of life, it was he. Sanborn commented with some reticence on Mrs. Hawthorne's letter, "I hardly think she understood her son's nature better than his teachers did; and this appeared later in his career." [85]

Nathaniel Hawthorne had written to his friend James Russell Lowell for advice about the best method of preparing his son for admission to Harvard College. Lowell replied from Cambridge on February 26, 1862:

> I think it would be very decidedly of advantage to Julian to be put under the training of a tutor here. Any clever man (like Mr. Sanborn) will begin to take what one may call *aesthetic* views of teaching after being for some time at the head of a school of his own. I mean that he will attach more importance to the *general* development of his pupils and less to their fitness to pass a special examination such as is needed here.

> I have spoken of the matter with Mr. Gurney, a thorough scholar, one of the best teachers connected with the College, and moreover a man whom you would like. Of course I made no definite bargain with him, but this morning he has consented to take Julian if you should wish it. It is very pleasant to me that he takes him because he is your son—when I first proposed it to him without mentioning names he declined. I don't suppose you will like him any better for it, but I confess *I* do, and moreover it is an augury that he will put his heart into his work. He does

not think it necessary that Julian should live here, which would be an expense to you, but would be able to decide about that after seeing him and finding out where he is wanting.[86]

Lowell's choice was a fortunate one. The brown-bearded Harvard classics professor and young Hawthorne became very friendly. In an amusing reversal of Lowell's expectations, the student stated that learning, under Gurney, was "delightful and endless," whereas with Sanborn it had been merely "an uneasy training for specific and transient ends." [87]

Julian looked forward to the examinations for Harvard College "with hope and fear." He wrote to his mother, "I am very well although I feel somewhat anxious about the examinations. If I get in, it will be by the skin of my teeth. I shall be very savage if I don't. . . . I shan't see you again till I have either triumphed or died in the attempt." [88] Luckily, the candidate returned with his shield instead of upon it. He scraped through, with, however, a "condition" in mathematics that was to plague him all during his career at Harvard. But his father, who had not wanted him to achieve high honors in the classroom but to measure himself against his fellows, was "deeply pleased."

The class of 1867, to which Julian Hawthorne belonged, numbered about sixty youths out of a total Harvard population of four hundred, a figure that included enrollment in the Law School and the Lawrence Scientific School. Three miles from Cambridge was Boston, which, to Harvard boys, meant Parker's Hotel on School Street, the Old Corner Book Store on Washington, the Boston Theatre, and Pell and Trowbridge's Negro Minstrel House. Cambridge was a "nice walk" from Boston, Hawthorne remembered, "with the river just across the meadows; and you saved the carfare, three cents, quite an item in one's expense account." [89] The walk must have been delightful to the lad, who, to the end of his life, enjoyed nothing more than a long stroll and who, during his Harvard days, would think nothing of the eighteen-mile journey from home in Concord to the house of James T. Fields for a pleasant chat.[90]

On weekends Hawthorne would return home to forage for books and read for his courses. "He stoutly hates the Mathematics," his mother wrote Horatio Bridge, "but is very fond of Latin, and friendly to Greek, and is the greatest gymnast in his class." [91] The formal portrait of Julian Hawthorne taken at seventeen, the first photograph of him extant, shows a figure of square, masculine ruggedness. The face is rather innocuously handsome: the forehead broad, the eyes and nose regular, the full moustache curling down around the mouth to the solid chin. This is the sturdy lad who struck down a sophomore in a brutal class battle on Harvard Delta, yet also the boy who impressed his mother as "aesthetic."

At the new collegian's room on the ground floor of the southeast corner of Hollis gathered several old Sanborn cronies like Frank Stearns, and many new friends, including two young men who were to play an important role in his later life: William Morton and William Peckham. A typical incident of his intermittent residence at Harvard (1863–66) is recounted in Hawthorne's *Memoirs*. He describes the joyous aftermath of passing the entrance examinations, when two equally victorious friends, Clem Fay and Eliot Clarke, joined him in an oyster stew, and the three

> strolled away on the Brighton road toward the setting moon, lighthearted and romantic. "Collegians!" we said to one another, gripping hands. We were in a high and happy mood. After some leisurely miles we came, in the luminous dusk, to a church; Clem said: "I play the organ in there sometimes. Let's go in—I know where they keep the key." And we entered the sacred interior. We felt reverent, stepping softly, hats off. Clem played a few low bars; the last of the moonlight came through a western window, and touched his red head: I had never felt more religious, thinking of God, and matriculation, and my coming years in Harvard and in the world. I have never forgotten that impression, and I record the episode here, as perhaps typical of home-grown New England youth in the year 1863.[92]

The avowedly romantic quality of this anecdote tinges the other recollections of Julian Hawthorne's college days that appear in his memoirs. The prayers at 6:15 in the morning; the cow that was deposited in a friend's room; the freshman who defied the sophomores by wearing a beaver hat; the undergraduate who journeyed down the Charles aboard a capsized shell singing lewd songs; the bread-and-water diet of the passionately committed Harvard crewmen, including Julian—all these reminiscences are recounted in ample detail and with an air of sentimental nostalgia. But they reveal very little of Julian Hawthorne himself. With the exception of his father's death, the really significant intellectual and emotional experiences of these early years remain unknown.

5. The Death of Nathaniel Hawthorne

In the years after the family's return to Concord, the father and son had grown closer, especially in the course of several trips they took together to Pride's Crossing, near Salem and the shore, in the summer of 1861, and to West Goldsborough, Maine, a year later. The intimacy of the two was accompanied by the growth of an affectionate humor.[93] "Our conversation had little relation to war-matters," Nathaniel Hawthorne's son recalled.

> He had begun to show himself to me as a friend, as well as a father, and sometimes spoke to me about my possible future. . . . "I suppose, when you are grown up, you will do so and so," he would say,—usually suggesting something so preposterous or distasteful as to stimulate me to define an alternative, which he would then criticize. But he always carefully avoided forcing upon his companion any wishes or expectations of his own; he would suggest, and then observe and perhaps modify the effect of his suggestions.[94]

In an unpublished sketch of later years dealing with his father's life in Concord, Julian was to dwell warmly on his father's friendship:

Our walks together were my chief education during my childhood years, an education all joy, wonder, and sunshine. For he not only found answers to my queries, but told me tales of great men and mighty deeds, of heroic valor and endurance, of the victories of Yankee patriots over British oppressors, of the glories of George Washington and Paul Jones. Or, in other moods, he would tell of witches and hobgoblins, and all the wondrous horde of Gothic and classic imagination. Would that they might have been preserved!—but they were always uttered under the open sky, as we walked side by side through the woods and meadows of Concord, or on the shores of Walden Pond, where the remains of Thoreau's hut still stood; afterward, along the green lanes and among the stately ruins of England; or on the Appian Way in Rome; or again beside the grey seas of Britain. It was only after our return to Concord that the sagas ended. . . .

But when the intercourse of Father and Child ceased, that of Father and Youth began—but its term was fated to be brief, a loss which I could not fully comprehend till long afterward. Our talks then were of realities, past or to come: wise counsel disguised and illuminated with his unfailing humor: deep questions, playfully put, but searching the depths of boyhood nature. Schooltime passed; college was at hand; but my father would still wear the bravery of jest and irony.[95]

As the Civil War continued, Hawthorne began to be aware that his son might very well be drawn into the conflict. Among Julian Hawthorne's earliest recollections, indeed, were "the lessons of vigorous patriotism which Hawthorne used to inculcate upon him. He told him the story of the Revolution until it was the most vivid and familiar part of the boy's life, and the latter went to England almost with the idea of carrying fire and sword into a hostile country." [96] While abroad, the boy had been fiercely patriotic; in Rome, where he was a ringleader of a little group of American boys, he had once stoutly defended his country with his fists against a juvenile Britisher.[97] Much of this fire remained in Julian Hawthorne when the Civil War began, and his patriotic hostility was easily transferred, it seems, from England to the South. His father wrote to Bridge in 1861 : "One thing as regards this matter [the war] I regret, and one thing I am glad of. The regrettable thing is that I am too old to shoulder a musket myself, and the joyful thing is that Julian is too young. He drills constantly with a company of lads, and means to enlist as soon as he reaches the minimum age. But I trust we shall either be victorious or vanquished before that time." [98] Certainly, the sights along the way to Maine in 1862 were calculated to inflame the young man; as the father observed, "At Hallowell, and subsequently all along the route, the country was astir with volunteers. . . . Every able-bodied man feels an immense pull and pressure upon him to go to the war. . . . The whole talk of the barrooms and every other place of intercourse was about enlisting and the war." [99] Perhaps only the death of Hawthorne, and the subsequent family responsibility that devolved upon his son, prevented Julian Hawthorne from going to the wars in 1864.

In the last winter of Hawthorne's life, his son began to be concerned about his father's greatly weakened condition. He tells of reading to him the passage in *Evangeline* in which the heroine finds her lover on his deathbed and holds him in her arms as he dies. "My father listened silently and intently," the son remembered; "and, as I read the last verses, a feeling came upon me that there was something in the occasion more memorable than I had thought of, so that I could hardly conclude without a faltering of the voice. That was my fore-glimpse of the truth; but afterwards I persuaded myself that he must, after all, be well again." [100] The following May, just before Hawthorne took his last journey with General Pierce, his son came down from Harvard to make some request of his father. "I said good-bye," he recalled afterward,

> and went to the door, where I stood a moment, looking back into the room. He was standing at the foot of the bed, leaning against it, and looking at me with a smile. He had on his old dark coat; his hair was almost wholly white, and he was very pale. But the expression of his face was full of beautiful kindness,—the gladness of having given his son a pleasure, and perhaps some-

thing more, that I did not then know of. His aspect at that moment, and the sunshine in the little room, are vivid in my memory. I never saw my father again.[101]

This image of the pale, kind, and gentle father, later to be joined to the vision of Hawthorne as a literary artist, was the one that Julian Hawthorne carried back with him to Harvard and throughout his own life thereafter. It was this image of the man and devoted father that most inspired him in the many books and articles he was to write about Nathaniel Hawthorne. The impression is inescapable that the elder Hawthorne, himself deprived of a father at the age of four, had sought to warm his heart at the fires of his childrens', and to be a loving father to them. In this role he could not share with them the stresses, the anxieties, the fears that his imagination had expressed in fiction and that he had thereby controlled. He could communicate to the children the affection that would make them feel secure and, of course, the literature and traditions of the past. But he could never communicate the inner sensitivity and greatness, the troubled vision of man's morally divided nature. The genius and the original imagination of the father were not, unfortunately, hereditary. Yet it is ironic that though Nathaniel Hawthorne sought, with great success, to substitute a warm and friendly family life for the gloomy evils of the Hawthorne heritage, he gave his children a heritage with which it was much more difficult for them to cope: himself.

2

A Student of Engineering

1. Julian Hawthorne and Franklin Pierce

On May 20, 1864, the day after Nathaniel Hawthorne's death in New Hampshire, his sister Elizabeth wrote to Una:

> Poor Julian, just entering the world, how much he will miss his father's care. You and Rose will be with your mother, and safe from evil; but a young man's life is full of peril. I hope General Pierce will counsel and have a care of him, for his father's sake.[1]

Pierce, the sincerely devoted friend of Hawthorne, was to attempt indeed to compensate for the loss of the young man's father, in accordance with Elizabeth's pious hope. He felt not merely a sense of responsibility toward the youth but a need for love himself, for his wife and young son were both dead.[2] In the summer after Hawthorne's death, he took his friend's son on a trip through the northern states. The two swam at Rye Beach and journeyed out to Appledore Island, where Hawthorne spent a blissful week admiring a young lady. On the way back Pierce told some stories about the boy's father and questioned his companion as to his own plans:

General Pierce asked me how I liked college. I replied that I liked the fellows (meaning my classmates) very well, that I enjoyed the gymnasium, and told him the fact that I had a larger chest-measure than any of the others, and that I didn't much mind the studies, except mathematics. I added that I had rowed Number Three in our class crew, and even had a chance of getting into "The Harvard" Crew. . . . But "now, of course," I remarked gravely, "I must give up Harvard and go to work to earn my living and support the family." [3]

The young student's plans for a profession were quite vague: to be an explorer like Livingstone or a naturalist like Agassiz or Thoreau; to do something, at any rate, that would keep him outdoors. Pierce countered that an outdoor life was not remunerative, and that he would be separated from his mother and sisters. He suggested a career in civil engineering, advice that Julian, despite his aversion to mathematics, was eventually to take.

After further conferences with his father's friends James T. Fields and George Hillard, Hawthorne decided to resume his college life, presumably in accord with his parents' wishes before his father's death,[4] "and to postpone meanwhile my grandiose project of being the Head of the Family and responsible for it. My short effort at being mature was over, and I was glad of it, for, whatever the Faculty might want or expect of me, there was no doubt about my being welcome to the class crew. My inclinations were more social and athletic than studious." [5] General Pierce contributed generously toward Hawthorne's expenses at Harvard as a further testimonial of his affection.[6]

The preservation of a series of letters from Julian Hawthorne to his benefactor enables us to discern more clearly the relations between the two in the year following the elder Hawthorne's death. In a letter of August 15, 1864, the student thanks the General for the good time they had had together on their trip, and notes that he has made an engagement with a college tutor for the last two weeks of August. A fortnight later, however, he writes in a different mood:

> I am almost ashamed to draw so soon on your generosity, but I received a bill of $22.00 from my tailor for several necessary articles, and as it seems to be the sort of thing you asked me to apply to you for, if it is convenient, whenever you please I shall be much obliged for it hoping to make it all right in the "good time coming." [7]

A letter from Hawthorne on September 11 acknowledges receipt of the money from the good Pierce, notes the recent "disturbances" at Harvard, and athletically boasts, "You need not be afraid of my being in any danger from the hazing operations."

The longest letter in the sequence was written on September 30. Hawthorne outlines in somewhat painful detail to his surrogate father his difficulties with the Harvard regimen in his second year:

> Mamma wishes me to give you an idea of my relations in regard to College, which are most unfortunate, and which to my mind and Mamma's are fatal to my continuance there. My embarrassments are these. First, I have all the ordinary work to go through with, which is supposed to be as much as an ordinary person can well accomplish. Except Mathematics, I can get along as well as the average. But in addition to this, I have the examinations for last year to make up,[8] which implies an amount of study which would fill up every cranny of spare time I could possibly obtain. Now, besides this, and worst of all, I have lost two weeks, and must lose another, by reason of sickness, which comes just in the most important time of the Mathematics, which I cannot go on with after coming back without first making up . . . , which, if I had nothing else to do, would take me from morning till night, studying all the time, and all the while the Class would be going further and further. The same is also true of Chemistry and Anglo-Saxon; so that I have an amount of work to do which would scare anybody, however smart. All this not mentioning the boating and Societies, with which I am intimately connected, and from which it would be

hardly possible to separate myself. Lastly, to crown all, this illness has left my eyes so weak, that I shall not be able to study at all for a considerable time, nor hard for a very long time. So far as I can see, College is knocked on the head. I need not say how sorry I am to leave the class, which I have found very pleasant, and doubtless in many ways profitable; but it seems unavoidable.

My plan is, to study under a private instructor for two or three years, and then if possible, enter the English University of Cambridge, which would be of immense advantage to me, if I can do it. At any rate I can study enough to fit me for it, which is about as much as one learns in College here. I think such a course would be the best as regards my Mathematics, which I cannot get satisfactorily explained at College.

In a letter dated October 13 and written from his home in Concord, Hawthorne goes on to explain that Professor Gurney had approved of his plan and had recommended Ferdinand Hoffman of Stockbridge as his private tutor. The writer concludes somewhat pathetically, "I know it is the best thing for me, though of course I do not look forward with great delight at being separated from every one I know for a year. However, I shall doubtless get used to it. I hope you will come down and see me sometimes." From another letter of April 25, 1865, however, it appears certain that young Hawthorne was still attached, at least nominally, to Harvard, because he thanks General Pierce for a "present" that enabled him to take care of "Society fees" at college.[9]

2. New Ambitions

In 1864, when Nathaniel Hawthorne died, Julian's sisters Rose and Una were thirteen and twenty, respectively. Sophia in this year described Rose as

blooming out vastly. She is nearly a head above Mama, and will be very tall. She is now discoursing music on the piano, for which she has a good faculty; and she goes to school, and has a talent for drawing figures. Una . . . feels excessively aged since her twentieth birthday, though Julian assures her she looks only sixteen. She has no tutor now, but studies by herself in the morning, and paints in the afternoon, and sews for the soldiers a great deal.[10]

Una kept up with her Latin and her music, sometimes practicing the piano for an incredible sixteen hours a day, and read history "and the literature suggested" to her mother. Despite their various skills, neither of the girls received the educational opportunities bestowed upon their brother. Rose attended several schools briefly, however: one in Concord, another at Lee, a "select academy for young ladies" in Salem, and Dr. Dio Lewis's gymnastic institute in Lexington; and Una, too, before Rose, had overcome her mother's objections and attended Dr. Lewis's school. Both girls were fond of visiting their aunt "Ebe" Hawthorne, their father's only living sister, at Montserrat, and Una was a favorite correspondent of the brilliant and acid-tongued spinster. Both sisters, too, looked up to their brother with something resembling reverence. "What a magnificent creature," Una declared of him. "He is not earthly! He certainly is the flower of ideal chivalry and trust." [11] To Rose he was her "Dearest Herculian boy." [12] The girls' temperaments were, however, radically different. Una was inclined to melancholy, whereas beautiful, red-haired Rose was high-spirited and seems to have been very much interested in the Concord young men.[13]

The years between her husband's death in 1864 and her removal abroad with her family in 1868 were particularly trying ones for Hawthorne's widow. The story of her financial difficulties, extending even to quarrels with her husband's publisher Fields, is a familiar one.[14] Toward her children she was fiercely protective, and was unreservedly enthusiastic about them in letter after letter. A few months after Hawthorne's death, she wrote to her sister Elizabeth Peabody, "The children join hearts and ring me round with a halo like the glory round the heads of saints. . . . They all seem to feel as if their father had silently bequeathed me to them to watch and ward—just as

I feel as if he had left me them to cherish"; [15] three years later she wrote Horatio Bridge that her children "are all so bright and good that my life is a thanksgiving for them. I live for them." [16] If Mrs. Hawthorne entertained any doubts about the excellence of her son Julian, they are unrecorded. We know her opinion that her son was "entirely of the aesthetic order," and she was proud of the fact that he "takes a father's place to his sisters with such a fine conscience." [17] Yet beginning soon after the elder Hawthorne's death, there began to appear certain flaws in this jewel of young manhood that might have disturbed any mother.

"The young man was unstudious," observes one writer on the Hawthorne family. "He showed too plainly that he had never been subjected to rigorous mental discipline. . . . He loafed at home, pretended to read philosophy, . . . and fell in and out of love." [18] Even before the end of his freshman year, Julian had had to resort to tutoring in his detested mathematics in order to remove the "condition" in his matriculation; and he continued this project through his second and third years at Harvard. During the long months away from his family at Stockbridge, and away also from his Harvard friends, Hawthorne indulged himself in much adolescent self-pity. In November, probably of 1865, he wrote to his mother of his homesickness; he felt somewhat hurt, too, that his mother had objected to his "showering" a local belle, Annie Bartlett, with letters, and added: "I should think people might be more considerate about absent acquaintances. But out of sight out of mind, I suppose. Frank Stearns is the only faithful friend I possess in this world. All women, yourselves excepted, are beneath contempt." [19] Whether Julian was being tutored in mathematics at Stockbridge, or studying logic and metaphysics at home, he was *not* very frequently in attendance at Harvard. In February, 1866, during his junior year, he was studying at Northboro, but planning to rejoin his class in Cambridge in March. At this juncture his old adviser, Professor Gurney, undertook to write frankly to his mother of the difficulties involved in the young man's accomplishing all the work necessary in the brief period remaining:

> Combined with this distrust of Julian being ready in March was the fear that rowing would so engross his energies next term, as I knew he would go into the Harvard, that he would once more be unable to do justice to his excellent powers in his studies. On the other hand I felt that the earlier he returned the more ready would the Faculty be to overlook his long absence from college, and to allow him to rejoin his class.[20]

Alluding then to a misunderstanding between Julian and him, Professor Gurney goes on:

> Julian was entirely mistaken if he supposed that I had in any degree lost my interest in him or his welfare. I like him very much as I have always done; I think most highly of his powers, and, in many respects, of his qualities [but] I do not think he has acted wisely or well at all times in the matter of his college career. . . .
>
> The very distastefulness of much of the routine of life here to Julian with his fastidiousness & ideals of what a student's life might be, made me none the less anxious that he should plod through the prose of Cambridge. I think hardly any form of self-indulgence more dangerous . . . than to fail to make the most of what circumstances have put within our reach because we see clearly its imperfections. As I said before, you will think me simply mistaken, not unkind or ungenerous if I say that this seems to me the way in which Julian is most liable to disappoint himself.

Professor Gurney's apprehensions proved to be well grounded. In the autumn of 1866, at what was to have been the beginning of Hawthorne's senior year, he "was told that he had been absent too often";[21] in a word, he was expelled. Sophia appealed personally, but without avail, to the president of Harvard. She finally blamed only the college and not her son, who, she declared, "bears this upsetting with his usual serene magnanimity—but it is very mortifying after telling all his friends that he was safely back." [22] Sophia confided to her sister Mary Mann that "it was Mr. Edwin Seaver who led him astray. He is one of the faculty and he assured Julian that he was all right." [23]

During the autumn and winter of 1866–67, the ex-Harvardian probably did loaf at home, doing nothing to aid the straitened family circumstances, even though his mother was in the grip of a "ferocious economy." Circumstances changed, however, very early in 1867. A new passion seized Julian Hawthorne. In a letter to his mother he wrote that a Dr. Loring had stirred his interest in an engineering career. Thus the old suggestion of General Pierce had finally flowered. Hawthorne went to Cambridge to consult with Professor Gurney, with whom he was presumably again on good terms. "He said he thought engineering would be a very good thing for me," Hawthorne writes, "that he thought I had better consult a good practical Engineer as to what I had better study, and then come to Cambridge to the Scientific School, and study it there." He had asked George Hillard if there was money for this new project, and the old family counselor had approved the idea heartily. "So," Hawthorne concludes, "I have decided to become a civil engineer, and shall make arrangements to be in Cambridge this winter." [24] But this fervent new resolution was temporarily sidetracked by another brilliant idea, which is first disclosed in Sophia's letter to her sister Elizabeth on March 3, 1867:

> Julian wants me and Una and Rose to go and live with him at Heidelburg [sic]. . . . Everyone says it is cheap to live there if you are once there. . . . You take tea in Edens, by the music of angels and pay six cents for that, and a few pennies for your supper. The climate is delightful, the grapes abound, and nothing costs anything.[25]

The idea of Europe as a new home must have been particularly attractive to all the Hawthornes, for, except for the Roman fever contracted by Una, the European sojourn of 1853–60 had been a long, golden idyl. But the "if" clause in Sophia's letter was temporarily decisive. In a later letter to Elizabeth, she wrote:

> All our European plans have fallen to the ground for want of money. We do not have a penny to go with, not even to send Julian. It was a terrible disappointment to him. . . . Seeing that he must make some money he will study civil engineering and be able to enter the Scientific School here this month. Oh how I wish it could be the technology school in Dresden—so splendid and free of cost too. But he must burrow down where he is. . . . There never was anything more divine than the way he feels and behaves. . . . When he has mastered his profession and made some money, he says he shall go to Europe with us.[26]

The Lawrence Scientific School had been established across the yard from the Harvard buildings just a few years earlier, with Josiah Dwight Whitney and Raphael Pumpelly assigned to the chairs of geology and mining. According to the historian Samuel Eliot Morison, the school in the 1860's "was full of sparkle, with Agassiz denouncing and Gray defending Darwinism, and Jeffries Wyman giving a course of lectures." [27] Though the faculty was impressive, the students were probably poor, for by 1869 the school was reputed to be "the resort of shirks and stragglers." [28] We may imagine Julian Hawthorne's dissatisfaction, also, at finding that the powerful Agassiz had made the Scientific School "an institution for individual study in research in Geology and Zoology," rather than an engineering school as was originally planned.[29] Hawthorne was probably in irregular attendance there for the whole of the 1867–68 academic year.

Meanwhile, in these years of 1867 and 1868, both Julian and Una had had unfortunate love affairs. The former, we learn from a letter of his mother dated March 24, 1867, had been jilted by one of the local belles, but had managed to keep up appearances; Sophia wrote that "his letter written to tell me and Una after he arrived in Boston is beyond all words in its divine tone of charity, pity, patience, and calmness." [30] Una's case, however, was far more serious. Early in 1868, she fell in love with Storrow Higginson, a young man who had served as a chaplain in the Civil War, but who had now given up his career in the ministry and was planning to go to South America. He had proposed to Una, and she had consented to marry him. [31] Unfortunately, powerful forces were working against the young couple. Sophia told her sister that "Storrow's mother and aunts had all confided that Una was far above him; they hoped, therefore, for her own sake that she would not marry him, though for his sake they hoped she would." [32] Emerson and Elizabeth Hoar, both drawn into this affair, disapproved of the engagement. Finally, Una, yielding, it seems, to these pressures, broke the engagement.

The effect of this decision on Una's somewhat unstable nature must have been great. We can understand Sophia Hawthorne's natural instinct to remove her daughter from the now melancholy Concord scene and far from the Concord gossips. Other forces soon entered to turn the family's faces toward Europe again, and, more definitely, Dresden. Lowell had been in that city in 1855–56, and so had Elizabeth Palmer Peabody, who "knew of comfortable, inexpensive lodgings there." [33] Julian Hawthorne recalled in later years that around this time a Miss Mary Vandevoort, a maiden lady of sixty, visited the family. "She had dwelt several years in Dresden. . . . It was due to her that we arrived in Dresden a year later." [34] The final impetus was provided undoubtedly by Hawthorne himself, who had been dissatisfied with his experience at the Lawrence Scientific School; it did not, he wrote, "minister to my self-esteem, or increase my fondness for mathematics." [35] He longed to enroll in the Dresden Realschule, "famous as the best in the world for training civil engineers." [36] In short, everything pointed to Dresden: the fact of Europe itself, the recommendations of friends, its usefulness as a retreat for the unhappy Una, its inexpensiveness, and its Realschule.

It was at this juncture that James Russell Lowell was able to render service to the son of his old friend Nathaniel Hawthorne.[37] Apparently, Lowell was convinced, as the student's family certainly was, that despite his unimpressive record both at Harvard and at the Lawrence Scientific School, Julian had at last settled on an appropriate enterprise. Lowell was induced to give young Hawthorne "a little preliminary insight into German; Lowell cordially undertook, for Hawthorne reasons, the mollifying of my barbarism." [38] These "Hawthorne reasons," it may be remarked, had already influenced Franklin Pierce and Professor Gurney, and were later to give Julian Hawthorne powerful friends in America, like Robert Carter, and in Europe, like Francis Bennoch and Henry A. Bright. The novelist's son sat with the eminent Harvard professor in his study at Elmwood two or three evenings a week:

> He would assign me a passage from the poem [*Faust*], courteously assume at our next meeting that I had mastered it, and would then proceed to read-out and construe it himself, giving me the benefit both of the great poet's visual, and of his own eloquent, comprehension of it; I have never enjoyed German so much since. . . . As a fact what I did learn was Lowell himself —as much of him as a boy could comprehend; he gave me generously whatever he thought I could assimilate. Ostensibly, we read Goethe's 'Faust' together—in reality he read and I listened.[39]

The final decision to leave New England was made in September of 1868. Sophia Hawthorne confidently expected that the trip could be financed through the publication by Fields of Hawthorne's English, French, and Italian notebooks, and by Putnam's publication of her own *Notes in England and Italy,* which was to appear in 1869. The Wayside was sold, and the Hawthornes sailed again for the Old World in October.

3. Dresden and a Love Affair

On board the *Deutschland* young Julian Hawthorne had his customary eye for the pretty girls aboard. "Once in a while," he confided to his journal, but perhaps not to his mother, "I capture a young lady, and elope with her to the bows, or behind the Pilot-House." [40] But of more significance is the extensive detail in which he discussed his fellow passengers and the events of the passage across the Atlantic. This was the first journal he had kept since the happy days with the family at Redcar almost ten years earlier; and these entries are so vivid, and written with such scrupulous care, that it is almost as if Hawthorne were taking notes for a novel, a purpose for which he was indeed to utilize this and other journals in the years to come.

The Hawthornes disembarked at Bremen, where "the cafes are very pleasant, and they have most excellent Bier, in very large glass tankards, with covers. Everything is absurdly cheap, and much better than in America. . . . So far, in spite of bad weather and unintelligible language, impressions of Germany are favorable." The family traveled by train through Magdeburg and Leipzig, and arrived weather-beaten but happy in Dresden. "Dresden!" Julian was to recall,

> with its Green Vaults full of treasures of antiquity; its great gallery of paintings, including Raphael's divine Madonna and Child; its opera house, where Wagner and all his mighty forerunners had their home; its nearness to Leipsic, where the toys were made; and its incomparable beer, foaming in hundreds of hospitable kellers and breweries.[41]

The contemporary journal preserves the excitement of the family's first winter in Dresden. True to the pattern of their earlier life in Europe, they visited the galleries frequently. Hawthorne indeed admired the Dresden Madonna, and rhapsodized about her for pages; but he was also candid enough to write:

> I am very much surprised to find so much beauty in the old pictures: for, judging from my boyish experiences in the Italian and French galleries, I did not anticipate much pleasure in these venerable works. But an eight years dose of America gave me many new and wise ideas, besides correcting many false impressions.

During that winter the young man also delighted in the opera house, the concerts in the "Bier Saloons," the open-air recitals in the Grosser Garten, the masked balls that abounded that season, and the fascinating display of German life and customs that included romantic duels on the one hand and unromantic peasant hardships on the other.

Meanwhile, the plans to attend the Dresden Polytechnic had not been forgotten, though it was to be almost a year before Hawthorne began formal studies there. First there was the problem of language, for the pupil of Lowell found his reading of *Faust* insufficient equipment; accordingly, the family engaged a tutor. Hawthorne planned to attend a few lectures at the Realschule before the beginning of the term, in order to familiarize himself with the technical vocabulary and the speed of lecturing. He used the good offices of a Mr. Meyer, who diplomatically approached the director of the school for him. On January 3, 1869, Hawthorne records that the director "told me I had better not enter there at present, but gave me the address of an individual by the name of Zschoche . . . who was in the habit of preparing men for entrance into the Institute." Herr Zschoche turned out to be "an elderly man, with a rusty gray shock-head of hair, rusty clothes, a deficiency of front teeth, pleasant brown eyes, and a fine square forehead. In his mouth was the butt-end of an execrable cigar." He must have seemed an extraordinary successor to such respectable and eminent New Englanders as Mr. Hoffman of Stockbridge, Professor Gurney, and James Russell Lowell. On January 7 Hawthorne made his "debut among the German schoolboys," as he called it. The American student was horrified at once by the age and filth of the classroom itself, and even more disturbed by the students. "The scholars are execrable," he declared, "and could not be worse. . . . Such unhealthy and hopeless looking creatures I never saw." By October 5, 1869, however, Hawthorne had presumably advanced sufficiently to be admitted to the Realschule. He writes in his journal that he is attending lectures there on mechanics, and vows: "I must get through by next fall and go home."

This ambitious statement was influenced by considerations other than his long-frustrated longing to receive a degree, a longing that was never to be satisfied. Julian Hawthorne was at last in love and deeply committed. In addition to the frivolous activities in Concord and on shipboard, there had been other brief romantic attachments in the American colony at Dresden. He was fascinated for a while by a Miss Sherman, a "perfectly pretty" girl, but "alarmingly correct in all her ideas." Charmed by her beauty, Hawthorne was yet provoked that it should be thrown away through an absence of a corresponding fineness of intellect. "I am even inclined to think," he adds in his journal, with one of many after-echoes of his father's ideas, "that if by any means she could be turned to evil courses, it would be an advantage to her; it might give her a certain form of intellectual development which she can never acquire as it is." Obviously, Miss Sherman was not very different from the everlasting progression of well-bred young ladies whom Julian had encountered ever since the days of Frank Sanborn's school. But suddenly, in February of 1869, he met a most extraordinary young lady, a Miss May Albertina Amelung, who was staying in Dresden with her mother and two younger brothers, Frederick and Lees. He spends pages of his journal recording long conversations between them, long intellectual banterings that clearly intrigued Hawthorne. His first descriptions of her show a balanced admiration and wry criticism:

Miss A is a very singular young lady. In appearance she is medium height and well and gracefully formed. She has flaxen hair piled on the top of her head, and flowing down behind. Her complexion is clear and bright, especially when she is excited; at times she is pale, especially about her lips. Her eyes are gray, and shaped differently from each other—the left eyelid sometimes sinks a little over the eye. She has a high forehead considerably concealed by her hair. Her mouth is small, and her

lips gracefully shaped, but thin; her chin curving out prominently. Her cheek bones are high, and give her whole expression
an air of experience and 'hardness'; but the impression wears off
a good deal after a while. She is twenty, but . . . looks two or
three years older. She is very handsome altogether.

In character she is quite different from what she tries . . . to
appear. She wishes to make herself out, an ordinary fast American girl. She wears the highest of heels, laces herself tightly,
lives in defiance of all rules of health and good sense. . . . She
advocates the idea that she is quite heartless, without any feelings, conscience or sense of propriety. . . . She is a girl of
unusual talents and power, and almost unconquerable spirit; and
will never think of surrender, unless she can freely acknowledge
herself quite overmatched and outdone. . . . I am pretty sure, if
she ever met an individual whom she feared and respected, and
for whom she would consequently entertain more or less regard,
she would be true as steel. . . . I imagine her to be a person of
peculiarly keen and delicate sensibilities, great power of will, and
a rather cynical cast of thought. . . . She is evidently not a
happy person.

(April 15, 1869)

Hawthorne continues in this vein for several pages, praising the
girl's devotion to her brothers, her keen sense of the ludicrous,
her brilliant and vivid conversation, and her "warm woman's
heart."

Throughout the rest of that year Julian and May, called
"Minne" by everyone, became closely attached. Hawthorne
writes on his twenty-third birthday (June 22): "I have one
present that should suffice to elevate and purify my life above
those of other men," but adds wryly, "Have I met more than
my match?" On July 20 Minne Amelung returned to America,
leaving Hawthorne lonely but contented in thoughts of her. He
commemorates her twenty-first birthday on August 15 by declaring: "Love will ennoble me, if anything on earth can." A
somewhat different chord is struck on November 8, when he
notes that he is "in the best of health," and "a marvel of
muscle," thanks to the fifty pound dumbbell he is using. "The
least thing I can do for my darling wife," he adds, "is to keep

myself in perfect physical condition: the more since she is far from well, though I truly believe that she will ultimately recover." This is the first we learn of Minne's poor health, which remained poor during the next decade but which did not prevent her from bearing an inordinate number of children.

Whether Julian Hawthorne and Minne Amelung became engaged in 1869 cannot be definitely established, though his allusion to her as his "darling wife" seems to point to that fact. The Amelung clan was a distinguished one, however, and neither Hawthorne nor his family need have feared a parallel with Una's engagement to Storrow Higginson. In 1784 John Frederick Amelung of Bremen had established a glass works at a community he founded and called New Bremen in Frederick County, Maryland. Aided by both German and American capital, Amelung set his German-trained crew of workers to producing some of the finest American glass of the period. The Amelung family finally settled in New York, where Frederick's grandson, John Alexander Amelung, was born. Minne was born to John and Mary Mildred Cardozo Amelung on August 15, 1848, the seventh of eleven children. On her mother's side she was a descendant of the Randolphs of Virginia.[42]

August of 1869, which marked Minne's birthday, was also the occasion of another important event in Julian Hawthorne's life. The name of "Hawthorne" exerted its first peculiarly talismanic effect on behalf of his writings. In that month two poems, "Yes" and "The Usurper," appeared in *Putnam's Magazine,* the same journal that was then serializing Mrs. Hawthorne's *Notes in England and Italy.* These are love poems, conventional but not insincere; and the coincidence of their publication and Minne's birthday is probably not accidental. These were Hawthorne's sentiments in "The Usurper":

> "Farewell, my Friend," I said, and went my way
> And thought, "Perhaps we shall not meet again,
> But meet or not, our Friendship shall remain."
> Yet, new lands and strange faces seemed to dim
> Her memory; a foolish, passing whim

Might make me half forget our parting day.
Thus first. Then, by degrees, and more and more,
Would thoughts of her among my musings stray:
At last they filled my heart from roof to floor;
Which questioning, I found, in Friendship's stead
The Tyrant Love established. Sorrowfully
I sought her presence: "Friendship has flown," I said,
"And Love usurped her kingdom utterly."
She raised her eyes to mine, in which, behold
Mirrored, the self-same tale I just had told.[43]

These poems mark Julian Hawthorne's first appearance in print under his own name; [44] and thus from 1869 may be dated the literary career that ended only with the appearance of the post-humously published *Memoirs* sixty-nine years later.

The chronology of the ensuing year is confused.[45] Minne seems to have returned to Europe in 1870,[46] and probably again met Hawthorne in Dresden. It is clear, at any rate, that after a semester or two, Hawthorne had absorbed all he was going to at the Realschule. Some time in 1870 he followed Minne back to New York, secured a position in the New York Dock Department, and married his loved one on November 15, 1870. Her parents were present at the wedding, but Julian Hawthorne's mother and sisters could not afford a trip to New York. The only extant comment on the ceremony is by Hawthorne's close friend Frank Lathrop, who wrote to Una Hawthorne on November 25:

> I was a witness to the great event in Julian's life, a week ago last Tuesday. He looked very grand and noble, and most of the young ladies in the congregation looked as if they would like to be in Minnie's [sic] place. . . . After the ceremony they went off to Boston and stayed about a week. This morning he called to see George [Lathrop] and looked as natural as he did before.[47]

The Hawthorne family's reaction to the wedding is not known beyond the fact that Sophia was "happy in his marriage," [48] and wrote her son wishing him "all the happiness which had been hers upon her own marriage." [49]

The years in Dresden had not been as fruitful and rewarding for Julian Hawthorne's mother and sisters as they had been for him. The teachers who lived in the American colony and who had seemed attractive to her sister Elizabeth only bothered Sophia with their incessant talk. For a time the art galleries were a source of delight, but Mrs. Hawthorne "took cold in the drafty marble halls and fell seriously ill." [50] Hawthorne's older sister found the language impossible and the customs revolting. In January, 1870, she wrote to a friend:

All the galleries and music of Europe can't make up for one's friends. Indeed I don't believe I am very artistic at all. Of course I always knew I had no talent to accomplish anything, but I did think I had latent seeds of appreciation, and perhaps they would come to something if I was not among these stolid, dirty Germans, who disenchant one of all ideas of beauty, and make one doubt if there is such a thing as spirit. [51]

Rose, still in her teens, was deeply involved in her drawing, painting, and piano lessons, so much so that she was not, perhaps, socially graceful. Her brother thought that she did not choose the right sort of friends, even going so far as to drink tea with elderly women quite insignificant socially. Elizabeth Hawthorne is our authority that Julian once

introduced her at a party, and as she was looking very pretty, he hoped she might effect something; but she held down her head, and only said "yes" and "no" and the nice young man (Herbert Browning, a son of the poet) after trying hard to draw her out, withdrew, thinking, probably, that she had not an idea in her head. Julian thinks she has a great many, and judging from her letters, that is my opinion. [52]

Just as romance had entered Julian Hawthorne's life in Dresden, so it entered the life of Rose in 1869. The Hawthornes had become acquainted with the Lathrops before November of that year in the Saxon city. The father, George Alfred Lathrop, was a physician, a distant cousin of Dr. Holmes and the historian

Motley, and then United States consul in Honolulu. The sons were Frank, the elder, a student of Whistler, and George Parsons Lathrop, a well-mannered, good-looking, and brilliant poet at nineteen who fascinated both of the Hawthorne sisters.[53] In later years rumors circulated that Una and George had been for a time engaged, and that George had broken the engagement in order to win Rose. Undoubtedly, Una was attracted to George Lathrop, but he was in love from the start with her sister.[54]

By the late spring of 1870, Sophia and Una had decided to leave Dresden and its generally unsympathetic atmosphere to return to the England that was now really "Our Old Home" to them. The outbreak of the Franco-Prussian War contributed to their desire to leave; but, curiously enough, Rose was left behind at a rigorously disciplined boarding school, and did not join her mother and sister in England until late in 1870. Since it appears unlikely that her mother would have left Rose, not yet twenty, alone in Dresden, especially in time of war (which began on July 19), there is reason to suppose that her brother was still in Dresden until the fall of 1870, and that he thus did not return to New York in pursuit of his bride until just before they married in November. Meanwhile, the Lathrop family had also left Dresden, Mrs. Lathrop and George returning to New York to rejoin Dr. Lathrop, and Frank going to London, at least for part of 1870, for we have seen that he was present at Hawthorne's wedding in America.

Thus the winter of 1870–71 began with Sophia, Una, and Rose happily reunited in London, Julian and Minne Hawthorne newly married after a romantic courtship, and everyone fond of the Lathrops. By the end of that winter, death and heartbreak had clouded the carefree spirit of the Dresden years.

5. The Brothers-in-Law

In February of 1871 Sophia Hawthorne fell seriously ill of typhoid pneumonia, a disease she had combatted successfully before the family left for Europe. But this time the outcome was to be fatal. Her two daughters nursed her faithfully for several weeks through bouts of excruciating pain and temporary relief. Una wrote:

> The least start or emotion was so liable to make her cough, that I seldom ventured to talk to her; and it was a day or two after a long letter from Julian came, that I told her of it. She smiled brightly, but did not speak till a good while after. She then said, "Julian." So then I gave her a sketch of the letter, and told her about Julian's arrangements in New York, and of his love for her.[55]

On Saturday, the day before her death, Sophia cried, "Have you telegraphed to Julian?"; and when informed that her daughters had not, she said reproachfully, "Oh, you should have telegraphed." Una was struck with sorrow that her mother should have felt the end imminent, but declared, "I could not but think it would have been a great mistake, and unnecessary pain to Julian." This tender regard for her brother's sensibilities was balanced by her feeling of incapacity after two weeks of the most severe mental anguish:

> I had the relief, for a little while, of passionate tears, down on the floor beside her, sobbing, and calling for Julian—Julian! It seemed as if I could not bear to have him away. And yet almost at once the revulsion came, "Oh, I am so glad this agony is spared him! He could be of no use to her." But oh, how I longed for him, to feel I had some one to do more than I! There was the bitter sense that mamma would never need my self-control or tender care again.[56]

Through the chloroform mists Sophia spoke very slowly: "I am tired—too tired—I am—glad to go—I only—wanted to live—for you—and Rose." The church bells sounded on Sunday morning, March 3, 1871, and Mrs. Bennoch, her old friend, joined the daughters round Sophia's bed. Sophia's last struggle for breath caused Una to hold her hand tighter.

In death, wrote Una, Sophia Hawthorne's face "looked more

and more like an angel's; a delicate color stayed upon the cheeks, a lovely smile upon the slightly parted lips; her beautiful white hair was brushed a little back from her face, under a pretty cap, and her waxen hands lay softly folded against each other upon her breast; the last day we took off her wedding ring and I wore it." [57] The following Saturday, Sophia was buried in Kensal Green, where Una was also to be interred only six years later.

Una Hawthorne's severe emotional upheaval during the weeks of illness left her unprepared for the ensuing emotional shock occasioned by the reentry of the Lathrops upon the scene. Back in New York Julian had been informed of his mother's death, but Minne was now pregnant, and the conditions of his engineering job might have contributed to the difficulty of his getting away to London to care for his sisters. Hildegarde, their first child, was born to Julian and Minne Hawthorne in the summer of 1871. But George Lathrop, his "kindred spirit" from Dresden days and Rose's admirer, was in New York also, studying at Columbia College, and it was arranged that George should escort the two girls back to America. This action should not be seen as an abnegation of responsibility on the brother's part, but rather as a necessary adjustment to circumstances. Yet there were problems beneath the surface, as a letter from Hawthorne to his sisters dated May 5, 1871, reveals. He had seen Osgood on a business matter, possibly concerning the publication of Nathaniel Hawthorne's late romance, *Septimius Felton,* which Una was now preparing with the assistance of Robert Browning. Hawthorne notes that George Hillard, who had long handled the family's financial matters, "proposes to entrust [the estate] to my care: but I cannot do it, at least at present, for every moment that I can work at all, must be devoted to my *family!*" And he goes on, "I am obliged to smile, my dears, at your persistent belief that I am going to draw on the estate for any more money. It belongs to you only, as long as I can use head and hands." [58] The tone of other letters from Hawthorne in these months is quite cordial; writing to Rose on

May 19, he indulges himself in long praises of her writing, noting incidentally that "my star in the Department is still in the ascendant." He might have been somewhat perturbed that George Lathrop remained in England so long and did not bring his sisters back; but it is likely that neither he nor Una suspected the romance between George and Rose. The two twenty-year-olds impulsively decided to get married in September of that year; George's brother Frank was a witness to that wedding as he had been to Hawthorne's, but Una was not present. She was ostensibly ill but in reality deeply grieved by the sudden ceremony. Sophia's sister Elizabeth, in a letter of this time, alludes to "Una's calamity," which may have been a species of nervous breakdown, perhaps even extending into insanity.[59] Una, we may be certain, spent an unhappy year, despite her work with Browning and her devoted settlement chores under Anglican auspices in London.

If Una was shocked by the marriage of George and Rose, her brother was somewhat more pompously aggrieved. He felt, of course, that he was the head of the family now, though separated from his sisters. He was exceedingly bitter toward George and Rose, and the animosities aroused in 1871 were not finally stilled until the 1880's; in fact, they were to erupt into a public quarrel between Lathrop and Hawthorne in 1876. And even though he and Lathrop eventually became friendly again, Hawthorne could still, after Lathrop's death, call the marriage "an error, not to be repaired." There is a certain mystery in the origin of this quarrel. Hawthorne may have shared his Aunt Ebe's annoyance that the young couple were to leave Una alone in England and return to America. He may have felt that George had played him a shabby trick in going to England under false pretenses. Other clues emerge from a letter Lathrop wrote to James Russell Lowell in 1876, wherein he speaks mysteriously of "the false position in which I was placed at the time of my marriage (partly through Julian's agency, too)," offers to explain to Lowell at some future date "the origin of Julian's wrath," and declares bitterly: "In the face of singularly intolerable treatment I strove a long time to prevent the breach which has now widened into publicity. Julian was my great admiration, before my marriage, and when he utterly disappointed my conception of his character, it did not rouse hostility in me. . . . But the other party has apparently cared not a fig for the idol [of friendship] . . . or for me, or for anything but his own powerful temper." [60] The new Mr. and Mrs. Lathrop crossed the Atlantic in December, 1871, and lived in New York for the first six months of their return. There is no evidence of any contact between the Hawthorne and Lathrop households in New York before the summer of 1872, when the Hawthornes again sailed for Europe and the Lathrops left for Cambridge, Massachusetts.

3

The Moorish Temple Rises

1. Gothic Foundations

Despite the shock that Julian Hawthorne undoubtedly felt at his mother's death in February and his sister's marriage in September, he nevertheless spent what must have been a joyous year, involved as he was both with his wife and new baby, on the one hand, and his first real intercourse with the world beyond the confines of the Hawthorne clan, on the other. That clan, to all intents, no longer existed, and Julian was for the first time thrown upon his own resources. He had his family to support, and a job of some importance as a hydrographic engineer working in the New York Dock Department under General George B. McClellan. One might suppose he would have been sufficiently occupied. But now his mind went back to the ease with which those poems of 1869 had been published in *Putnam's Magazine*. And Minne, too, was there, as a silent source of encouragement; in fact, Hawthorne wrote somewhat ambiguously a few years later that if it had not been for Minne, he would not have begun a literary career at all. He himself describes the feelings of 1871 :

> Years before, I had received parental warnings—unnecessary, as I thought—against writing for a living. During [1871], how-

ever, . . . I amused myself by writing a short story, called "Love and Counter-Love," which was published in *Harper's Weekly*, and for which I was paid fifty dollars. "If fifty dollars can be so easily earned," I thought, "why not go on adding to my income in this way from time to time?" I was aided and abetted in the idea by the late Robert Carter, editor of *Appleton's Journal;* and the latter periodical and *Harper's Magazine* had the burden, and I the benefit, of the result.[1]

Robert Carter, whom Julian was to characterize in the biography of his parents as "a man of rare sagacity and wide learning," [2] was to be a steadfast literary friend during the next two years. He had been Lowell's partner in the editorship of the brilliant but ill-starred journal *The Pioneer* in 1843, and he had printed Nathaniel Hawthorne's tales "The Hall of Fantasy" and "The Birthmark" in that publication.[3] In 1833 he wrote at length to the elder Hawthorne commenting ecstatically upon the writer's *Wonder-Book*.[4] In 1870 Carter took over the direction of *Appleton's* from E. L. Youmans and edited the magazine for two years. It seems likely that Nathaniel Hawthorne's son might have become personally acquainted with Carter through the good offices of Lowell; but however the connection was established, Carter was undoubtedly delighted to help along the son of an author whom, he could congratulate himself, he had also been one of the first to appreciate. During the two years of Carter's editorship, *Appleton's* published five short stories, two sketches, and two slight poems by Hawthorne; and in the following year, 1873, Carter was instrumental in persuading the new editor of *Appleton's,* Oliver Bell Bunce, to serialize Hawthorne's first novel, *Bressant*. This was a considerable tribute either to Hawthorne's story or to Carter's influence (or both), for "most of the serials were by English, French, and German novelists, the editor having a very low opinion of the American novel." [5]

If Hawthorne at first only suspected the value of the Hawthorne name in the fictional marketplace of the day, he quickly came, in the year after the anonymous publication of his first story, on March 11, 1871,[6] to recognize its worth. Certainly, he began by wishing to write anonymously and *not* to present his work to the public with the glorious Hawthorne name attached to it. A strong argument in favor of using his name was put forth by Carter, who wrote to him on June 22, accepting his second story, "Dr. Pechal's Theory," for *Appleton's* as a tale "quaint, original, and told with dramatic effect," and adding:

> I suggest that you let me put your name to it. I appreciate your objections to this, but am sure it will be wise to disregard those objections. Your name will give additional value to the story, and I can assure you that the tale itself is not unworthy even of your name. A nom de plume is almost always absurd and embarrassing and the incognito can never be preserved. Sooner or later you *must* write under your own name, and there is really *no* reason why you should not make the plunge at once and begin boldly *now*. Knowing your father as I did personally . . . I am satisfied that the course I advise will be judicious.[7]

Julian must have found this argument convincing; or perhaps he really wanted to be convinced. At any rate, he was henceforth always to publish his name, except under unusual circumstances.[8]

The appearance of "Dr. Pechal's Theory" in the August 19 number of *Appleton's* with the magical name of Hawthorne beneath it quickly stirred up interest among several of the other editors of leading magazines. Richard Watson Gilder of *Scribner's Monthly* invited a Christmas story from Julian in September and accepted the quickly written tale "The Oak-Tree's Christmas Gift" on September 30, at the rate of ten dollars per one thousand words. Richard Henry Stoddard also wrote to Hawthorne in that month:

> I have undertaken to edit a magazine entitled the 'Aldine,' the specialty of which so far has been pictures, and very good most of them have been. I want to have its future literature at least as good. With this end in view I am looking about among my friends for help, and I feel sure of obtaining it from them. I

want a story from you—I need not say as good an one as you can write, but a fresh, bright short story, not to exceed, if you can help it, 3 columns of the magazine. . . . I have, of course, no advice to give you, as regards choice of subjects. That I leave to your father's son.[9]

The outcome of this request, with its frank invitation to imitativeness, was Hawthorne's fanciful "The Real Romance," which appeared in *The Aldine* in January of 1872. Another tale and three slight sketches also appeared in *The Aldine* in 1871–72. At this time H. M. Alden, editor of *Harper's Magazine,* had also jumped at the chance to use Hawthorne's work, and he published four of the new writer's stories. Hawthorne was one of the few American authors whose novels were to be serialized in *Harper's* in the 1870's and early 1880's, at a time when English novelists held sway in the pages of that periodical.[10] Alden exercised something of a restraining hand on the writer's first productions. On April 3, 1871, for example, he wrote to Hawthorne:

> I think that "Star and Candle" is a very strong story, and with some modification I should be glad to publish it. It is not necessary, it seems to me, to make the heroine a fallen woman. . . . No artistic requirement makes it necessary that she should have lost her purity of soul; and the *pathos* of the story is rather diminished than otherwise if she is thus represented.[11]

Hawthorne acceded to this genteel purification of his story and received fifty dollars for "Star and Candle" on April 17. He was obviously a rapid rewriter. Alden noted blandly, "I am glad that you agreed with me as to the propriety of the modifications suggested." [12]

There was one exception to this general rush, however: the august *Atlantic Monthly,* edited by William Dean Howells. Scribbled on a letter from Howells of June 20, 1873, rejecting a story Hawthorne had submitted, is the author's important comment: "My first refusal!" Julian Hawthorne's brother-in-law and now his enemy, George Lathrop, had become, in 1872, a staff critic for the *Atlantic,* and his influence on the magazine may have been considerable by 1873; for the *Atlantic,* which was then concentrating on publishing the work of Howells himself, DeForest, and James, chose not even to take notice of Julian Hawthorne's first novel, *Bressant,* and commented on it only in the course of a scathing review by Henry James of Hawthorne's second major work, *Idolatry* (1874). When Howells wrote in October, 1872, that "the whole varied field of American life is coming into view in American fiction," [13] he clearly did not consider Julian Hawthorne's work visible.

At the outset of any consideration of the younger Hawthorne's fiction, his relation to the mainstream of Gothic literature ought to be looked at briefly. For better or worse this was one of the principal literary traditions within which he worked. Although he knew Gothic literature well enough, it would be more accurate to say that he came to it at second hand through his reading of his father's fiction; certainly, his first attempts at writing showed a rather gross interpretation of the elder Hawthorne's imaginative works, a grasp of the more obvious, melodramatic, "Gothic" aspects of those works.

The genre of the Gothic tale, which flowered in Europe from the time of *The Castle of Otranto* (1764) to that of *Melmoth the Wanderer* (1820) and which found expression subsequently in such American tales as those of Poe and Nathaniel Hawthorne, is only part of the more inclusive genre of the "tale of terror and wonder" whose fascination has persisted from the narrative of Odysseus' descent to Hades to the assorted horror stories of Yoknapatawpha County.[14] As a genre, the Gothic tale is customarily identified both by a limited group of stock images, characters, and devices used in combination and by the principal aesthetic intent of arousing pleasurable, nonmoral horror.[15] Historians of the Gothic mode have isolated the various "stage props" of the Gothic tale, generally with an eye to establishing Gothic tendencies in a particular writer or group of writers. Lionel Stevenson selects the following aspects of Gothic romanticism as an a priori basis for the deduction that

Hawthorne was a markedly Gothic writer: "fondness for the supernatural and the horrible, violence in the depiction of uncontrolled emotional frenzy, selection of a hero who is a superman in physique, intellect, and passion, and indulgence in . . . the 'pathetic fallacy' of natural phenomena as responsive to human moods, . . . They are handled with gusto and often seem to be the very embryo of the plot." [16] Certainly the most important of these structural and thematic devices, many of which clustered around the Gothic tale from the broader Romantic movement, is the use of the supernatural and the Black Art. Ghosts, witches, wizards, sorcerers, and incubi and succubi are among the figures from the lore of witchcraft and demonology who make their appearance. Enchanted objects, magic potions, and amulets are found in great profusion. As part of the Black Art, there is found a cabbalistic laboratory, in which the bounds of knowledge are shattered and the spirit solves the basic problems of existence. By extension of this idea, "science" is developed as a crutch for the romantic plot, and we find resulting an interest in the phenomena of clairvoyance, mesmerism, and somnambulism. Here too enters the familiar Faustian theme of the compact with the devil in order to transcend human limitations.

Hawthorne's characteristic, even compulsive, use of the supernatural both as theme and technique, although allied to the tradition established by the romancers of the Gothic school, nevertheless links him also with the romancers of all ages, from the writer of "Saul and the Witch of Endor" to his own father. The marvelous was indeed to be introduced into *Bressant, Idolatry, Garth,* and later works; but it is only in the preface to *The Laughing Mill and Other Stories* (1879), a collection of four tales dealing in one way or another with the supernatural, that Julian Hawthorne lays bare his great reliance upon superstitious fancies as a bedrock for his fiction. "The marvelous," he declares, "always possesses a fascination, and justly; for while it is neither human nature nor fact, it ministers to an aesthetic appetite of the mind which neither fact nor human nature can gratify." [17] He goes on:

> He who would mirror in his works the whole of man must needs include the impossible along with the rest. *Tom Jones, Adam Bede,* and *Vanity Fair* are earth without sky, without that unfathomed mystery opening all around us—the sky of Shakespeare and Dante, of Goethe and George Sand. . . . The storyteller, sensible of the risk he runs of making his supernatural element appear crude and ridiculous, exerts himself to the utmost, and his style and method purify and wax artistic under the strain.[18]

Although the "purifying" aspects of Romantic technique may be questioned, the remark defending the supernatural as symbolic of "that unfathomed mystery opening all around us" embodies a high and noble aim for Hawthorne's romances.[19] The relation of this aesthetic doctrine to Hawthorne's view of "spiritual reality," derived in a debased form from Plato and Emerson, was clarified in a passage at the opening of *Kildhurm's Oak* (1880). He declared:

> I am not at this moment concerned to enter upon a discussion of supernatural phenomena, so called, beyond remarking that no physiologist can pretend to any right to be heard at all on the subject, the credulity which can believe witchcraft and sorcery to be the bugbears of a diseased imagination being too gross to command attention. Reasonable people believe that the human body has a soul; that there is a spiritual sight answering to the bodily sight, and that when the spiritual sight is opened it must inevitably behold the objects of a spiritual world. . . . Concerning the spiritual world only the laws of the mind can hold sway there; it is therefore free from the trammels of space and time. Further, it is a world of real substance in contradistinction to the apparent substantiality of the world of matter. Thus far logic carries us.[20]

The terminology and point of view of Hawthorne's statements on the supernatural and the spiritual world suggest an inheritance not only from Emerson but from Emanuel Swedenborg; and indeed, the latter writer greatly helped to shape Julian Hawthorne's "religious" ideas, which were integrated with his aesthetic and political theories. There survives from the 1870's a manuscript article called "The Swedenborg Philosophy," leaning in part on Emerson's chapter on Swedenborg in *Representative Men,* which seeks to replace the Kantian and Hegelian metaphysic with the Swedenborgian view of spiritual reality. Kant and Hegel, Hawthorne wrote, had separated man from the face of the deity by all the breadth of nature and length of history. He goes on:

> Swedenborg's analysis restores man to the fellowship of God. Consciousness claims two disproportionate generative elements: one universal, passive, organic; the other human, active, free. The former element gives us fixity, or identifies us, by relating us to nature; the latter element gives us freedom, or individualizes us, by relating us to the infinite or God.

In another passage in this essay, Hawthorne states more clearly the Transcendental doctrine that underlies the creation of his Gothic fancies:

> The natural world is a necessary implication of the spiritual, and the spiritual the only safe or adequate explication of the natural. . . . Nature is not in the least absolute and independent, but an effect of spiritual causes as contrasted and yet as united as God's infinite love and man's unfathomable want.[21]

In his writer's notebook of 1871–72, Hawthorne discusses in detail Swedenborg's Language of Colors, the Law of Correspondences, and such occult matters as the Adramandoni, the Garden of Conjugal Love. He displays a fascination with the problem of duality and argues (with himself) for the preeminence of the Spiritual. "True symbols," he writes, "are representatives of divine things, in material form, which are symbols of no arbitrary manufacture, . . . but are grounded in the deepest, most primitive nature and essence of Existence." These banalities indicate, perhaps, a kind of delayed reaction to "great ideas" in the years when Hawthorne was attempting to teach himself what he had never learned at Harvard and what he felt he needed as novelist's equipment.[22] Intoxicated with spurious metaphysics, he became an Inebriate of Air and produced an *olla podrida* best described as Swedenborgian Gothic.

Despite the fairly coherent philosophical basis of his theory of the supernatural in fiction, Julian Hawthorne lacked the ability to make his supernatural elements graphic, in the manner of Poe; unlike the elder Hawthorne, he neglected the tremendous possibilities of a *suggestion* of supernaturalism, with the final "reality" left ambiguous. In a typical early review of Hawthorne's fiction, for example, the *Saturday Review* found "inherited" from Nathaniel Hawthorne the love of "relieving the workaday aspect of the tangible world by casting over its actors and events a mist borrowed from realms fantastic, imagined, or even supernatural." But the younger Hawthorne, the journal went on, concealed the improbabilities of his narrative but poorly, and made the connection between his real and fanciful worlds too gross.[23] Finally, Hawthorne did not let his ghosts fulfill their destinies as ghosts, but felt obliged to intrude and explain; and this is an explanation of his relative failure, despite his frequent use of the supernatural and other Gothic devices, to achieve pure horror effects. Stevenson puts the case well:

> His handling of the supernatural lacks the pristine assurance of the Gothic tale of terror, from Mrs. Radcliffe to Poe. The second half of the nineteenth century witnessed the first invasion of the mesmerists, mediums, mahatmas, . . . [who] brought the practice of black magic up to date by investing it with a technical vocabulary, and expounding it in abstruse theses. In short, even superstition had to follow the new fashion and become scientific. Julian Hawthorne, therefore, whenever he introduced an apparition or a spell or a curse into his story, felt impelled to comment upon it in the best scientific terminology.[24]

The generalized use of the supernatural in Gothic fiction accompanies numerous other typical scenes and devices. Of these the most important is the use of a castle, which customarily contains secret cabinets and corridors, and a labyrinthine network of subterranean passages. There are haunted wings, secret chambers, and the occasional terrifying spectacle of immurement. In the castle one frequently finds mysterious works of art, such as sinister ancestral paintings with figures that step out of their frames or roll their eyes and utter fateful words. One hears throughout a Gothic narrative strange shrieks of terror, mysterious voices, and dismal groans; and natural phenomena, in accordance with the pathetic fallacy, are stressed in order to serve the terrifying purpose as lightning, storms, and darkness attend the crucial events of the narrative. Heroes and villains follow a predictable pattern. The former are generally of Byronic lineage, characterized by defiance of convention, potentialities for great evil as well as great good, and frenzied inward conflicts; and the latter are most frequently "dark" personages in holy orders, whose crimes, which may include illicit or incestuous love, often form the basis for an ancestral curse. Other miscellaneous Gothic phenomena include prophetic dreams, double personality, and the use of a manuscript that has been transcribed or translated by the author.

The reader of the discussions of Julian Hawthorne's novels, romances, and stories that appear later in this study will have little trouble finding significant examples of the writer's use of Gothic paraphernalia. The Gothic castle appears, for example, in *Garth* and *Archibald Malmaison*;[25] witches and wizards in *Idolatry* and *Garth*; the Byronic hero in all of Hawthorne's early novels; double personality in *Archibald Malmaison*; the cabbalistic laboratory in *The Professor's Sister*; the ancient manuscript in "The Mysterious Case of My Friend Browne" and "The Trial of Gideon"; and so on. But of Hawthorne's major novels and short stories viewed as a whole, only three— *Archibald Malmaison*, "The Laughing Mill," and "Ken's Mystery"—have both the aesthetic intent of arousing pleasurable horror and a significant combination of Gothic devices used to that end. Only these, then, can be considered as Hawthorne's genuine additions to the genre of the Gothic tale. Certain other works of fiction bear what may be called a Gothic flavor. The greatest influence of Gothic romanticism was exerted between 1874 (*Idolatry*) and 1880 (*Kildhurm's Oak*); from the latter date to 1888 ("Ken's Mystery") there is a rapid turning away from Gothic elements; and finally, between 1888 and 1896, Gothic features, with the exception of the perennial supernatural elements, disappear almost entirely from Hawthorne's works. One must reject as too sweeping Stevenson's categorical assertion that Hawthorne was "primarily . . . a devotee of . . . Gothic romanticism," and that "its distinguishing features are to be discerned in every one of the younger Hawthorne's novels, and not as superficial trimmings but always innate in the very heart of the story." [26]

2. First Stories and Sketches

The short stories written in the first years of apprenticeship (1871–73) seem singularly different from the important modes of writing in the period. In the first place, Julian Hawthorne's fiction does not seek to exploit the new vein of local color being richly worked by Bret Harte, Sarah Orne Jewett, and George Washington Cable. Although his settings range from quiet New England towns to New York City, from Cape Ann in Massachusetts to the Dead Sea in Palestine, Hawthorne never explores the life and folkways of a single regional setting. More important, his settings do not bear an integral relation to the themes of the tales. Third, the realistic mode of fiction, as coming to be defined by Edward Eggleston and Howells, is deliberately eschewed in favor of rather old-fashioned romance, with, frequently, a supernatural twist. We may already see at work the critical theory that Hawthorne was later to expound; but since there is no evidence to show that that theory was already clearly developed in his mind, we must draw conclusions about the temper of his early work solely from that work itself. Perhaps at first Hawthorne had really been interested in catching the flavor of contemporary life; such, at any rate, seems to be the main point of his parable "The Real Romance" (1872), in which the only character in his story that the fictional author finds not to be a "mis-formed, ill-balanced, one-sided creation" is the housemaid, whom he had patterned after a real person. This is theory, certainly, but not the kind that Hawthorne could live up to; for fifteen years later he was to write:

> In two or three cases I have tried to make portraits of real persons whom I have known; but these persons have always been more lifeless than the others, and most lifeless in precisely those features that most nearly reproduced life. The best results in this direction are realized by those characters that come to their birth simultaneously with the general scheme of the proposed events.[27]

Indeed, "The Real Romance" is completely fanciful, does not exhort by example, and is quite as much concerned with poking fun at romantic stereotypes as in advocating a realistic mode. Hawthorne seems to have restricted his portraiture of real persons and events to such sketches as "A Golden Wedding in the Best Society," which stemmed from his careful observations in Dresden in November, 1872, and which was printed by the faithful *Appleton's* in January of the following year. The golden wedding ceremonies are those of the king and queen of Saxony, celebrated with six days of festivities and attended by the German emperor and his retinue. Hawthorne allows himself a certain scorn of the aged royal pair, who,

> here, in Saxony, amid the dangers, turmoils, and revolutions of the nineteenth century, . . . have been living their royal little lives, doing their formal little duties, making their stiff little visits, enjoying their sober little glories, suffering their unimportant little misfortunes, worshipping according to the tenets of their bigoted old religion, and loving and relying upon each other in their courteous little way.[28]

This is rhetorical sarcasm, not analysis; but Hawthorne's eye is a sharp one, and his descriptions as he looks from his study window, mingles with the crowds in the streets, and attends a ceremony, betray a keen if not impartial observer. The attitude here resembles Una's ("these stolid, dirty Germans"); indeed, Hawthorne made a loutish German officer the villain of his first, but inconsequential, short story, "Love and Counter-Love," and he portrayed another evil German, Herr Rauber-kerl, in "Mrs. Suffrin's Smelling-bottle." Later in the year 1873, *The Galaxy* printed "A Feast of Blood," in which Hawthorne surveyed the custom of dueling. Again we have the same shrewd perceptiveness and caustic tone that had marked "A Golden Wedding," and that prefigures the later, full-scale attack upon things German in *Saxon Studies* (1876).

It was to the romantic and supernatural mode rather than to the realistic that Julian Hawthorne turned in these first years of short-story writing. His imagination in his early tales, even the humorous ones, was directed to the mysterious, the spiritual, the fanciful; and he made extensive use of romantic coincidences. He looked to the past for his inspiration—in particular, to that segment of literary past dominated by his father—rather than to the present or the future. The young man's first "writer's notebook" of 1871–72—there were to be many such notebooks in the years to come—opens with lines that are vaguely familiar:

Personify Ruin, and the various forms under which he undermines victims.

Two persons make their wills in each other's favor, by agreement. Hoaxed by a false report of each other's death.

The mood in which a person soon to die would visit familiar persons and things.

A popular individual in Society to be traced by some one who has a grudge against him. Finally comes across his mossy tombstone.

These hints for stories are obviously in the Nathaniel Hawthorne manner, and the imitation of the elder Hawthorne's journals seems highly conscious. In another early passage we find an anecdote that suggests the kind of wretched material to which young Hawthorne could be drawn:

> A man in England had married a woman from somewhere in the West Indies, I think. They lived in Sussex, near the sea. The woman was not, apparently, more than half civilised: she had some kind of a temple built for her, out in the grounds contiguous to the house, and here she used to go to perform the rites of her pagan religion. On what terms she lived with her husband is not known: but when he died, she exhibited great grief, and after his funeral she disappeared. Search being made for her, she was found—or rather, her burnt ashes were—in her temple. She had built a funeral pyre and immolated herself upon it, according to the custom of her people.

The tone is unfortunately that of Rider Haggard—not Virgil; although, had Hawthorne written a tale based on this sketch, he would undoubtedly have called it "A West Indian Dido." [29]

In "The Mysterious Case of My Friend Browne," Hawthorne takes up the Gothic properties of an old manuscript, a poisoned ring, and even a palpable ghost escaped from Trinity Churchyard to wreak his revenge on the descendant of a man who had wronged him. In this story there is a precise reenactment in present-day New York of events that had occurred one hundred and fifty years earlier; and this very theme of deliberately created "wonder" is exploited again in the fantastic narrative "Mrs. Suffrin's Smelling-bottle," [30] in which the characters play out in modern dress a tragedy that had taken place fifty centuries earlier at the destruction of Sodom.[31] The phenomenon of clairvoyance, which had fascinated Nathaniel Hawthorne in *The Blithedale Romance,* makes its first appearance in two bizarre tales, "Dr. Pechal's Theory" and "Mr. Maximilian Morningdew's Advice." [32] In the former, Dr. Pechal, a "frowzy precise foreigner," has "evolved the law which regulates the time, place, and circumstances, of the death of every human being"; but his attempt to stave off his own death succeeds only through a lucky coincidence. In the latter story a youth is deeply troubled by a dream in which his immediate future has accurately been foretold. Hawthorne does not focus on whatever sense of wonder can be extracted from this rather stale situation; he merely requires us to accept the fact of the revelation and proceeds to recount the lad's disillusionment at the hands of the cynical Mr. Morningdew. "The Strange Friend" foreshadows a whole rash of later stories in which a skeletal plot is made to serve as a springboard for extended metaphysical speculations, in this case on the distinction between earthly and heavenly love. The humorous tales of this period, "Why Muggins Was Kept" and "The Mullenville Mystery," show an ingenious handling of the surprise ending, but even these are not free of romantic improbability. Much more successful than any of the tales so far mentioned is "A Picturesque Transformation," which deliberately recalls the father's story "The Prophetic Pictures." Tremaine, a penniless painter, is in love with Hildegarde, who is also loved by her rich guardian, the Professor. Tremaine paints a great picture, and the Professor, seeking to exploit his rival's cupidity, offers to pay him handsomely for copies of the original. The painter performs this work for two years, meanwhile postponing his marriage to Hildegarde; and as time goes on, the three faces in the picture become changed, hardening into the portraits of "three condemned souls." Seized with horror at the change, Tremaine offers to forfeit the Professor's money if Hildegarde will marry him; but she and her guardian have become engaged, and, it is implied, the Professor's punishment will swiftly follow. In all these stories Julian Hawthorne does not explore very deeply the sense of horror possible in the melodramatic incidents he contrives; nor does he effectively use the supernatural as a means of moral insight. He scarcely dwells upon his ghosts, in fact, and the "unvariegated hue of common circumstance" (a phrase from "The Real Romance") is freely mixed with the wilder fantasies. Even "A Picturesque Transformation," with its symbolic concern about the evils of the prostitution of artistic talent, is weakened by its melodramatic and mechanical structure.

More serious and carefully wrought than the above tales are "Star and Candle," "The Bronze Paper-Knife," and "The Minister's Oath," which are linked both by their attempt to study the consequences of sin and by the use of unduly melodramatic incidents to further this attempt. "Star and Candle," which was the seed of the long novel *Sebastian Strome* (1879), presents a hero whose selfishness is gradually transmuted into self-abnegation.[33] Honslow, the sinner in "The Bronze Paper-Knife," finds that his bastard son Jim is stalked by the ghost of his friend's wife, who had died believing her own husband to be Jim's father. Alice, the woman's daughter, grows up a peculiar child, very much recalling Pearl in *The Scarlet Letter:* she was, Hawthorne writes, "an exquisite monstrosity as regarded mankind." She has a strange predilection for the paper-knife that Honslow had presented her mother, as if the "cold and bitter soul of that lady, when it left her body, had slipped into the hard, metal image, and perhaps found it quite as congenial an abiding-place." When Alice sees the branded letter "H" on Jim's forehead, she is impelled by some supernatural force to stab him; but she is forestalled by Honslow, who burns the dagger and banishes the curse. The concern with the consequences of sin is scarcely central to this long story. Hawthorne seems more interested in the figure of the revengeful mother, in Alice's inherited hatred for Jim, and in the symbolism of the knife: that is, in the melodramatic, rather than the moral, elements of the tale.

With some modification the same point may be made of Hawthorne's most ambitious story of 1871–73, "The Minister's Oath," which seems deliberately to invite comparison, on the basis of the title alone, with the elder Hawthorne's "The Minister's Black Veil." The heroine, Ellen Barret, jilts Harry Pelmore at a ball; and even though he quickly forgets his vow of eventual revenge, his former fiancée does not. Years later, Ellen is married to Pelmore's former rival, the young minister

Frank Morley. Their son falls ill, and Pelmore, now a physician, is called in to attend him. When the child dies, the wife, convinced that Pelmore had deliberately murdered him, makes her husband swear to kill whoever injures her, even though she never reveals her suspicions of Pelmore to him. Years again pass, and a girl has been born to the Morleys. One night, as the minister completes a sermon on "Sudden Death," Ellen seeks to have him withdraw his oath, but Morley refuses. The mother, going in to her baby girl, meets "sudden death" when a pair of scissors clasped by her child pierce her brain in the dark. Her husband becomes deranged at the sight of his dead wife and bloodstained child, and, true to his oath, attempts to kill the baby. But before any injury can be done, his brain weakens completely. The years again pass. Pelmore has raised his own son with Sallie Morley and has lived near the insane minister. The two youngsters chance upon the old sermon, and Morley, hearing Sallie read it, is seized with his old frenzy. His renewed attempt to kill the child is thwarted by Pelmore, who loses his life in the process, while Morley recovers his sanity.

The original oath itself, the motivating force of the story, seems absurd, for the husband did not vow to punish the "murderer" of his son but only whoever harmed Ellen. This seems a transparently obvious "setting up" for the events to follow, like the misunderstanding at the heart of "The Bronze Paper-Knife." The violent passages of time in a reasonably short story are likewise troubling; the materials here seem more than sufficient for a novel, and no single emotion or idea is long sustained. Hawthorne again seems most concerned with the melodramatic surface of his tale: the terrible night scene when the mother dies and the child plays in her blood, and the pathetic murder attempt at the close. The author does attempt to do something—very little, to be sure—with the effect of the oath on the minister's character; and the reader feels that surely here, if anywhere, the primary interest of such a story must lie. Hawthorne, however, merely describes something of this effect:

His whole life, since the night he took the oath, had been an unnatural and morally unhealthy one. Human and divine love had been at continual war within him, and he had beheld the demoralizing spectacle of the divine continually worsted in the struggle. To one of such exceptional fineness and delicacy of feeling as he nothing could be more destructive of all balance and proportion. . . . The integrity, purity, and truth of the minister's nature were deeply compromised, the corruption having eaten into the very weapons and armor with which alone he could have hoped to keep corruption away.[34]

This sort of analysis is good as far as it goes. But Hawthorne has not yet developed the ability to go beyond melodrama, to dramatize such internal conflicts, or even to focus his narrative properly upon them as static forces, a model for which is a chapter Hawthorne knew well: "The Interior of a Heart," in *The Scarlet Letter.* Too much plot gets in the way, and the final impression one has is an incoherent blur of merely sensational events. If "The Minister's Oath" is a decided failure as a short story, it is nevertheless not a serious failure for an imaginative young writer who has yet to learn to compress his tale and to satisfy his readers' aroused expectations for a narrative of conscience. Although Hawthorne continued writing short stories to the end of his life, he learned to structure his more abundant fancies into novels and romances.

The impression is inescapable that in the twenty tales and sketches written between 1871 and 1873, Julian Hawthorne was deliberately working the vein that had, in the elder Hawthorne, produced fiction of great power and beauty. To invite, even challenge, comparison on his father's own ground was, at this point in his career, foolhardy. To begin with, his style was hasty, slapdash, and, in diction, inexact. He lacked, and was indeed never to acquire, the historical imagination that had produced such tales as "The Gray Champion." Some of his themes seemed either unnecessarily crude or unbearably sentimental. Finally, his compulsive supernaturalist fancies were frequently handled carelessly or with a rather vulgar humor:

almost, sometimes, as if young Hawthorne scarcely believed in them and scarcely expected the reader to.

The difficulty in interpreting these early tales is not one of evaluation. One may state at the outset, categorically, that with one or two exceptions Julian Hawthorne's best stories are not as good as Nathaniel Hawthorne's poorest. But evaluation aside, the question of deliberate imitativeness remains puzzling. Two answers suggest themselves. The first is that Julian Hawthorne was attracted by a reasonably easy way of making a living; if magazine editors and publishers expected a Nathaniel Hawthorne-esque story of his "father's son," then that was what he would supply them. The second, more flattering, and equally probable answer is that the young writer produced his tales as a form of homage to his father's name and memory. Perhaps both answers are in some measure true; to the end of his life it may be said that Julian Hawthorne both revered his father's name—and exploited it.

The romantic directions apparent in these early stories were momentarily, in the writing of Hawthorne's first novel, *Bressant* (1873), to be bypassed in favor of a stricter realism. In his second long work, *Idolatry* (1874), however, the Gothic and supernatural reasserted themselves; and for the next twenty years, the fiction of Julian Hawthorne evidenced this dichotomy between the realistic and the supernatural modes, in his "novels" and in his "romances."

3. "Bressant: A Novel"

In the spring of 1872 Julian was "rotated" out of office in the New York Dock Department.[35] He was then offered another engineering job in South America. The alternative was to develop beyond literary dilettantism, which had thus far been greeted with the success of immediate publication, and to attempt to support his family as a professional writer. He chose the latter course, bought twelve reams of large letter paper, and began his first major work, *Bressant*.[36] In later years Haw-

thorne was frequently to express regret that he had not remained an engineer—especially when, in the early years of the
twentieth century, he was to rally friends to the support of his
mining schemes in Canada.[37] But despite the hardships he and
Minne were to undergo in the 1870's, there is every reason to
believe that Hawthorne was not at first displeased with his
choice. Authorship is certainly "a blessed profession," he wrote
in his journal for March 22, 1873.

The genesis of his first novel was recalled by Hawthorne in
Confessions and Criticisms:

> I finished it in three weeks; but prudent counselors advised me
> that it was too immoral to publish, except in French; so I recast
> it, as the phrase is, and, in its chastened state, sent it through the
> post to a Boston publisher. It was lost on the way, and has not
> yet been found. I was rather pleased than otherwise at this
> catastrophe; for I had in those days a strange delight in rewrit-
> ing my productions; it was, perhaps, a more sensible practice
> than to print them. Accordingly, I rewrote and enlarged 'Bres-
> sant' . . . but—immorality aside—I think the first version was
> the best of the three.[38]

Bressant's lineage is Byronic, and he is endowed with
strange magnetic powers. When he appears at the opening of
the novel, he is a dedicated and ascetic young intellectual,
unsophisticated and almost primitive in his social relationships.
His mentor, Professor Valeyon, finds him a product of a theory
of education that "aimed rather to give the man power in
whatever direction he chose to exercise it, than to store his
mind with greater or less quantities of particular forms of
knowledge. The only faculty to be left uncultivated . . . was
that of human love—this being considered destructive, or, at
least, greatly prejudicial, to progress and efficiency in any other
direction." [39] At first Bressant regards love only as a "delicious
weakness," refusing to believe that it can coexist with lofty
aims and strenuous effort; but before the end of the narrative,
he declares: "Love is study enough, and work enough, for a

lifetime. Mathematics, and logic, and philosophy—all those things have nothing to do with love, and couldn't help me in it. . . . It has laws of its own." [40] Bressant's emotional and sexual awakening is dramatized in his alternating love for Valeyon's two daughters: the "earthly," dark, sensual Cornelia, and the fair, "spiritual" Sophie [41]—the latter, in name, invalidism, drawing skill, and spirituality of temperament recalling to the reader the young Sophia Peabody. Although the stress on the redemptive power of love recalls a recurrent theme of Nathaniel Hawthorne, Julian Hawthorne's concurrent stress on the power of sexual attraction is both coarser and more frank and worldly than anything to be found in the elder Hawthorne's novels.

Bressant presents three themes that are to be dominant in the major fiction of the ensuing decades. The first is the primacy of love over selfish intellect. Hawthorne's heroes, beginning with Bressant, are afflicted with the Faustian lust for knowledge and power, boundless ambition, and an egotistical contempt for their fellow creatures that isolates them from humanity. Julian seems to have taken for his text his father's often-repeated views about the dangers of intellectual ambition, which had been expressed as early as his first volume of short stories. Discussing the painter in "The Prophetic Pictures," Nathaniel Hawthorne had written:

> Like all other men around whom an engrossing purpose wreathes itself, he was insulated from the mass of human kind. . . . His heart was cold. . . . It is not good for man to cherish a solitary ambition. Unless there be those around him by whose example he may regulate himself, his thoughts, desires, and hopes will become extravagant, and he the semblance, perhaps the reality, of a madman. [42]

There appears in Julian Hawthorne's heroes the same grave imbalance between head and heart that afflicts such familiar figures as Aylmer, Chillingworth, and Ethan Brand. In the younger Hawthorne's stories, these heroes tend to begin their lives in quest of learning in a serious profession; they are scientists, divinity students, or, very commonly, artists. Their intellectual self-absorption inevitably fades, however, as they learn, through the development of their affections, to accept a humble lot. One may view this thematic material as a by-product of an overly sentimental interpretation of standard Christian doctrine, especially if one views humility as a poor substitute for unfettered rational inquiry.

A related theme dramatized in *Bressant* is the necessity for a choice between sacred and profane love, a problem that Hawthorne had first explored in "The Strange Friend," and that was later to face such characters as Lancaster in *Dust,* Boardwine in *A Dream and a Forgetting,* and Merlin in *The Professor's Sister.* Artistically, however, Hawthorne was unmoved by the spectacle of the "good" women, his nominal heroines, who, from Sophie in *Bressant* onward, are unmitigated bores. Women with a little bit of the devil in them, on the other hand, like Cornelia, stir his pen to individualizing creativity.[43] Cornelia, the beautiful, passionate sister, is the lineal antecedent of such brilliantly portrayed Hawthorne women as Madge Danver in *Garth,* Mary Dene in *Sebastian Strome,* and Perdita Grantley in *Dust.*[44] Unfortunately, Hawthorne's use of the dual-heroine convention as a dramatic form for his investigation of sacred and profane love is not successful. It results generally in a sacrifice of dramatic force, in a vapidity of treatment; one wishes that his heroes would not always wind up in the arms of the fair, and patently insufferable, angel.

A third theme introduced in *Bressant* and repeated unvaryingly in every succeeding novel and romance is the contrast between the purity and innocence of small-town life and the wickedness and corruption of the big city. Hawthorne was not, of course, a reformer complaining of the evils of urbanization; his view is sentimental rather than intellectual, and falls into the stereotype that was only rarely to be questioned before the appearance of Ed Howe, Hamlin Garland, Edgar Lee Masters, and Sherwood Anderson.[45] The village town in *Bressant* is portrayed with the deep affection we may expect from a writer who grew up in Concord; and the country scenes of such novels as *Garth, Fortune's Fool,* and *Beatrix Randolph* are handled with the same loving attention to detail. The evil contrast in this first novel is supplied by New York, where Cornelia is exposed to wicked society life. Even granting Hawthorne's easy adoption of a literary convention, one may question his sincerity here, even more than in the use of the themes discussed above, or certainly more than in his use of supernatural themes. He loved society, adventurous women, and life in such great cities as New York and London. On the other hand—and again granting the convention—one may suspect in this glorification of simple country life a sincere but suppressed longing for the recovery of his childhood.

Hawthorne's own copy of *Bressant* (preserved in the Julian Hawthorne Collection at the University of California, Berkeley) contains scores of the author's changes penciled into the text—changes that, it would appear, were designed for a second edition in 1875 that never was published. Not only is the language tightened and many trite passages omitted in this revision but the melodramatic plot (as distinguished from the narrative of the hero's emotional development in contact with the sisters) is greatly altered and improved. As the plot stands, Professor Valeyon, at whose parsonage Bressant is studying for the ministry, believes the young man to be the son of Abbie, his old love, who had left her husband and now keeps a boardinghouse in the nearby village. Bressant learns the truth from his real mother, the New Yorker Mrs. Vanderplanck, however: that he is her illegitimate son, who had replaced Abbie's dead child in his father's household.[46] In the most powerful scene in the novel, which anticipates the soon-to-be fashionable truth-telling scenes of Ibsen, Bressant savagely berates Abbie for her life of supposed purity, which, he declares, has been the fraudulent cloak of her unforgivable sin in abandoning her sickly child in order to live independently.

Bressant, who had planned to marry Sophie and become a

country parson, finds that in order to fulfill his plans he would have to give up his claim to his father's fortune. Ashamed of his own brutal motives, and shamed even more by the revelation of his true birth, he decides to run away to Europe with Cornelia, who has won his love by "dishonorable intriguing and reckless self-desecration." On the train to New York, a young lad talks to him, and when the boy evidences a mystic acquaintance with the situation, and even goes so far as to point out the lessons of the tale, Bressant realizes that it is the spirit of Sophie, who is lying gravely ill at home, speaking to him. He returns to the parsonage; and although Sophie has died, a ray of sunshine descends from heaven at the close and shines on him, presaging better days. These days will be spent, after all, with Cornelia, for the spectral boy had proclaimed: "Let it be the work of your lives—a work of penitence and punishment—to elevate and refine your love, which has been degraded, until it becomes worthy of the name of love, in its highest sense. You have lowered each other, and now each must help to raise the other up." [47]

Yet *Bressant* is a surprisingly unsentimental work of fiction, despite its "ideal" portraits of Sophie Valeyon and her absent-minded old father, and its tedious conclusion. The unabashed carnality of the love between the hero and Cornelia; the attack upon hypocrisy; the exploration of the phenomena of innocence and sophistication: all of these mark the work's considerable originality. The psychology of love interested Hawthorne, and even though its dramatic form is fairly primitive, its manifestations in the sexual and emotional awakening of Bressant are recounted with great power. Certain scenes, also—Cornelia's rage at losing Bressant's love, Bressant's attack on Abbie—indicate artistic skill in tracing the subtleties of emotional states. These are valuable things to find in a first novel. But the defects of *Bressant* are at least as obvious as its virtues. The style is undistinguished; the ponderousness of Bressant's utterances is rarely offset by the author's wit or anything that can be called a sense of humor. The mechanical contrasts of character, the overly involved and melodramatic plot, the disfiguring elements of the marvelous that enter at the most inappropriate moments, betray an immaturity of dramatic treatment that marks the novel's distinct failure as a work of art.

Equipped with letters of introduction to Henry S. King and other London publishers, and with the manuscript of *Bressant* in his trunk, Julian Hawthorne left New York for Europe about June, 1872. Minne's mother and her two brothers Frederick and Lees either made the journey with the Hawthorne family of three or else joined them later in Dresden. Robert Carter had advised seeing King about the simultaneous publication of *Bressant* in England and America; Carter was to take care of the publication arrangements with *Appleton's,* and Hawthorne's old Harvard friend William G. Peckham, Jr.,[48] was to handle his financial arrangements in America, much as Hillard had managed Hawthorne affairs for the family earlier.

For Hawthorne the trip to England was a sentimental pilgrimage, for he had not visited the country in his second trip to Europe (1868–70). Here his mother had died, and his sister Una was still living, alone, but surrounded by old and steadfast admirers of the Hawthorne family like Robert Browning, Francis Bennoch, and Henry Bright. The Hawthornes landed in Liverpool, on a hot, close June day, and Julian promptly revisited the familiar scenes of his youth, such as Mrs. Blodgett's boardinghouse. It was "unaltered," he said, "but she and her captains were no more. I began to feel very old." [49] He called also on an old college acquaintance named Dudley, now occupying the elder Hawthorne's former position as American consul. The trip to London was exhilarating: "My memory of England flowed back to life once more. The train slipped fast and smooth through this serene beauty: grey castles peeped at us over tree-tops, but habitations were few, small though the ancient island be. . . . The River Trent, like a lusty porpoise in a tranquil nature, neighbored us along the valleys. . . . The deepest solitudes were peopled with the history of a thousand years." [50] From the Queen's Hotel in London, Hawthorne walked out to see the city on a rainy day. "The street names," he recalled, "were a benediction from my forefathers." [51] The names and the magic associations of Old London—Drury Lane, Cornhill, Fleet Street—were to be some of the magnets that eventually drew Hawthorne and his family back from the Continent. Meanwhile, he undoubtedly spent some time with Una in order to introduce her to Minne, now pregnant with their second child, and little Hildegarde, who was just a year old. Then the family was off to Dresden again. Despite the excitements of London, to which Hawthorne was to return within two years for a seven-year sojourn, Dresden still held out the lure of inexpensive living. Besides, perhaps Julian and Minne wished to recapture something of the romance that had first flowered in Saxony three years earlier.

The third and final draft of the 115,000-word novel *Bressant* was completed in Dresden on September 17, 1872, about three months after the Hawthornes moved there. By September 26 King in London had received the book for consideration. On November 9 he accepted it, paying £100 outright. King had been cordial to Hawthorne, and there were to be no difficulties attendant upon the English publication of his first novel, which appeared with the King imprint, "robed in crimson and in two volumes," as Julian Hawthorne put it, on April 22, 1873. But Hawthorne soon ran into difficulties with *Appleton's,* in which magazine he had hoped to serialize *Bressant* before its appearance in book form. On November 14, 1872, Carter wrote to him that after receiving the final draft, William Appleton and Oliver Bell Bunce had decided not to publish *Bressant* in the periodical:

> As a serial in the Journal I confess to a little fear of it. While there is nothing that can be quoted as positively objectionable there is a tone to which some scrupulous readers might demur. W[illiam] A[ppleton] thought it had not incident enough and he doubted its moral tone. Mr. Bunce next read it and came to about the same conclusion as Willie.[52]

On January 30, 1873, Carter reported a turn of events:

> After much effort I have succeeded in getting [Bunce] to accept "Bressant" for the Journal. . . . The Appletons will not only pay for its use in the Journal but a copyright on the volume when reprinted. . . . Write to King and tell him to send proofs of his edition as fast as possible, for I want to make the two editions conform as much as I can.

Carter still retained a few doubts about the tone of *Bressant,* however, and he offered Hawthorne some advice on altering one of his minor characters. The novelist could take such advice in stride; and anyway, he would have been more than willing to oblige the friend who not only got his work printed but wrung his money out of the unsuspectedly tight-fisted Appletons. Hawthorne had published "A Golden Wedding in the Best Society" in the January number of *Appleton's,* and Bunce had promised Carter to send Hawthorne his check promptly. But Carter soon discovered that Bunce was remiss in his promise, and was forced to "stand over him" until he procured the check, which he sent on to his protégé.

Further troubles with *Appleton's Journal* were in store. By May 4, 1873, the novel had concluded its run in the magazine, and Hawthorne was anxious for payment at the agreed-on rate of fifteen dollars a page. On June 27 Carter wrote him of Peckham's difficulties in acting as his agent:

> Peckham some weeks ago began negotiations with Bunce to get pay for "Bressant's" appearance in the Journal. Not succeeding, *why* I can't understand, as Bunce was more than usually incoherent on the subject, he called on me for aid and by vouching for him and his authority and making explanations generally I got a cheque for him for $610, that is 61 pp at $10 a page. I think you ought to be satisfied with $610. The Appletons will not like to pay more as they do not think the novel helps the journal any, but on the contrary rather hurt[s] it by its immorality, of which, really, a good many complaints have been made.

Carter goes on to note that two thousand copies of the first edition of June 7, 1873, had been printed, to be sold at $1.50 a copy, and that since Hawthorne was to receive ten per cent of retail sales, he should be receiving $300 soon. "As the sale has only just begun," Carter concludes, "you will doubtless get much more than that. The English notices are very good and the Appletons have quoted freely from them in their advertisements. I have helped you what I could in a notice in The Sun. George L[athrop] I suppose will send you the Boston notices. None have appeared in the New York papers except a sneering one in the World. . . ." [53] On August 12, 1873, Carter wrote Hawthorne that *Bressant* was continuing to sell, and that the Appletons were certainly advertising it sufficiently.

Despite their reservations about the novel, which Carter had been quite frank in describing, the Appletons obviously hoped to help create a market for Julian Hawthorne's writings in the future through the heavy advertising they poured into *Bressant*. A letter from *Appleton's* on September 12 makes this very point and indicates that the book had already gone into a second printing. Thirty-four hundred copies had now been printed, and five hundred and fifty were left: "It is selling much better than at first, about 750 being sold during last month." Yet Hawthorne was deeply chagrined, first, over what he considered the penny-pinching rate of serialization, and second, at the difficulty Peckham was encountering in securing his checks. A month after the fairly cordial letter from *Appleton's* just cited, Hawthorne wrote to his agent, Peckham, "tearfully grateful" for checks that Peckham, after long delays, had just sent to Dresden, and superimposing a sketch of the Hawthorne family traveling from "Poor House" and "Pawn-Broker's" to a new house and the bank. Hawthorne comments cholerically: "I find no redeeming traits whatever in the Appletons. I have written to them . . . courteously informing them that I should abstain from business relations with them in future. O is there no way of wringing from them their ill-gotten gains?" [54] Hawthorne had become incensed enough to offer his second work, *Idolatry*, to Osgood in America,[55] and persisted in his plan despite a cautionary note from Carter on March 3 of the following year:

"The Appletons seem to feel a good deal disappointed at not getting that great work [Idolatry] and I still think you would have done better to have let them have it. I have an impression somehow that Osgood is not in a sound condition." Later in the 1870's, Hawthorne and the Appletons again joined fortunes. But 1873 marks the first year of real poverty in the Hawthorne household, and the agonizing weeks of waiting upon a publisher's checks.

In April, 1873, Hawthorne had made a brief visit to England in order that he might be present at the taking out of his copyright for Bressant. Henry King greeted his newest novelist with "silken courtesy," invited him to spend the night at his home, and arranged for the English copyright. Hawthorne saw his sister, "who is very thin," he wrote in his journal, "and has a cough: seems happy, however. She is dressed in a black cloak very much as a sister of charity." [56] Back in Dresden, Hawthorne and his family—which now included Minne, Hildegarde, John Francis Bennoch Hawthorne (born December 7, 1872), Mrs. Amelung, Minne's two brothers, and Emma the nurse—were living in a large, handsome house with about a dozen rooms. Hawthorne described Hildegarde in the summer of 1873, when she was not quite two years old, as "highly intellectual, but flat-headed, curly-haired, pretty, and healthy." The firstborn son, "Jack," whose godfather was Francis Bennoch, had "much of the old sea-captain in him. He is bluff and hearty. . . . He is a German, and has something of German ponderousness." [57] Hawthorne's study looked out over a stone church with a massive spire. In a corner stood his father's writing desk, easy chair, and cane-bottomed arm chair.

This year, 1873, was one of exhilaration at the publication of his novel in both England and America, but also one of somber anxiety, primarily financial but partly artistic. Hawthorne's feelings are fully documented in his contemporary journal, and in letters to Una and his Aunt Ebe. The new sense of duty appears in a letter to his sister of February 17, 1873, when he writes that "life has ceased being a picture and a song to me:

truly it is a mighty responsibility." He calls Una and Minne his "gentle-readers," adding that he never should have written anything but for his wife. He is expecting a good public reception for *Bressant,* then running serially.[58] A few days later, Hawthorne wrote at somewhat greater length to his sister that the experience of seeing his first book in print

> has been somewhat dulled, for me, by my previous indulgences in periodical literature. [*Bressant*] is rather morbid, and not crisp and telling. . . . Minne thinks it fine; but, were it not for the consideration of lucre, I would suppress the edition at once. . . . The next book shall be a breeze to blow away the heavy vapors of the first, and make people forget it ever lived. . . . You would be awfully impressed could you behold the accumulation of my notes and reservoirs for the forthcoming work.[59]

In June, three weeks after *Bressant* was finally published in America, its author wrote candidly to Aunt Ebe:

> By this, you have received and read that book of mine—"Bressant". . . . [I] consider it . . . a good book spoiled. But it is not so bad as to forbid the hope that I shall do better: and it was written under many disadvantages, both physical and mental, not likely to be repeated. Meanwhile, the critics are uniformly well disposed towards it and me, and one or two are even incoherently laudatory: for nine tenths of which I have my name to thank—not my work. People would willingly persuade themselves that my "father's mantle has fallen on my shoulders"—as they express it: but I shall never wear mantle of his: it will be cut to another pattern, and woven from quite other material. This I prove, not from the internal evidence of "Bressant," . . . but from the internal evidence of my own mind and tone of thought. . . . I can not reach the serene power and purity of his level, [but] I shall make a respectable place for myself, and one that no one else will [be] likely to contend with me.[60]

The statement as to his own work in relation to his father's is at once modest and confident. It is echoed in Hawthorne's journal of that month:

People are rather desirous than otherwise that I should prove worthy the name I bear : and will cling as long as possible to the belief that I yet may. I may succeed—nay, I will, if I have life and faculties spared me : but my monument will be to the elder Hawthorne's as—a Moorish temple to the Parthenon. I can never reproduce nor even imitate the simple grandeur and pure intuition of that man. And so I shall wisely walk in as divergent a path as is possible, consistently with self-respect and truth.[61]

Hawthorne did not yet understand fully the incredible difficulties that were to attend the attempt to walk in a "divergent path." He was conscious of the problem, obviously, but he felt confident enough in his own powers to surmount it. Yet he could have applied just as well to himself the advice he gave his sister Una when he learned that she had written to the London *Daily News* appealing for funds for her charity work. "Remember," he cautioned her, "that those who send subscriptions are paying you, not for carrying on a charity school, but for being Nathaniel Hawthorne's daughter." [62]

Hawthorne marked his twenty-seventh birthday in his journal in substantially the same sober, sanguine mood :

Yesterday 27 years ago I was born in Boston. I had there a father who was a man of genius. . . . Now I have neither father nor mother ; my sister is living alone in London ; another sister might be dead for all she is to me. . . . I am poor and likely long to be so. . . .

Here I am living in Dresden, married, with two children : and supporting myself and my family on no better prop than this pen. I certainly never was so happy as now, though entirely removed from that world of friends and relatives where twenty-three years of my life were passed. I have no sense of loss, of homesickness, of longing : save the ever-present longing to be a man honored by men, for having done them good that no one else could have done quite so well.[63]

4. *"Idolatry: A Romance"*

Despite the new conditions under which he took up residence in Dresden in 1872, Julian Hawthorne's life there in the ensuing two years was in some respects akin to the carefree days he had spent there earlier. In December of 1872, for example, he attended "the first party of the season" at the home of his friends the Hales, and there were other social events that must have been *de rigueur* for the Hawthornes. There were the functions of the American Club, which he visited occasionally, but which he now found "paralysing and palsying. It is like a stale burial vault, haunted by the memory of past gentility." [64] In May, 1873, the novelist reported to Una that a crew had been formed, consisting of Hawthorne and four Englishmen, and that they often spent the day rowing up the river to a nearby beer garden. Christmas, 1873, was a happy season, for Una journeyed down from London to spend the holiday with the Hawthornes. The Hawthorne physique was not neglected either in this period. The former star of the Harvard gymnasium ran four or five miles every morning, and exercised with a twenty-seven-pound dumbbell; he proudly records, on March 19, 1873, that his upper arm measures $14\frac{1}{4}$ inches, his forearm $11\frac{3}{4}$ inches, and his chest, inflated, 45 inches. "Am thinner than ever before," Hawthorne wrote that March, "but hard and solid all over." Only his smoking seemed to disturb the health-minded young man, for he confided to his journal that he sometimes smoked as many as fifteen cigars a day.

Finally, Dresden was enlivened by the visits of friends. Fred Wilmerding, with whom he had worked for a year in the Dock Department, appeared in Dresden, suddenly developed, Hawthorne says somewhat enviously, "into an agonising swell, with $10,000 a year and unlimited expectations." [65] A college friend named William Morton,[66] with whom Hawthorne was to act out the major tragedy of his life forty years later, also appeared, on his way to the African diamond fields. Morton, who was to become an eminent physician and surgeon, was, like Hawthorne, the son of a powerful and original father. Julian describes him as handsome, quiet, outwardly lazy but inwardly resolute and energetic, and currently involved in a love affair whose outcome was to be unhappy. Another visitor, probably in the early part of 1874, was a college friend identified only as "Damon," who wrote a long and interesting dispatch to the Springfield *Republican* about his encounter with the sometime expatriate. Recollecting that Julian Hawthorne had been advised by his father to earn his living in any field other than authorship, and recalling too that at Harvard Hawthorne had not been of a studious cast of mind, Damon expressed the widespread surprise of his college acquaintances at the new direction of his friend's ambitions. After a long separation Damon found Hawthorne in one of the best houses of one of the finest streets in Dresden, amid luxurious surroundings. He was struck, the newspaper dispatch reads, by the change in his appearance:

> There was the same massive, broad-shouldered form, with limbs like small doric columns, and the head large as Franklin or Webster's surmounting it; but the hearty fullness of face and waist had disappeared, as well as the sun-burnt complexion, and, instead, the sharply chiseled lines and white forehead that told of the hard-worked scholar and writer. Still, the general bearing could not be described as one of debility, or ill-health.

Hawthorne was eager to learn of America "and all the people and things in it," but seemed newly attracted by England. The favorable comments of the English press on *Bressant* had surprised him, in contrast to the rather sharp criticisms, on the grounds of indecency primarily, leveled at the book by such American sources as the Boston *Advertiser* and the New York *Nation*. Though believing that the English were strongly partisan and insular, he felt that they seemed even readier to acknowledge merit in an American author than in one of their own. He had even "quite determined . . . to leave Dresden, and go to live in London, where he would make friends and be supported in his writing, as well as checked in a proper manner by the best literary opinion of the age." Damon's conversation with Hawthorne ranged over such topics as the superiority of Nuremberg beers and the identity of Bacon and Shakespeare, a view that was part of the Hawthorne family inheritance. Julian Hawthorne discussed his reading in philosophy and especially metaphysics, which was to be a lifelong concern, and noted his particular admiration for Goethe, Emerson, and Thackeray.[67] Damon found his discussions of authors full of a "readiness of expression and nicety of criticism that nearly equalled the manner of an essayist." [68]

As early as February, 1873, Hawthorne was hard at work on *Idolatry*. Probably he had begun gathering materials for this romance as early as November, 1872, a few months after he had completed the last version of *Bressant*. Most of 1873 and part of 1874 were devoted to this new work, which eventually was rewritten four times,[69] and completed on April 8, 1874. By March 10, however, King had received almost all of the manuscript, and it is thus possible that Hawthorne made final changes and corrections. *Idolatry* was dedicated warmly to Robert Carter, the man, Julian Hawthorne declared, "responsible for its writing. Your advice and encouragement first led me to book-making." In his preface to the work, Hawthorne modestly pleads his case for the acceptance of *Idolatry* as a simple Gothic entertainment:

> The first duty of the fiction-monger . . . is, to be amusing; to shrink at no shifts which shall beguile the patient into procrastinating escape until the moment be gone by. The gentle reader will not too sternly set his face against such artifices, but, so they go not the length of fantastically presenting phenomena inexplicable upon any common-sense hypothesis, he will rather lend himself to his own beguilement.[70]

The "artifices" of *Idolatry* are little short of extraordinary. Taking a different tack from the essentially realistic *Bressant,* this work introduces a wildly romantic tale, complete with many discernible Gothic manifestations, into a peaceful New Jersey landscape. It is one of the worst of Julian Hawthorne's stories, despite the inordinate amount of time and creative energy poured into it. The biggest difficulty with *Idolatry* is its mixture of the serious and the ludicrous, the never-quite-sublime and the patently absurd. A brief account of the plot will clarify this difficulty.

The opening chapter of *Idolatry* immediately creates the mood of a strange and mysterious, and also somewhat ridiculous, enchantment. In a Boston hotel, asleep, lies Dr. Hiero Glyphic. He is wearing a magical diamond ring, in whose depths the author deciphers his previous history for the benefit of the reader. Dr. Glyphic had, many years before, brought to America an Egyptian youth named Manetho, who chose to become a priest. His intended bride fell in love with, and married, a man named Thor Helwyse, and bore him twins before she died. Having vowed vengeance on the Helwyse clan, Manetho, with the aid of a disfigured nurse whom he did not recognize as his old inamorata Salome, stole Helwyse's supposed daughter Gnulemah.[71] In Dr. Glyphic's strange house on the New Jersey Palisades, he brought her up—"poisonous" in her innocence of wrong—as a supposed incarnation of evil.

Elements of Gothic romanticism begin to emerge most clearly when Balder Helwyse, Thor's son, seeking to claim his share of the Glyphic fortune and not knowing that the old Egyptologist is dead, arrives at the mansion. In the oak-paneled hall "the essence of mediaeval England lingered," but each room in this castle with a Gothic exterior is decorated in the style of a different country. In a tomblike Egyptian chamber, Helwyse finds the mummy of Dr. Glyphic himself. Leading off from the Egyptian room is the priest's secret retreat, reached only through a sliding panel. The old nurse Salome possesses "an eye which, two hundred years ago, would have convicted its owner of witchcraft."[72] But the most unusual Gothic feature of the tale is the nature of Manetho's revenge, for he plans to marry the unsuspecting twins, Gnulemah and Balder, to each other. This Romantic incest theme is partly negated by the ironic revelation that Balder's twin sister actually had died in a fire when a year old, and that Manetho had thus brought up as the instrument of his revenge his own illegitimate daughter by Salome. Yet, since much is made of Manetho's own passion for Gnulemah prior to the revelation, perhaps the theme is more subtle than may at first be supposed. A deep darkness attends the crucial events here, for as the romance ends, with Manetho dying, Gnulemah is blinded by a great lightning storm. Hawthorne intrudes: "Had that vast cloud come to shut out [Manetho's] soul from heaven, and was its mighty voice uttering the sentence of his condemnation?" [73]

Gnulemah is interesting only in so far as she is allied to the persecuted maidens of Gothic romanticism, and like Rappaccini's daughter, to the poison-maid motif in folk literature. In such passages as the following one describing her, Hawthorne descended to the nadir of his talents: "Womanly she was—instinct with that tender, sensitive power, the marvelous gift of God to woman only, which almost moves the sick man to bless his sickness. A holy gift,—surely the immediate influx of Christ's spirit. Man knows it not, albeit when he and woman become more closely united than now, he may attain to share the Divine prerogative." [74] Helwyse is a more successful character. He is linked with Hawthorne's Byronic heroes, for "he aimed at knowledge and power beyond recognized human reach." At one point the figure of Raskolnikov is superimposed upon the Byronic ideal: "Possessed of a strong, comprehensive mind, [Helwyse] had made a providence of himself; confounded intelligence with integrity; used the moral principle not as a law of action but as a means of insight." [75] Helwyse is ruled by his intellect, his aesthetic sense, and his search for power. "God," declares the author, "was his elder brother—himself in some distant but attainable condition." Manetho's view of sin points up the spiritual kinship of hero and villain: "I will admit," he tells Balder, "that the vast majority of criminals are weak and foolish; but that does not affect the dignity of the true sinner,—he who sins from exalted motives. Ignorance is the only real crime, polluting deeds that, wisely done, are sublime. Sin is culture." [76] Against these values Hawthorne places the primacy of love and the universe of feelings within, a universe where "the cockle-shell of mental attainments is lost like an asteroid in the abyss of space." The hero's egoism is finally conquered by his love for Gnulemah; but for Manetho there is only retribution.

Despite minor virtues, such as the character of the believably villainous Egyptian priest, the romance is enervated not only by the absurd plot but by the interminable and sentimental digressions. The critical reader must agree with the self-deprecatory Hawthorne in his preface to *Idolatry,* when he states, "Not seldom does it happen that what he [the writer] proffers as genuine arcana of imagination and philosophy affects the reader as a dose of Hieroglyphics and Balderdash." [77] Yet in some ways *Idolatry* marks an advance over *Bressant;* it is much more ambitious in its attempt to fuse philosophy with romance, somewhat in the static, moralizing vein of *The Marble Faun.* The young man was obviously entranced by new, large, vaguely Swedenborgian ideas. He could not, however, dramatize them successfully with his essentially foolish plot and characters; the latter lack the nobility and depth of perception of even the weakest of Nathaniel Hawthorne's major figures. In other respects it is clear that *Idolatry* showed an unfortunate direction for Julian Hawthorne's muse to take. The glimmerings of supernaturalism in *Bressant*—the clairvoyance of Sophie, the hero's "magnetism," and the spectral appearance of the boy— are here succeeded by all the outpourings of the romantic fancy: enchanted rings, tombs and crypts in the Gothic castle, immurement, the incest motif, murder and revenge, Byronic hero and dark priestly villain: in a word, all those barefaced sensational things that were so to cheapen Julian Hawthorne's art in the ensuing decades. In the long view the failure of *Idolatry* could be minimized if it were merely a way of working youthful excesses out of the writer's system; but unfortunately, the tone and compulsive themes of the fiction stemmed unerringly from Hawthorne's view of spiritual reality and his dubious interpretation of his father's art. The *Atlantic Monthly* commented sagely that "the author seems less to be working off his likeness to his father than working into it," and added that *Idolatry* even verged occasionally upon a "burlesque" of the elder Hawthorne's "exquisite fantasies." [78] Hawthorne's later fiction was to be memorable only—but alas, even then not always—when the supernaturalist excrescences typified by the themes, characters, and setting of *Idolatry* were abandoned.

Julian Hawthorne's romance was reviewed by at least forty newspapers and magazines in America and England, many more than had noticed *Bressant*. Reviews ranged from the rhapsodic to the damning, with almost every reviewer making the already stale comment about the father's mantle descending (or not descending) upon the shoulders of the son. The following portion of the intelligent review in the influential *Athenaeum* of London may be considered fairly typical:

All of us who have either known Nathaniel Hawthorne personally or through his works, are watching with keen interest, and no less keen jealousy, Julian Hawthorne's literary career. Has the cloud woven mantle of the father really fallen on the shoulders of his son? Are the rare and special gifts which men call genius an hereditary possession? . . . Or, on the other hand, have we here only literary aptitude and facility, which, though good in their way, are of inferior worth, and will but dim the lustre of a great name? . . . There are reminiscences, as it were, of Nathaniel Hawthorne in the book. There is something of the same fantastic imagination. But the contrast is greater than the resemblance. The power is not restrained. The moralizing, which, in the father, took the form of a suggestive hint or stray misgiving, too often becomes a wild and random declamation. The imagination runs riot, and the fantastic element is at times exaggerated into the grotesque. . . . A sensual coarseness peeps out at times. . . . In Julian Hawthorne's book there are passages a woman should hardly read aloud. . . . There are passages of almost exquisite beauty here and there. . . . Careful work and self-restraint are what are mainly needed; with them, Julian Hawthorne will do much; without them, each novel he writes will be more extravagant and less powerful. [79]

These themes were all repeated with variations in the other reviews. Thus the New York *Times* found the book "extravagant, audacious, imperfect, but fascinating," and the *Academy* censured its "morbid and unhealthy" moral tone. The *Sun* was severely critical, largely of style, condemning the "boldness, recklessness, want of discrimination, and bad taste in the use of words." The *Galaxy* praised Hawthorne's "inventive power," and the *Saturday Review* attacked his use of the romantic mode as excessively improbable. Hawthorne's aunt, Elizabeth Palmer Peabody, writing in *The Western,* was all idolatry: "Besides cultivated senses, brilliant imagination, and spiritual insight, there are sentences indicating a reflective wisdom and moral and religious experience, hardly to be looked for in combination with the other gifts of so young a man." Francis Bennoch was moved to write the author: "The deep, daring soundings of human passion, and general human nature, have so far as I know, never been sounded so deep before. . . . The style is admirable, the language clear, terse, idiomatic and wonderfully varied. . . . *Bressant* was great. *Idolatry* is ten times greater." [80] Henry A. Bright, in another letter to Hawthorne, was more restrained: "I have read both your novels greedily. —I am obliged to say that I don't like 'Idolatry' as well as 'Bressant,' but it is impossible not to recognise the very considerable power both novels show,—a power which with the necessary restraint is, I am sure, capable of great work." That Hawthorne was himself conscious of the defects of *Idolatry* is betrayed by a significant remark in his journal on the tenth anniversary of his father's death, in 1874. "This tenth anniversary," he notes, "reaches me far below the point I ought to have attained." [81] Two years later he wrote to Carter, the man "responsible for its writing," who had reacted to *Idolatry* with frigidity. "The execution," he declared, "is in some places atrociously bad—I suppose because I could not help feeling that I was writing in the teeth of the general sympathy—a very dismal weakness in me. It was also written five years too soon." [82] The most charitable judgment today would be that the novel had been best not written at all.

5. "Saxon Studies"

From the weird and absurd fantasy of *Idolatry,* Julian Hawthorne turned to the rich fabric of contemporary manners. On June 6, 1874, he first noted his plan to write "a dozen chapters on German life." Actually, however, he had already written several sketches based on his earlier and later Dresden experiences. The first of these were articles printed in the form of letters to the London *Times* late in 1872; and two sketches, "A Golden Wedding in the Best Society" and "A Feast of Blood," appeared in American magazines in 1873. By July of 1874 he was writing to Una that "I am busy . . . writing that Book on German life, which flowers beneath my hand quite promisingly. I think it will be more popular than my unfortunate novels. I am also making notes for my next romance." [83] *Saxon Studies* began appearing in Alexander Strahan's *Contemporary Review* in November of 1874 and ran through the issue of August, 1875. Serial portions also were printed in *Living Age* and the *Eclectic Magazine.*

Hawthorne's preface to *Saxon Studies* indicates that he was not writing a "travel book" or a detailed and objective evaluation of Saxon life itself. He admits that his "interest in Saxony and the Saxons is of the most moderate kind,—certainly not enough to provoke a treatise upon them. They are as dull and featureless a race as exists in this century, and the less one has to do with them, the better." [84] His declared aim was to find a concrete nucleus around which he could group his thoughts, fancies, and observations of human nature. He notes that the chapters of *Saxon Studies,* while appearing serially, were bitterly denounced in the Dresden journals, but adds that he himself would be "hugely diverted to find himself masquerading in a character so alien to his ambition and capacity as that of a patcher-up of dilapidated manners and morals." [85] These protestations may be sincere, although there is a good deal of the disgruntled visitor shaking the dust of an unhappy experience from his feet in the pages of *Saxon Studies*. The book, patched as it is from notebook jottings and from memory, has a mixed tone. Many of its observations of human nature are trite and sentimental, on a par with the typical pseudophilosophical passages of *Idolatry;* but the descriptions of Saxon life and customs are vivid and telling, and through these descriptions runs an irony (occasionally vindictive) that is itself uneven—sometimes heavy-handed, sometimes subtle.

Hawthorne surveys this "flattened swarm of mean-featured houses spreading dingily on both sides of a muddy river"—its streets and squares, its beer gardens, its masquerades, its opera performances—and finds the whole panorama wanting in grace, in distinctiveness, in beauty. Thus he observes that "the Saxons have a less correct ear for music than any people with which I am acquainted"; [86] that Dresden's "only distinctive characteristics . . . are its ubiquitous evil odor and its omnipresent dirty plaster"; [87] and the like. These remarks are, to be sure, tempered with others that give some credit to the quality of Dresden life. But typically, as in describing the Saxon soldiers, Hawthorne praises with his right hand while smiting with his left:

> Saxon soldiers are the best in the world. They can swallow most discipline. They submit to so much stuffing with rules and regulations, great and small, that little of the original creature is left save organic life and uniform. They are a docile sort of Frankensteins. . . . Much is signified in the fact that their captains address them as "children," while we Americans, and our English friends, try to inspire our warriors by appeals to their "manhood." Men, forsooth! Such is the fruit of illogical sentiment. But persist in calling a person child, and treating him so, and presently he will share our view of the matter, and thus become fit for the camp. [88]

Hawthorne's final judgment in the book is probably the same that he imposed when the Hawthorne family left Dresden forever. It is a summary of the attraction that the city had held for him, and of the final disappointment he came to feel:

> The city charms at first sight—at a distance—or mirrored in the glass of the imagination. There is a mirage of grace and neatness about it that captivates us unawares. Howbeit, a nearer acquaintance dispels all illusions; we discover various unlovely traits, intrinsic no less than accidental. The place is in bad hands—vulgarly companioned and beset—invested with a questionable atmosphere—and what is worse, does not seem to mind it. It is impossible to enjoy its beauties apart from its defects: the latter are innate, the former purely superficial. It is the more disappointing from having bid fair to interest us; but the parting disappointment is the saddest of all,—that so few and slight regrets attend our last farewell! [89]

Although *Saxon Studies* was widely read serially, it quickly slipped into oblivion, primarily because both the English and American publishers, Strahan and Osgood, went bankrupt in 1876, and thus circulated only review copies of the book. Hawthorne himself is authority for the fact that the book was banned in Germany by order of the emperor.[90] This oblivion is all the more unfortunate because Hawthorne thought *Saxon Studies,* which was part of the not-so-innocent-abroad tradition, "the best book I ever wrote." [91] It reminded some reviewers of the elder Hawthorne's *Our Old Home,* others of Emerson's *English Traits,* a book Hawthorne greatly admired, and still others of Henry Mayhew's *German Life and Manners* (1864), a book equally critical of the Saxons but founded more solidly on factual observation. The *Academy* conceded to the book certain picturesque passages and some truthfulness, but deplored the total denigration of Saxon taste and public behavior, and the excess and exaggeration that gave a misleading impression of German life. The *Dresdener Nachrichten* reviewed viciously this "outrageous libel" by a "bumptious American" against not only Dresden but the whole of Germany and, in a curious parallel to English-language criticisms, traced the son's xenophobia to certain remarks made by Nathaniel

Hawthorne in *Our Old Home*. The most interesting review of the book appeared in the *Nation,* which, after having dismissed *Bressant* as containing "a morbid fingering of unclean emotions," [92] had ignored the apppearance of Hawthorne's next novel. The review was written by Henry James, who had already been negative about *Idolatry* in the columns of the *Atlantic.* James found in *Saxon Studies* a pervasive "immaturity of thought" and "combined ill-humor and conscious cleverness." The critic regretted Hawthorne's failure to report on private manners and morals, on opinions, conversations, and the theater, literature, press, and the arts. [93] He had obviously missed the point of Hawthorne's preface.

By the end of 1874 the Hawthornes were in England at last. They had probably wanted to move earlier, if we can credit Damon's interview with Hawthorne on this point. But Minne had again been pregnant during the early part of 1874. Henry, the Hawthornes' third child, was born in Dresden on June 8. In July, Hawthorne wrote to Una that they were "of course in extreme pecuniary distress," but that Minne was "painting silk fans like a maniac" to add to their income. The family, which, with Mrs. Amelung and her boys, now numbered eight, left for England in September, and by January 1, 1875, had moved to their permanent home there, Ways End, Belmont, Twickenham.

4

The English Years

1. Twickenham and London

The feeling that had led Nathaniel Hawthorne to seek out his "Old Home," and that had led Sophia and Una Hawthorne to return to London in 1870, was probably still viable in the romancer's son when he began his seven years' residence in England. Added to this impulse—which was not one of unqualified admiration, as we shall see—was Julian Hawthorne's own realistic view of his place in the socio-literary milieu of the time. He was to write, in 1887, that "the true rewards of literature, for men of limited calibre, are the incidental ones,—the valuable friendships and the charming associations which it brings about."[1] Forty years later, in *Shapes That Pass*, his opinion had scarcely changed. He felt that his chief profit in writing his early books

> was the introduction to English society which my name gave me. The literary profession is always good for that, and if the writer's father was also a writer, and distinguished, so much the better. A man's third and fourth decades are his society period, or so I found them, and it was both pleasant and fortunate for me that I passed the better part of them in England. For not often in English history have more men and women worth

knowing been gathered in London than during the last quarter of the nineteenth century.[2]

There were other reasons for Hawthorne's choice of England, in addition to those of sentiment and a perhaps craven exploitation of the prominence of the family name there. He planned, for example, to offer a home to his sister Una. He thought that his income would increase;[3] and even though he did not expect his financial difficulties to disappear, perhaps he felt that life in London could not be more impoverishing to his spirit than life in merely "inexpensive" Dresden. He had grown very weary of that city, as *Saxon Studies* attests, and desired, as Damon had recorded, to be "checked in a proper manner by the best literary opinion of the age." There was, finally, a good business reason for Hawthorne's decision to make England his home. Several years before, in May, 1868, the House of Lords had "concluded that an alien became entitled to copyright by first publishing in the United Kingdom provided he were at the time of publication anywhere in the British dominions. . . . The best means of securing a valid British copyright was, of course, to be in England when one's book appeared."[4] Hawthorne had made the long trip from Dresden to London twice already, in order to secure the copyrights for *Bressant* and *Idolatry;* in England, he now certainly felt, he could more closely superintend his business affairs. An authority on American writers in England during this period declares that such authors as the two Hawthornes, Henry James, James Russell Lowell, Bret Harte, and Joaquin Miller "profited by residing in Europe at a time when certain of their works were first published in London, and thus enjoyed, along with royalties presumably greater than the average for Americans, publication in a more dignified and expensive format and so, often received, through the business connections of their publishers, more favorable attention in the review columns of newspapers and magazines."[5] In short, all roads led to London.

On October 11, 1874 Minne wrote Una a long letter[6] (with

a scribbled greeting from Julian to his "Dear Old Unus Vicu-
nas San Salvador") that gives a pleasant picture of the discovery of the family's new home. Minne first alluded to her plan
for a long lease, adding with unconscious irony to Una, "So
you see you have the prospect of a long life in England before
you." She went on:

> We found a most delightful little detached villa in Twickenham,
> situate (to be English) at the end of a cul de sac, so that there is
> no noise of passing carriages to annoy Julian; with a most
> charming little lawn planted with standard roses, in front, a
> small conservatory at the side and another garden at the back.
> . . . Inside we have on the ground floor (there is no basement)
> a good-sized drawing room, dining room and study, kitchen, scul-
> lery, larders, &c. Upstairs there are four large rooms, for nurs-
> eries and bedrooms and one little room that is to be a morning
> room for you and me; in the attic are four rooms. . . . The rent,
> my dear, is but £55 a year! $275 in our money! [7]

The Hawthorne home at Twickenham was some twelve miles
south by rail from Waterloo Station in London. But frequently,
after a night of London dinners and revelry, Hawthorne would
walk home through Richmond, and over Richmond Bridge:

> The Thames here [he recalled] is at its most lovely; to the left
> embowering trees overhang the river-bend and the path that
> leads to Kew Gardens; on the right, topping the hill, was the
> Star and Garter Inn, with a rearward of vigorous oaks. . . . It
> was often my fortune to cross the bridge about sunrise of a June
> morning. . . . The shadows streamed far westward from the
> brightness. . . . The rowboats moored along the banks hardly
> swayed in the glassy stillness; even the anglers were not yet
> abroad, and the colours were rich and sweet on sky and stream.
> From the bridge the reaches of the road passed a grey old
> church amid its gravestones, traversed the little town with its
> sleeping shops, and leaving the residence of the French princes
> on the left, with cedars of Lebanon rising above its high wall,
> came out in the open, with Pope's villa in the distance, and the
> fantastic castle which Horace Walpole built at Strawberry Hill. [8]

The road then opened into a region of stuccoed dwellings, each in its little walled garden; at the end of the road was Hawthorne's home, Ways End, the name inscribed in capitals on the square gatepost. The landlord, Captain Sleasby, had a "poisonous predilection" for Hawthorne's society, a feeling not reciprocated; nearby also lived a Dr. Diamond, a venerable figure who operated a private lunatic asylum on the premises and who proved a gracious and hospitable friend. Another acquaintance in nearby Teddington was the novelist Richard D. Blackmore.

The Hawthorne entourage had settled at Twickenham attracted by the low rent and by the seclusion. It was "a good place for story-writing," Hawthorne recalled, "and for visits of friends who were friends enough to come out from London." [9] The daily routine was simple, and was recorded in Hawthorne's notebook as the "Order of Exercises":

8	Out of Bed. Bath. Coffee.
9–2	Write 5 pages of fiction.
2–5	Lunch, read, or write reviews.
5–7	Exercise. Dress.
7:30–8:30	Dinner
8:30–11	Ad Libitum. Bed.[10]

Hawthorne's reading at Twickenham continued, as it had earlier in the 1870's, to range over the whole of literature. In 1880 he compiled for his own amusement a list of the authors he had enjoyed reading. Nathaniel Hawthorne, Emerson, Carlyle, and Thackeray figure most prominently in his list. Of Dickens he enjoyed only "pages here and there," and of George Eliot, "*Romola,* perhaps." The list, while enormous and varied, is nevertheless rather predictable: Shakespeare, Heine, and Poe; Balzac, Dumas, and Sand; Sterne, Fielding, and Smollett; "Monk" Lewis; Tennyson and Browning.[11]

There was always time for the nursery, however, and Julian and Minne enjoyed writing down the "Sayings of the Children." [12] Hildegarde, wrote her father when she was about four years old, "laughs and tells little stories in the most affectedly vivacious style, throwing her head on one side, casting down her eyes, laughing lightly. Sometimes is excessively impertinent without really meaning to be so. . . . She is very sweet with Henry, taking quite a maternal interest in him. . . . But Jack and she quarrel dreadfully; one always wants what the other has; only yesterday she made a great mark under his eye with a pencil." But she was also "growing quite poetical, makes little rhymes, likes to hear Tennyson read." The father noted in 1876 that "Henry is growing a bright fearless boy, Hildegarde is portentously clever and old womanly; Jack still timid but very witty." At Christmas of that year there were two horses for the boys, but Hawthorne writes, "I had to punish [Hildegarde] for hurting Jack. She pleaded that he had teased her, saying 'No, Miss,' and making faces at her. She also said, 'Well, I kissed him afterwards; I always kiss him after I slap him.' " A fourth child, Gwendolyn, was born to the Hawthornes in October, 1877; their fifth child, Beatrix, in 1878; and Frederick in 1880. The last child born to them in Europe, Gladys, lived only two years, and died in America.

The friends who were "friends enough to come out from London" were numerous, and the house at Ways End echoed with discussions far into the night. Hawthorne's closest companions in England were Richard Halkett Lord, William Jerrold Dixon, and Charles Dickens the younger—all, it is to be noted, sons of famous men like Hawthorne himself. The first, Lord, a stepson of the founder of *Punch,* was under forty, black-haired, and full-bearded; his was a strong, sensual, intellectual nature, Hawthorne thought. His vigorous and adventurous life appealed to the American's imagination, as did his broad knowledge and biting conversation. Lord was poor, and escaped the debtor's law only by having a room at the Temple. In 1887 Lord and Julian Hawthorne met again in America, and the old English friend was adopted into the Hawthorne residence at Sag Harbor, Long Island, for the next six years. Willie Dixon was a gentle man habitually bullied and wronged by his father, the now-forgotten writer Hapworth Dixon. He was attracted to the stage, and he and Hawthorne once collaborated on a four-act comedy of English art and society life designed for Ellen Terry. Dixon died suddenly in Ireland in the summer of 1879.[13] The third close friend was Charley Dickens, who had inherited from his father the editorship of *All the Year Round,* and perhaps some of the same problems that Julian faced as the son of Nathaniel Hawthorne. Charles Dickens the younger was "plain and likable, and had no small literary ability," Hawthorne wrote, "but his father's renown took his own breath away." [14] Dickens wrote a popular yet erudite *Dictionary of London,* and was one of the lively group that congregated at the Savage Club, which had been "instituted for the association of gentlemen connected professionally with literature, art, the drama, or science." The club was the center of well-bred Bohemianism in the 1870's: the Savages "demanded brains, talent, genius even, but not mastership; and nothing would do if the applicant were not a good fellow. Tennyson, Browning, Millais, Tadema, for instance, were not on the roster; but the Club mothered and nursed men less effulgent, but of wit, humour, and capacity; not of the heights nor depths, but of the middle parts of fortune which Shakespeare approved." [15]

Another excellent friend during Julian Hawthorne's English sojourn was the poet Coventry Patmore, whom he met for the first time in 1877 at Hastings, the ancient Channel town. Patmore was then about fifty,

> his grey hair thick and wavy, his young, dark eyes sparkling, laughing, piercing, sympathising under that great four-cornered forehead, his face tapering to the pointed chin. . . . He stands on the hearth-rug, . . . and from him come waves of speech, joyous, meditative, tender, ironic, philosophic, or mere sparkling narrative.[16]

Patmore graciously welcomed the son of the novelist he had met in 1859, when he was assistant librarian at the British Museum. In the late 1870's he had become something of a

Swedenborgian, and thus found a common ground of thought with Hawthorne, who had studied Swedenborg intensively. The two men also enjoyed tramping over the downs near Hastings, and along the beach. Occasionally, at Patmore's house, Hawthorne would meet Monsignor Capel, who had guided the poet into the Catholic church. "Capel had great qualities," Hawthorne wrote, "and his conversation was soothing and beguiling, especially after . . . Madeira. 'I have told Hawthorne,' said Patmore, 'that a man with a mind and imagination like his has no business to be out of the Church'; and Capel said: 'He is like some others—he is in the Church without knowing it!' The truth was, I thought, that the chief attraction of his faith, for Patmore, was that it kept his imagination and poetic faculties ever at work making its fallacies appear logical and true. And I fancy the Monsignor perceived this, and took care not to disturb him by insisting upon points of dogma." [17]

The roll call of the great and near-great whom Julian Hawthorne also knew in his English years is impressive. His first book, *Bressant,* had been benignly noticed in the London *Spectator* by its editor, Richard H. Hutton, who began his review, "Here is a case for Mr. Galton!"—an ominous chord, perhaps, but not an unfriendly one for Hutton to strike. Hawthorne wrote requesting to see Hutton, whom he found in his dark, book-littered den on Wellington Street in the Strand. The novelist thought Hutton a man of profound literary erudition, with a kind of "fierce, shy heartiness" in him. He and Hawthorne became good friends; he was "for ten years a rock in the maelstrom for me," the latter recalled. [18] At the time of Hawthorne's first appearance at the *Spectator* offices, it was probably the most influential of the weekly journals, and the American writer was undoubtedly delighted at his appointment to its book-reviewing staff. Hutton took Hawthorne around to his club, the Garrick, where he renewed his acquaintance with Eustace Clare Grenville Murray, the writer, diplomat, and founder of the London *World,* whom Hawthorne had first met in Dresden when Murray was an honorary member of the American Club. Julian was also befriended by the delightful family of Thomas Henry Huxley, whom he visited in their home at St. John's Wood. There were the already venerable figures Anthony Trollope, Wilkie Collins, and George Eliot, whom Hawthorne met briefly in drawing rooms or newspaper offices. Matthew Arnold, whose social graciousness Hawthorne admired quite as much as his chilly intellect, was a somewhat closer acquaintance. At the house of Baron Trübner, the publisher, Hawthorne met George Meredith, whom he came to know very well; Hawthorne joined in the "Sunday Tramps," led by Leslie Stephen, editor of *The Cornhill,* and emanating from Meredith's home at Box Hill. At the drawing rooms in Mayfair, in Bloomsbury, and in Kensington, Hawthorne also met and admired Whistler, DuMaurier, and such lesser artists as Fred Leighton, Sir Lawrence Alma-Tadema, and Howard Helmick; it was DuMaurier, Hawthorne recalled, who made him at home in English society. Hawthorne came to know well Richard Monckton Milnes, Lord Houghton, an old friend of his father, and thus as reliable a bulwark to him as those other close family friends Bennoch and Bright. There were lively receptions held by Christopher Murray,[19] and more humble ones at the home of Robert Edward Francillon, a once popular novelist and journalist, "steady, standardised, meritorious, uninspired." [20] He and Hawthorne, five years his junior, met probably late in 1876; Francillon's preoccupation with the occult, which extended to casting elaborate horoscopes for his friends, undoubtedly interested Julian Hawthorne. He was also flattered by such letters from the "established" Francillon as the following:

> I am very glad indeed that you wrote "The Rose of Death" and "Calbot's Rival," not only for my own sake but for the sake of the Dream Literature which is in need of a master. That Third Presence in the latter is the most fascinating of all nightmares.

. . . My hope and belief that you are destined to be our guide through Dreamland is not altogether comfortable concerning what we may find there.[21]

At the home of George Smalley and his wife, Hawthorne conversed amiably with Robert Browning, another old friend of his father and his sister Una. "Browning had become another Browning," Hawthorne remembered, quite different from the figure of the Florence days. "His silver hair was brushed close to his head, his short, pointed beard was carefully barbered, his silk hat and all below it were of Piccadilly and Pall Mall, he was staid, grave, urbane, polished; he was a rich banker, he was a perfected butler, no one would have suspected him of poetry." [22] An affinity for port wine, rather than for literary discussion, drew the two men together.

Within the inner circle of his English friends, then—Lord, Dixon, Dickens, Patmore—and also within the outer circle, which included the illustrious company just enumerated, Julian Hawthorne moved comfortably and easily, enjoying the high art of conversation in a conversational age, and mingling, perhaps always with an eye to his literary fortunes, with the most important figures in the world of publishing, literature, and the arts. At the teas, the dinners, the receptions, and the balls, his name, and also his work, served as immediate assurance of acceptance and warm hospitality. None of Nathaniel Hawthorne's shrinking timidity in social intercourse had descended to his son.

Yet there is a darker side to the picture, one that fails to emerge in the charming English recollections in *Shapes That Pass* written some sixty years later. As a child, we recall, Julian had been anything but a partisan of the English. Now that childish hostility had a more concrete basis. He wrote to his good friend Edward Carter in January, 1876—just a year after he had settled in Twickenham:

Now that I have begun to get the better of Fate, I am beginning to look towards home. . . . I want to tread on these English before I leave them, and I think a year will be sufficient. England, unless, as Landor says, you have a solar system of your own, is a dreary place. If you can afford to knock every body down that you meet, and drink whiskey with them afterwards, you can be happy. If not, you meet them on the uncongenial side, and are depressed. When I leave here, I shall like them much better than I do now.[23]

The departure, however, was to be delayed six years; and in the meantime the continuity of Hawthorne's feelings may be observed in his calling the English "detestable" two years later in a letter to—of all people—Henry James. One shudders to think of Hawthorne actually having written, as he planned, a study of the English as a successor to *Saxon Studies*.

With most of the well-known Americans in London at this period, Julian Hawthorne was on the friendliest of terms.[24] There was, for example, Joaquin Miller, a fellow member of the Savage Club,

> a licensed libertine, charming, amiable, and harmless, amusing the Club and himself by costuming his part as Poet of the Sierras: sombrero, red shirt open at the neck, flowing scarf and sash, trousers tucked into spurred boots, long hair down over his shoulders, and a great blond beard. 'It helps sell the poems, boys!' he would say, 'and it tickles the duchesses'. . . . The Club understood him and approved his dramatisations and Munchausenisms.[25]

At his home in Twickenham, Hawthorne entertained such American visitors as Charles Dudley Warner and the Shakespearean editor Richard Grant White, with whom Hawthorne took several memorable walks in the neighborhood.[26] The greatest of the American writers in England in this period was, of course, Henry James, whom Hawthorne met at the homes of Wemyss Mackenzie, George Smalley, Lord Houghton, and others. When James came into a London drawing room, Hawthorne recalled, he "would be surrounded by group after group of admirers, in whose presence he could not overcome a naïve embarrassment. He talked hesitatingly, as if seeking the right word; his rather prominent brown eyes, the eyes of the seer, avoided the questioning gaze, turning aside, turning to the ornaments on the ceiling; he smiled deprecatingly at all compliments, making a bon-mot in self-defence; and after half an hour, he would leave with some excuse about getting back to his books." [27] Hawthorne had known James from his teens in New England, having gone to school with two of Henry's brothers. Since then their careers had followed singularly divergent paths, Hawthorne's in the direction of the popular and romantic, James's in the direction of the intellectually and emotionally refined, the artistically dedicated.[28] James, it will be recalled, had written a rather cruel review of Julian Hawthorne's *Saxon Studies* for the *Nation* in 1876.

In 1878 James was asked to prepare a study of Nathaniel Hawthorne for the Macmillan series, and he turned to the novelist's son for firsthand information. After a cordial exchange of notes, the following letter was received by Hawthorne at Hastings, where he was spending the winter of 1878–79:

> I must thank you without delay for your very liberal response to my appeal, and your kind allusions to hospitality. . . . I am well aware that it will not be an easy matter to give an account of your father's life and genius save on a very modest scale. I have undertaken the task reluctantly, and chiefly for three reasons: —I. The Editor desired greatly it should be done, and was evidently determined it should be by some one. II.—It seemed to me that, this being the case, it should, if possible, be done by an American. III. I could think (in all modesty) of no American who didn't seem likely to do it worse than I.—For, with 1000 thanks for your compliment to my own critical powers, I must say that I don't think we *are* a race of accomplished critics,—I feel as if, also, I ought to notify you that I don't find the circumambient people a "detestable" one. On the contrary! I could never bring myself to live, regularly, among a people I should distinctly dislike,—it would be too gross a wrong both to myself and to them. But we will talk of that too.[29]

James did go to Hastings, "in doubt and distress," Hawthorne recalled. They took long walks together along the downs and the beach, and James repeated, "I don't want to do it. I'm not competent: and yet, if I don't, some Englishman will do it worse than I would. Your father was the greatest imaginative writer we had, and yet, I feel that his principle was wrong. . . . Imagination is out of place; only the strictest realism can be right. But how can a barely known scribbler like me offer criticism on him?" [30] When the book appeared, Hawthorne spoke justly of it as "an honest and painful piece of work, [which] will endure." Aside from the visit at Hastings, the meetings in the drawing rooms, and Hawthorne's occasional calls on James in "his little room secluded from the city's uproar," there seems to have been little that could be called friendship between these two American contemporaries.[31]

2. Una Hawthorne

When the Hawthornes arrived in England in 1874, Julian's sister Una had temporarily abandoned her settlement work in London to pay a visit to Rose and George Lathrop in New York. The estrangement between her and her sister had clearly not been as severe and long-lasting as that between Julian Hawthorne and the Lathrops. Una wrote proudly to the Hawthornes in December, 1874, that she had met John Greenleaf Whittier at the Lathrops' home, and that he had complimented her on a poem she had recently published in the *Independent*; "One feels," Una noted, "that what he says means something." Of far more significance than the compliment from Whittier was her meeting a young man named Albert Webster, "ambitious for recognition as a writer . . . [and] interested mainly, it appears, in her name." [32] That Una met Webster in 1874 and not on her next and last visit to the Lathrops in 1876, as earlier biographers have declared,[33] is proved by her unpublished diary for 1875 and by Julian Hawthorne's biography of his parents, in which he writes:

> After leaving London [probably at Christmas, 1873] she lived
> for a time with her brother in Dresden; and then made a visit to

her married sister in New York, where she became acquainted with Albert Webster. . . . When I moved to London, she rejoined me there; and Webster wrote, offering her marriage. She accepted him.[34]

Una joined the Hawthornes in their new home at Twickenham on the first of March, 1875. Her diary records that she went to church regularly, paid and received calls with Minne, and illuminated books; and she notes her brother's brief trip to Paris in 1875. Then suddenly, in the midst of trivial observations, she cries out (August 12): "Wrote to Mr. Webster. Oh I am heartsick and sorrowful. How can I wait to hear from you, Bertie, my love, my love! Shall I ever be able to tell you the love that stifles my heart?" [35] It was no doubt to see her fiancé again that she crossed the Atlantic in 1876, again staying with Rose and George. Webster, it appears, was in the last stages of consumption, and George Lathrop recommended to him the climate of the Sandwich Islands. Besides, there he could have the expert medical attention of George's father. So he and Una parted again. We hear of Una happily working on her wedding dress, unaware that just as she had lost Storrow Higginson and George Lathrop, so she was to lose Albert Webster too. He died on shipboard a few days out from San Francisco, and a friend wrote to Una, telling her the news:

> The letter came one afternoon [wrote Julian Hawthorne], as we were all sitting in our little library. She began to read, but after a moment quickly turned over the page and glanced on the other side. "Ah—yes!" she said, slowly, with a slight sigh. She made no complaint, nor gave way to any passion of grief; but she seemed to become spiritualized,—to relinquish the world, along with her hopes of happiness in it. She made no change in her daily life and occupations. She was a "district visitor" in the church, and she continued to make her regular rounds as usual. But before the end of the year her dark auburn hair had become quite gray, and her vital functions and organs were (as the physician afterwards told me) those of an old woman.[36]

Una's Aunt Ebe was troubled, as were all the members of the family: "Una cannot go on from day to day," she wrote to a

friend, "as I have always done, when there was no reason why I
should not, finding interest and a moderate degree of pleasure
in what did not at all concern me personally. Neither is she
particularly fond of reading." [37] But Una Hawthorne did go on,
for a few months at least. In the late summer of the following
year, 1877, she visited friends in a Protestant convent that she
was thinking of entering at the town of Clewer. A few days
after the parting from her brother and his family, Hawthorne
received a telegram saying that Una was dangerously ill. He
arrived too late. His notebook for that day, September 10,
records simply, "Una died about half past ten o'clock this
morning, at Clewer, in St. Andrew's Cottage." On September
13 his entry is equally brief: "Una was buried today beside our
mother in Kensal Green Cemetery, at about three in the afternoon. She was 33½ years old." [38]

So ended the unhappy life of Una Hawthorne, the firstborn
of Nathaniel and Sophia. In worldly terms she had accomplished nothing; as a human being she had succeeded. "No
occasion for the manifestation of truth, charity, generosity,
self-sacrifice, ever found her wanting," [39] her brother observed,
with a brother's genuine love and admiration. Unfortunately,
Una's death only served to increase much of the old gossip
concerning her insanity, gossip that her brother-in-law George
Lathrop churlishly confirmed in a letter to the New York
Tribune on June 25, 1879. He wrote that he wished to set the
record straight concerning Una's supposed engagement to him
before he and Rose were betrothed. No such engagement ever
existed, he declared. In an egregious display of bad taste, he
added that Una had indeed had a recent attack of insanity,
having also had one ten years earlier. [40]

3. The Hawthorne-Lathrop Quarrel

Although his remarks about her sister Una Hawthorne must
have pained George's wife, Rose, they were only part of a
continual display of bad manners between the Lathrop and
Hawthorne clans. It has been noted earlier that the two families

had fallen out originally over George's supposed betrayal of Julian Hawthorne's trust in 1872; the Hawthorne-Lathrop feud was to continue for ten years longer, with only a temporary armistice. The most serious phase of the quarrel began with Lathrop's publication, in 1876, of *A Study of Hawthorne.* Lathrop was then only twenty-five, but even now his maturity of judgment is admirable. The work was primarily, as the title stated, a study, rather than a biography; but it was nonetheless irritating to Nathaniel Hawthorne's son, who perhaps was already planning the definitive biography of his parents, which appeared eight years later. Certainly, that the first major work on his father should be written by this pretender to the family reputation, and not by *him,* was infuriating; and it was doubly so since Lathrop thus became a Hawthorne authority of sufficient prestige to be invited to write the introductions for the volumes of the great Riverside edition of Hawthorne's collected works. Julian Hawthorne fired the first gun in the battle in a long, bitter letter to the New York *Tribune* of July 8, 1876.[41] He cited his father's aversion to being made the subject of a biography, and noted that many of Mrs. Hawthorne's papers, including letters of a "peculiarly private and delicate nature," which had been given to the son as a "legacy," had fallen unexpectedly into the hands of Lathrop, who had "connected himself with [the family] by marriage." Ever since 1872, Hawthorne declared, he and Una had

> used every means at our disposal to prevail upon Mr. Lathrop to surrender the papers of which he had thus accidentally got control. Mr. Lathrop at first maintained that he had an equal claim to them with myself; but subsequently he agreed to return them after having had opportunity to make himself familiar with their contents. To this condition I was obliged to accede. . . . When at length the papers in question began to be given up, it appeared that Mr. Lathrop had considered it justifiable to retain copies of all such passages in them as had specially interested him; and furthermore that he proposed using the information gained from their perusal to fill out the pages of his "Study."

Hawthorne flailed his brother-in-law for "imbibing" the private letters and memoranda, and taking the objectionable course of paraphrasing them in his narrative. Lathrop was accused of having created a hero in his book who was little more than an enlarged picture of Lathrop himself. More seriously, he had violated unspoken family wishes: "He was attempting a work which no member of Mr. Hawthorne's own family would have ventured to undertake." There is even an outright, though cunningly expressed, attack upon Lathrop for forcing himself "into prominence by attaching himself to a famous name." Hawthorne concludes:

> If the testimony of one who knew his father well, and has diligently studied his writings and meditated upon his mind and character, and whose opinion is substantiated by those of his own sister and of the sister of Nathaniel Hawthorne,—if such testimony carry any weight, then Mr. Lathrop's "Study" will not be taken at its own valuation. It was composed and published in violation of a trust and in the face of repeated warning and opposition; and after all it conveys no just or truthful representation of its subject.

It was thus that Hawthorne unburdened himself of four years of resentment against his brother-in-law. The reaction of the newspapers, however, was almost universally hostile to Julian Hawthorne. One journal typically observed that "Mr. Hawthorne has added strength to the performance which he seeks to discredit by telling Mr. Lathrop's readers what they did not know before, that his work is founded upon authentic family papers. . . . It is a pity that Nathaniel Hawthorne's memory should be made the theme of a family quarrel conducted in the public journals."

Lathrop's rejoinder came on July 13, 1876. In contrast to the long, vituperative letter he was answering, his was short, modest, and firm. He denied knowing that the surviving papers in question belonged exclusively to Julian Hawthorne, and asserted that he had actually used only half a dozen of them, and those "not, moreover, of a confidential nature." Lathrop stressed that the biographical passages of his work were subordinated to the prevailing critical emphasis: this, he says, "all unprejudiced and discriminating persons will perceive." The *Study,* he concludes circumspectly, "was not undertaken with any expectation of injuring any one, least of all any member of Nathaniel Hawthorne's family, but with a sincere love and reverence for his memory." The defense is ably presented and is borne out by a textual examination of his work.

The following newspaper account of the quarrel summarizes the general public dissatisfaction with Hawthorne's performance and stresses Lathrop's respectable credentials. First the *Study* itself is quoted:

> "It will be seen, therefore, that my book makes no pretension to the character of a life. The wish of Hawthorne on this point would alone be enough to prevent that. If such a work is to be undertaken it should be by another hand, in which the right to set aside this wish is much more earnestly vested than in mine."
>
> If Mr. Julian Hawthorne is meant by this [the newspaper goes on], let us hope that the father's wish never will be set aside. . . . It must strike a sensitive reader that Mr. Julian Hawthorne is the last person to treat of his parent's genius and work, . . . because his writings, so far published, argue him extremely unsympathetic. Unless a great change should come over the spirit of his literary ventures, he would be sure to exasperate a large number of his father's admirers and hurt his own position in their eyes. . . . The violent and personal letter which he has written to the New-York press about this little book and its author proves very conclusively how unfit he himself is to attempt what Mr. Lathrop has pleasantly and modestly carried out. Mr. Lathrop is widely and favorably known, is the assistant editor of the Atlantic Monthly under Mr. Howells, and cannot be hurt by the unveiling of a family quarrel which Mr. Hawthorne's letter would seem to promise.

Julian Hawthorne's hearsay evidence about the numerous quarrels and reconciliations of Rose and George Lathrop had not been calculated to increase his esteem of his brother-in-law.

Perhaps rumors had already crossed the Atlantic, too, about Lathrop's alcoholism, which, in the late 1880's, was rapidly to ruin his once promising career. But in 1876, the year of Una's second visit and the public quarrel, a child, Francis Hawthorne Lathrop, was born. George and Rose bought the old Hawthorne home, the Wayside—and then George quarreled unexpectedly with Howells and lost his position on the *Atlantic*. He was unemployed for several years, until 1879, when he went to work for the Boston *Sunday Courier*. Two years later, on February 6, 1881, Francis Lathrop died of diphtheria, an event that caused Julian Hawthorne to write the following sincere letter of condolence to his sister on March 15:

> I remember how you and I used to be children together here in England, five and twenty years ago; we had our childish quarrels then, and made them up before nightfall. Is there any quarrel so just that it may not be made up before the last nightfall of all? . . . I have never lost the feeling that you were my sister, or the wish to be to you all that a brother could be. You and I are all that is left of us now; and it is strange that we should stand apart.

He then offered her husband any service he could perform for him in England: "I say that in no conventional sense, but with all my heart. It is a favor which I ask, not offer." [42] It was on the basis of this letter, and Rose's undoubtedly warm answer, that a reconciliation was effected between the families. George and Rose went to Europe in the summer of 1881, and were received kindly by Julian and Minne in their temporary home in the little artists' colony of Bedford Park. Rose wrote to Elizabeth Palmer Peabody on August 28, "As for Julian, you may be sure my gratitude for the reunion with him is great. . . . He is lovely to George, . . . and is in fact the dearest brother!" [43] While Rose stayed with the Hawthornes, George traveled briefly in Spain, gathering material for his *Spanish Vistas*. Both families returned to America in 1882, and Lathrop cordially offered the Hawthorne clan his home at the Wayside while he and Rose lived in New York. But this was to be only a momentary interlude of peace.

4. Financial Problems and Twice-Told Tales

Except for acting as hostess to her husband's frequent visitors at Ways End and, later, Bedford Park (after a fire at the Twickenham house, during which "she pulled the babies out of the flames," according to her husband), Minne Hawthorne does not seem to have taken part in Hawthorne's social adventures in London. There were the children to look after, and the household accounts to keep, and quite as much worry on the latter score as the former. Financially, these were trying years for the Hawthornes. Although he attempted to write four or five pages of fiction a day, Julian Hawthorne's production varied with the exigencies of the household. In some years he would write virtually nothing save a few stories and articles; in such a year as 1879–80, however, when he composed most of *Fortune's Fool,* he would, to avoid noise and interruption, begin writing at eight in the evening and continue until six or seven o'clock the next morning.[44] Then there was the problem of magazines and publishers who printed Hawthorne's works but were remiss in payment. The novelist had encountered this phenomenon early in his career while *Bressant* was being serialized; and *Appleton's* was the villain in another sharp maneuver by Oliver Bell Bunce, who, Hawthorne discovered in February, 1877, had been underpaying him since the previous July at the rate of five shillings sixpence a page, since the *Appleton's Journal* page contained 1,120 words and not 1,000, as Bunce had estimated.

Hawthorne's opening journal entry for the year 1875 is cheerful. "We begin this year deeply in debt; but with many blessings, such as a roof that we call our own for seven years, health and strength, three handsome children, and a few true friends. My literary reputation is on the increase, and my writings command the largest market price." [45] The tone of a letter to Edward Carter a year later is more somber:

Since my family has attained its present respectable dimensions, I have heard something of the howling of the wolves in the forest; and more than once have been forced to stand hard to my defence. This may surprise you; for the general impression (which I am by no means concerned to efface) seems to be that I am . . . rolling in gold. The truth is that like many other men of transcendent genius and worth, my reputation is much sounder than my bank account. [46]

Full household and business records have survived for the year 1877, and the picture they give is of a struggling, frequently impoverished family. Hawthorne wrote the following rather grim entry in his household book in January:

We begin operations [for the year] with 6^d ready money in hand; a pierced sovereign, which we shall try to change at the Bank of England, and a five shilling piece, a rare impression, which we must also try to get changed. Also a thousand pounds and upwards of debts. [47]

The January accounts show receipts from the sovereign, from Una and Mrs. Amelung, and from Chatto and Windus for a story, a total of over eighty-four pounds; the expenses included amounts for the loan installment, fire and life assurance, household accounts, and sundries, amounting to over sixty-seven pounds, which should have left a balance of around seventeen pounds; but, Hawthorne continues,

This exhibit shows what we have received, but gives no trustworthy idea of what the current expenses of the month actually are. Nor can we know this until we are out of debt; because we pay instalments on our debts as often as we have money in hand. . . .

We have a total of necessary expenses of about £534 a year. By writing four pages a day on the average, I should make over

£1000 a year, which would leave us over £400 balance. Take £200 of this for incidental expenses, and we have £200 to pay debts with. By publishing magazine articles in both England and America, the income would be enlarged to at least £1500, and the percentage on copies of books sold, and on interest on American investments, &c, ought to bring at least £500 more, making £2000. If this can be realised, we ought to pay our debts by the end of the year, and have something in hand.

Hawthorne added that he had bought about fifty pounds worth of clothes—unpaid for, of course—and that Minne had spent the extraordinary sum of two pounds for clothes, the first she had bought since her marriage! As a matter of fact, Julian Hawthorne did not make even a thousand pounds that year of 1877, the year which saw the death of his sister Una and the birth of his child Gwendolyn. He made 778 pounds, of which only about half was earned by his literary work in England. The rest dribbled in from his American sales and investments supervised by Peckham, from Una and Mrs. Amelung, and from Bennoch and Bright. Of the amount received, the records reveal that 774 was spent, leaving a balance of four pounds, and the burden of debt practically intact. Another problem was that the amount of income fluctuated wildly from month to month, from a low of £35 for May to a high of £152 in November. The situation was certainly close to desperate for the family, and remained so through 1881. The pattern of poverty that had been established as early as the days in Dresden and that continued through the English years did not disappear when Julian Hawthorne took his family back to America. The house at Sag Harbor was as much a fortress against creditors as the Twickenham home had been. It was of this latter era that Hawthorne's son Fred wrote years later, but his words are surely applicable to the 1870's as well:

[Hawthorne] was always hard pressed to support, by pen alone, his family. . . . No matter where we lived, . . . I still have indelible memories of tradesmen wearing out the 'Welcome' mats at our various residences, looking for payment for groceries, butchers and bakers, etc. We were generally in that situation, but it made the days when publishers finally came through with checks, and bills were paid, all the happier and temporarily carefree.[48]

It is in the light of these straitened circumstances that one may choose to see the unsavory episode that followed the publication of Julian Hawthorne's story "The Rose of Death," in September, 1876. It was a natural temptation for Hawthorne, as well as other writers of the time, to prevent the pirating of their stories abroad by the relatively simple expedient of rewriting those stories for the overseas market. The New York *Sunday Times,* the victim of this literary charlatanism, opened the discussion of the issue with a blistering attack upon the American writer:

> We find that the story entitled "The Rose of Death," republished in THE TIMES of Sunday from the Cornhill Magazine originally appeared in Harper's Bazar some five years ago under the title of "Otto of Roses." The story was purchased by Messrs. HARPER & BROTHERS from Mr. JULIAN HAWTHORNE, and that versatile person would appear to have slightly expanded and touched up this early production and resold it to the publishers of the Cornhill. We have had some similar experience of the sharp practice of the novelist of the period in regard to stories purchased from Mr. BRET HARTE, and to a story for which we were on the point of paying an agent of Mr. WILKIE COLLINS. It is perhaps natural that authors who are appreciably poorer because of the lack of an international copyright law, should be tempted, now and again, to indemnify themselves by selling the same wares twice.[49]

Hawthorne's reply to the *Times* is at once critical of their hypocrisy and defensive as to his own literary honesty. He writes:

> You gave the story in your Sunday issue as if it were contributed by me directly to you, and did not credit it to Cornhill at all. . . . I submitted my story to the editor of the Cornhill, advising

him that the idea upon which it is founded had been before treated by me; and further observing that after doubting whether or not to throw it into the form of a short novel, I had finally decided to fix it in its present form. And this form let me say, is widely different from that of the earlier version in Harper's Bazar. The whole subject has been conceived afresh; the tone and sentiment are modified; much new matter is added, much omitted; while of what remains scarcely a paragraph in the two versions is identical. It was altered, moreover, not from any motive of concealment . . . but in accordance with the demands of maturer critical and intellectual experience. . . . I am not superior to pecuniary considerations; but neither are they so potent with me as to induce me to foist stale work upon the public, or to descend to empty and gratuitous self-repetition.

Let me add that in the course of the next few months I intend publishing in English magazines, several short stories, some of which own a more or less distant relationship to tales printed some years since in America. I would counsel you not to "republish" these stories in THE SUNDAY TIMES.

To the New York *World* Hawthorne wrote a similar letter, but one much more critical of the "piratical" *Times*. "It may have intended to compliment me," he declares, "by plundering my story, but it is certainly a graceless proceeding to attack me because its knavish profession was in danger of exposure. I would recommend the Times either to cease stealing or quit its assumption of tender innocence." Under the ironic heading "Twice-Told Tales," itself an implied criticism of Julian Hawthorne, the New York *Evening Post* commented succinctly that "the whole affair appears to have grown out of the absence of international copyright laws." [50]

In the late 1870's the Hawthornes had even been reduced to selling their silver, and word of their monetary problems got back to Mrs. Amelung, who had returned to New York with her boys. She wrote to her daughter that her son John had volunteered to take over Julian Hawthorne's business affairs from his old friend Peckham, who seems to have been a little put out by Hawthorne's "extravagance." Mrs. Amelung first seems in agreement with Peckham, then has a change of heart a few lines further on, and says, "Who knows better than I how self denying he is." She has advice, also:

My dearest child do not be offended at anything I say but do you not think that it has been proved by experiment that Julian cannot support his family by literature—would it not be better to try and get a position as assistant on a magazine or paper—if it paid but a small salary it would be certain—tangible.[51]

But Julian resisted this and various other appeals through the years to abandon his free-lance career. He believed no doubt, that he had poured too much creative energy into active apprenticeship to abandon his profession entirely. And a career in literature was much more adapted to his social inclinations than would have been a career in, say, civil engineering. Even a regularly paying job would have robbed him of much of his hard-won sense of freedom.

5. Romancer and Novelist

By the late seventies Julian Hawthorne had become firmly established on the English literary and journalistic scene. England had, as we have seen, welcomed him as the son of Nathaniel Hawthorne, as the author of two somewhat promising long narratives, and as the sarcastic delineator of Saxon customs. Soon after Hutton of the *Spectator* had adopted him as book reviewer, Hawthorne was reviewing and writing fiction for almost every newspaper and magazine in London: the *Examiner, To-Day,* the *World,* the *Standard,* the *Pall Mall Gazette* (which he served for a time as assistant editor), the *St. James Gazette, Temple Bar, Cornhill, Time,* the *Contemporary,* the *New Quarterly,* the *Daily News, Belgravia,* and *University.* Despite his numerous appearances in print, and the various literary and family controversies—with George Parsons Lathrop and with the *Sunday Times*—that kept his name in the forefront of discussion, Julian Hawthorne was not, it seems, regarded as a major writer of fiction. In identifying the most significant fictional production of this period by American writers, critics pointed primarily to the "new school" of social realism led by Howells and James. The vein worked by Julian Hawthorne, the bizarre and fantastic intermixed with realism, was too idiosyncratic to attract the imitation of fellow writers, and no single imaginative work by Hawthorne, not even the impressive *Garth* or the Poe-esque fantasy *Archibald Malmaison,* was an unqualified critical success. In turning to Hawthorne's major fiction of the 1870's, one must remember that it was professedly commercial, yet, paradoxically, dedicated to an ideal of fiction that had no major adherents in the period.

The important works of the English years fall naturally into two distinct groups determined by emphasis. The first group is the lineal descendant of *Idolatry* and the early short fantasies. In *Archibald Malmaison, Kildhurm's Oak,* and *The Laughing Mill and Other Stories,* and in his juvenile tales, Hawthorne gave free rein to his penchant for Gothic-style narrative and mysterious supernatural phenomena. The second group of narratives descends directly from *Bressant:* there is a realistic, densely plotted frame in the novels *Garth, Sebastian Strome,* and *Fortune's Fool,* and supernatural events are either relegated to a minor role or are carefully avoided. By turns—for the stories in the groups mentioned did not appear in sequence —Hawthorne was romancer and novelist. The dichotomy that had been established in the years 1873–74 thus persisted, not only throughout the 1870's, but to the very end of his fictional career in 1896, when the two directions of his genius were illustrated in, respectively, *Love Is a Spirit* and *A Fool of Nature.*[52]

The best of the romances of the seventies is *Archibald Malmaison* (1879), Hawthorne's most melodramatically effective work of fiction. Crowded with many Gothic manifestations, it arouses still the horror intended; in contrast to the crude Gothicisms of such a story as "Calbot's Rival," which elicit smiles more readily than shudders, the Gothic effects of this romance are stirring, especially in the climactic scenes. The story proved to be one of Hawthorne's most popular, both in England and America; as he himself explained, with his familiar touch of irony, "It was the horror of 'Archibald Malmaison,' not any literary merit, that gave it vogue,—its horror, its strangeness, and its brevity." [53]

The framework of the story is purposely made realistic, for, though the author acknowledges in his introduction that "the artistic graces of romance are irreconcilable with the crude straightforwardness of fact," [54] he insists that his story is not a romance at all but literal truth, transcribed from the recollections of a friend named Dr. Rollinson. Archibald is the second son of a baronet, retarded until his seventh year, when he seems to awaken and undergo rapid development. His life then proceeds in seven-year cycles of atrophy followed by intellectual growth; in neither phase does he recall anything of the other, but his affections and enmities are reversed. A modified "ancestral curse" explanation is offered tentatively: "There was a hoary tradition to the effect that the son or grandson of the first emigrant had made some compact or other with the Evil One, the terms of which were that he (the grandson) was to prolong his terrestrial existence for one hundred and forty years by the ingenious device of living only every alternate seven years, the intervening periods to be passed in a sort of hibernation." [55]

During his first waking period, Archibald falls in love with Kate Battledown; but when, at the age of twenty-one, he wakes again from the torpid state that had caused Kate to reject him, he finds her, now an heiress, married to his enemy Richard Pennroyal. After Archibald's brother's death from the effects of a duel with the vicious Richard, the latter sues for the Malmaison estates. In a secret room in the house, Archibald discovers some old papers that negate Pennroyal's claims and uses them to ruin him in court. He also steals Pennroyal's wife from him, and, surprised with her, he kills the drunken husband in a duel and sinks him in the fish pond. His plan is to hide Kate away in the secret chamber until such time as they can escape together. But after he locks her in, Archibald's cycle changes, in a chilling scene, and he loses all memory of recent events. Seven years later he is suddenly again conscious of Kate waiting for him in the room, and hurries to her. The scene is handled with some restraint:

> He went close up to her, and laid his hand on her shoulder: he seemed to grasp nothing but the empty stuff of her dress. With a terrified, convulsive motion, he pulled her round, so that the head was disturbed from its position on the arms, and the ghastly mystery was revealed to his starting eyeballs. The spectacle was not one to be described. He uttered a weak, wavering scream, and stood there, unable to turn away his gaze.[56]

Malmaison House serves as an excellent Gothic castle. It is over two centuries old, "an imposing pile of graystone"; there are "secret passages hollowed out within the walls themselves, and communicating by means of sliding panels from room to room." [57] Ancient swords and breastplates adorn the great hall, and in the secret chamber is a suit of medieval armor. A portrait of Archibald's great-grandfather hangs in the east chamber, and the painted eyes look out with "a slightly frowning glance" at his heir. The hero, we read, "probably had a few of Mrs. Radcliffe's romances . . . on his shelves, and he may have cherished a notion that a treasure . . . was concealed in the vicinity." [58] Through experimentation Archibald discovers the secret room in which the main horror of the romance is to take place. "Henceforth Archibald was as much a wizard" as his forefather, Hawthorne writes. The immurement of Kate is also a familiar adaptation from Gothic romance, like a corresponding scene in *Idolatry*. Despite the pasteboard characterizations and coincidental plot of this romance, it does manage in its final scenes to achieve its primary artistic effect: a sense of horror. In fact, since *Archibald Malmaison* is one of Hawthorne's very few stories in which the aesthetic intent of arousing horror is paramount, and Gothic devices are used in significant combination to achieve this end, we are justified in speaking of it as part of the genre of the Gothic tale.

Another exaggerated neo-Gothic tale of these years in England is *Kildhurm's Oak* (1880). A descendant of the Kildhurm family tells the author a tale that begins in Elizabethan times, when a much-injured wife plants an oak and waters it with her heart's blood. Through the centuries this oak grows to monstrous proportions overhanging a cliff near the Kildhurm Tower, whose dark, brooding aspect makes it a fine, Gothic-like castle. A curse has been attached to the oak by its first gardener, the wife, and it is known to mutter and grumble just prior to someone's death; at one crucial point, "From the grinding together of the mighty boughs were generated shrieks and human-like outcries, and noises like weeping and like mocking laughter, as though a knot of evil spirits were tearing each other to pieces in the central darkness of the tree." [59]

Although the tale is episodic, the most important events are clearly those that surround Sir Norman Kildhurm's murder of a guest, Colonel Banyon, for his jewels. On an appropriately dark and stormy night, Kildhurm does away with the Colonel and ascends the screaming oak to cache his haul for the evening. But later he is found dead by his wife beneath the tree, with the flesh of his hand torn away. In a manner recalling Mrs. Radcliffe, this horror is carefully "explained," at the end of the story, as the result of his catching his hand in a crevice of the oak; but the supernatural interpretation—the personification of a malignant spirit in the tree—is not denied as a possibility, and constitutes one of Hawthorne's rare uses of the ambiguous terror. Lady Kildhurm, deranged by her husband's death, becomes something of a witch, a "sibyl, acquainted with supernatural lore." The melodramatic recovery of the lost treasure in the tree fulfills the ancestral prophecy and closes the tale.[60] *Kildhurm's Oak* is interesting for its use of the recurrent Hawthorne version of the Gothic, but it cannot be taken very seriously as a work of fiction.

The Gothic group of Hawthorne tales of the late 1870's includes, finally, *The Laughing Mill and Other Stories* (1879). The title story [61] uses a very common technique of Hawthorne's, the narrator who is himself involved in the events described. A lawyer named Firemount recalls how, twenty years earlier, he had heard the strange tale of the Laughing Mill from both the stout Mr. Poyntz and a wraith, the Scholar Gloam. The latter was the legitimate, and David an illegitimate, son of Squire Harold; the half-brothers lived with David's mother at the Mill, which was wont to make horrible unexplained noises. The Scholar brings up, and grows to love, a little child named Swanhilda, who had been washed ashore one day with a pearl-shell necklace at her throat; but she is attracted to the worthless David and bears him a child. In a ghastly night piece at the howling Mill, Gloam murders his half-brother and, unwittingly, Swanhilda. The narrator, it transpires, and Swanhilda's daughter Agatha are descendants of two branches of a Danish family that had feuded centuries before; he marries her and thus resolves the ancient quarrel. In this genuine Gothic tale, the aesthetic intent of producing horror is manifest (as demonstrated in two major episodes: the spectral appearance of Gloam, and the murder scene); and the Gothic devices are used to promote this effect. The same Gothic cloud hangs over two other stories in this collection, "Calbot's Rival" (an Anglicized version of the early tale "The Mysterious Case of My Friend Browne") and "A Christmas Guest."

The most lively story in this collection of 1879 is *Mrs. Gainsborough's Diamonds.* Despite a glancing reference to mesmerism, the tale is a non-Gothic mystery story foreshadowing the detective stories of the late 1880's. As an after-dinner story, Gainsborough tells how in his youth in Europe, he found a Mr. Birchmore and his beautiful daughter Kate seemingly under the influence of Birchmore's evil valet, Slurk. The latter can mesmerize Kate, and has stolen papers from his employer that have put the man in his power—or so Gainsborough is told. By several clever tricks Hawthorne makes the revelation of the conspiracy a real surprise. The three had plotted from the beginning to seem to befriend the young Gainsborough only reluctantly, and then to steal the fortune in diamonds that he was carrying on his person. Here, in other words, are several purely romantic elements—the father and daughter under an evil influence, and the youthful resolve of Gainsborough to "rescue" the two of them—given an ironic reverse twist. The reader is kept from suspecting the trio, because elements in the description of Kate correspond to those in the person of Mrs. Gainsborough, who appears at the beginning of the story. The young man comes down to reality when he is robbed; he is rescued, however, by a farm girl, and the thieves captured. This slick, melodramatic story was published separately four times in the decade after its first appearance in 1878, and translated twice.

An equally successful work of the English years was Julian Hawthorne's book of children's stories, *Yellow-Cap and Other Fairy Stories for Children* (1879). The supernatural contrivances in such tales do not appear as clumsy or forced as they do in the adult narratives. The best of the stories by far is "Rumpty-Dudget," [62] whose hero is an evil dwarf and whose scenes evoke a sense of wonder and enchantment. For many years the stories that were most closely identified in the public mind with Julian Hawthorne were three of these romantic tales published during his English residence: *Archibald Malmaison, Mrs. Gainsborough's Diamonds,* and "Rumpty-Dudget."

In contrast to the romances, mysteries, and juvenile stories of this period, the three works most accurately called novels— *Garth, Sebastian Strome,* and *Fortune's Fool*—are long, serious, plot-heavy books with few outcroppings of Gothic sensationalism. The first major work of Julian Hawthorne to follow *Saxon Studies* was *Garth* (1877), dedicated to his friend, and the friend of his father, Francis Bennoch. This, Hawthorne's most carefully wrought longer work, is an analysis of the effects of heredity and environment upon young Garth Urmson of New Hampshire. Few of Hawthorne's novels are so firmly rooted in "place": the Urmsons' ancient house and the village of Urmhurst. As the community events, such as church gatherings, picnics, and fish fries, take place, the sense of background is solidly filled in with the best descriptive writing in any novel by the young pretender.

The glaring weakness in this portrait-of-the-artist-as-a-young-man (for Garth is an untutored painter) is the central figure. Garth is viewed melodramatically as the descendent of a long line of Puritan Urmsons, with the devil and angel in him battling for ascendancy. His *Sturm und Drang* period at Bowdoin College,[63] his rather muddled views on art, and his "doubts and broken beginnings and marrowless compromises" are carefully explored; but the last of the Urmsons is, unfortunately, a bore. He is also a fool, for the main plot is centered upon his love for beautiful Madge Danver, a love that he carries on out of a sense of responsibility years after he has ceased to care for her.[64] Madge, one of Hawthorne's finest creations, is a combination of sweetness and storm in an inconsistent pattern. Like Mrs. Cartaux in the later *A Dream and a Forgetting,* she admires the animal part of man, and she loves and remains true to Garth only so long as he seems to her the most powerful of men. We even believe her refusal to tend her lover in a desperate illness that to her appears "un-manly." Her strange personality is thus summarized by Garth's father to the hero's friend Selwyn: "You see the subtlety and perverted principles beneath the beauty and fascination, but you've taken no account of the goodness and sincerity that are mixed up along with them. That is what makes Madge so hard to deal justly with. . . . Her love seems to come and go with the tide; but, in fact, it is her opinion as to the identity of the man with her ideal of him that varies." [65] Madge's self-revelations in her scene with Selwyn are dexterously managed, and show the reader some of Hawthorne's most penetrating insights into the relationships of men and women.

Several of the minor characters are brilliantly drawn. Eleanor Golightley, the sensitive, haughty young violinist, who contends almost against her will for Garth's love, and who, unlike Madge, understands the hero, comes off almost as well as

Madge herself. Cuthbert Urmson, Garth's father, is a winningly gentle ironist. His prodigal half-brother Golightley, who has swallowed up the family fortune in Europe with his aesthetic and speculative tastes and returned to Urmhurst with a stolen fortune in his pockets, is a creature of elegant falsity who is never merely despicable. Parson Graeme must be mentioned, Hawthorne's most full-blooded character, a huge, ancient, rambling, and utterly delightful figure cut from the same cloth as Dickens's grotesques. The fat, pursy Mrs. Tenterden is a good foil for Eleanor, as is the cynical Selwyn for Garth. Only in the characters of the half-breed villain Sam Kineo and his grandmother Nikomis, an Indian witch who represents symbolically the ancient Indian curse on the clan of the Urmsons, does Hawthorne's compulsive romantic method manifest itself, and here his inspiration fails him.

The characters of *Garth* are infinitely more interesting than the narrative. The setting and story bear some obvious resemblances to those of *The House of the Seven Gables*. In commenting on that novel, Hawthorne later wrote that "the idea of a house, founded two hundred years ago upon a crime, is a thoroughly picturesque idea"; [66] and perhaps he had thought it picturesque enough to use in almost the same way as his father had done. The blood feud in *Garth,* however, is not between families but between races. The theme of "reenactment," which had appeared in the early stories, is here utilized to portray the hereditary consequences of sin; Garth inherits his ancestor's disposition to commit murder, and his battles with Kineo reenact the drama that had taken place at the founding of Urmhurst. The artistic development of Garth, from his early theorizing about the immorality of Art painting an already perfect Universe,[67] is intertwined with the working out of the family history of the Urmsons and the detective hunt for Golightley and Kineo, the thieves who had robbed Mrs. Tenterden and Eleanor of their money in Europe. The concluding chapters of the novel are crowded with the accidental murder of Cuthbert by Golightley, the capture of Sam, the flight of Madge to

Europe to realize her wild dreams of life, the subsequent marriage of Garth to Eleanor, and the laying to rest of the ancestral curse by the burning of the Urmhurst mansion.

Julian Hawthorne's handling of the general problem of sin in man is reminiscent of his father's treatment, but he makes a qualifiedly optimistic distinction, redolent of sentimental, non-Puritan Christianity. "The secret sympathy with sin," he writes, "lies nearer to the natural heart of man than sympathy with virtue, and an evil influence affects him more positively than many good ones—for he recognizes more of himself in it. Good, nevertheless, if the man acknowledge it not of himself but of God, may outweigh all the evil in the world." [68]

The general consensus of the reviewers was that *Garth* had more purity and beauty of prose style, but less force, than its two predecessors, *Bressant* and *Idolatry*. Thus Edward L. Burlingame, writing in the *North American Review,* professed himself delighted with the first hundred pages of narrative, but then found the plot wandering aimlessly. Hawthorne, he declared, lacked a clear conception in beginning his work, and a "staying quality"; his novels ended as if he were tired of them, and were disfigured at the close by slovenly writing. Though giving Hawthorne credit for a distinct literary conscience, he thought that the writer lacked "a reverent ideal of work," and took the occasion to compare Hawthorne with Henry James:

> In precisely that direction in which Mr. James is strong lies Mr. Hawthorne's greatest weakness. Were the two painters, one would use his rather cold, gray tints to fill out perfect drawing. . . . The other, conscious that he had some warm colors on his palette, would seek . . . to make them do duty on his canvas in place of all the patient toil and care of art, . . . lacking that which compels a man to finished and faithful performance.[69]

In writing *Garth,* Julian Hawthorne had finally come to grips with the Hawthorne tradition, much more than in his early stories or his first two imaginative works. *Garth* may be considered the logical successor to Nathaniel Hawthorne's great series of romances; the themes, the setting, and some of the characters, for example, are unmistakably linked with *The House of the Seven Gables*. But the differences are far greater than the similarities in this novel. As Burlingame noted, a sense of proportion and symmetry is absent. After the easy, charming narrative of Garth's early years, the subsequent chapters become cheaply melodramatic, and the conclusion is crowded and tedious. The delicious humor of Nathaniel Hawthorne is nowhere apparent; in its place are lengthy philosophical discussions rarely relieved by a flash of wit. Without enumerating all these marked differences, one more, the frequently inelegant diction, may be mentioned. No novel could have displayed more clearly than *Garth* that Julian Hawthorne's "monument" to his father was indeed but a bizarre Moorish temple.

Sebastian Strome (1879), Hawthorne's next major novel, has for its hero the lineal fictional descendant of Bressant and Balder Helwyse. Strome, a young divinity student, was "instinct with a sense of personal triumph and invincibility that seemed to lift him above human limitations." [70] Strome's emotions are greatly exacerbated by his agnosticism, for he is the son of a pious clergyman incapable of understanding his aspirations. He is a hypocrite as well: he has seduced a girl named Fanny and soon afterward engaged himself to a young neighborhood heiress, Mary Dene. In certain respects, then, the plot repeats some of the central elements of *The Scarlet Letter*. Despite his problems Strome's plans are grandiose: to become not only a Jesuit but another Ignatius Loyola, and to rule by the human motives stressed by Machiavelli.

Like other Julian Hawthorne heroes, however, Strome finds his egoistic plans ground into dust both by circumstances and a regained personal nobility. His small fortune is dissipated by gambling; and when Fanny bears his child and dies, he forces himself to break his engagement to Mary, even though it means that she will fall to his old enemy, Selim Fawley. Abandoning his studies and subduing his spiritual pride, Sebastian descends into the slums of London to earn his living by woodworking and to bring up his little daughter. Mary, who had indeed married Strome's rival, becomes the baby's godmother. Fawley kills the child in an ostensible accident, but even though the "new" and now truly Christian hero abjures revenge, a brain attack carries off the slayer. A melodramatic exploit in the Crimea is introduced to patch up the plot.

Sebastian Strome is an essentially realistic novel of the interplay of character and environment, and although marred at times by an oppressive Christian sentimentality and by the introduction of stock figures in minor roles, it is marked by several stirring scenes and by the creation of two extraordinarily lifelike human beings, Mary Dene and Selim Fawley. Mary is a proud young tigress of a girl, beautiful and moody, whose intellect and nobility recall the qualities of Mrs. Casaubon in *Middlemarch*. Her pride and love are shattered in the great scene in which Sebastian confesses his unworthiness to marry her. She goes so far as to contemplate the murder of her husband in retribution for her months of agony with him as well as for his slaying of the baby. Partly demented as a result of her husband's death and her recognition of her own motives, she allows her passions, long held in check, to rise to the surface as she meets Sebastian, in a scene that is Hawthorne's greatest triumph in this novel. Selim Fawley's Semitic origin and characteristics seem to have made him, for Hawthorne, a perfect villain.[71] He is a speculator, a cruel husband, a murderer, and something even darker that is hinted at only vaguely; but his love for Mary, frustrated by her contempt for him, and his inconsistencies of speech and action make him convincing.

Sebastian Strome utilizes a tragic dissimilarity between father and son as a basic structural device. It would perhaps be unwise to attempt to establish overly close analogies between the themes of Hawthorne's fiction on the one hand and his attitude toward his father on the other. But the facts remain these: that the writer felt deeply the disparity between his father's genius and his own talents; and that in a half-dozen of the novels and romances this disparity of ideals or interests or capabilities between father and son is made an important element of the plot. This projective theme appears also in *Garth, Fortune's Fool, Archibald Malmaison, Beatrix Randolph, Dust,* and *A Fool of Nature.*

Sebastian Strome was one of Hawthorne's greatest critical successes, perhaps partly because it was, for once, completely free of supernatural ornamentation. It reminded some reviewers of the old-fashioned, "muscular" novels of Charles Kingsley, while others viewed its themes as a deliberate rejection of those expounded in Eliot's *Daniel Deronda.* The *Scribner's Monthly* critic was most enthusiastic. "It holds the attention like a vise," he declared. "It abounds in ideas, new views of daily matters, bold and original declarations." [72]

This survey of Julian Hawthorne's fictional production in England may conclude with a brief account of one of his most ambitious productions, *Fortune's Fool* (1883), and a summary of his artistic accomplishments thus far. Hawthorne began the story late in 1880 and wrote the first ten of its twelve serial installments in three months. But the two remaining sections were not written and published until 1883, after he had returned to America, and this delay probably spoiled the book. In *Confessions and Criticisms* Hawthorne explains at length the genesis and composition of this novel. He tells candidly how he lost his sense of correct proportion as the writing of the tale advanced, in much the same manner as he had lost control of the earlier *Garth* and *Sebastian Strome.* The story, he declared, "lacked wholeness and continuous vitality. As a work of art, it was a failure. But I did not realize this fact until it was too late, and probably should not have known how to mend matters had it been otherwise." [73]

In the slow, unhurried opening chapters, Hawthorne describes the primitive forests of northern New England where the hero is born early in the nineteenth century. The familiar aura of wonder and mystery is cast over the "Witch's Head," a large boulder "invested . . . with a semi-supernatural importance," beside which the hero, Jack, grows up. He is the son of Floyd Vivian, lord of the Castlemere estates in England, who had died uncertain of his heir's existence. Vivian had drawn up two wills: one giving all to Madeleine, the daughter of his younger brother, and the second, which has priority, giving all to Jack, should he be found. Unknown to each other, Jack and Madeleine meet one day beneath the Witch's Head, become friends, and exchange keepsakes. Jack's is a locket, containing a portrait of Madeleine that is to inspire his search for beauty and love throughout his life. Jack is an untutored mystic, as attuned to the mysteries of nature as Leatherstocking. He goes West in order to live with the Indians, steals a chieftain's daughter, and develops his considerable skills in the clay portraiture of animal figures.[74]

Madeleine, meanwhile, had returned to England, where she is brought up by her aunts. During the years of Jack's adventures in California, she becomes a beautiful, sophisticated heiress, whose artistic temperament draws her to the stage. She is encouraged in this direction by Bryan Sinclair, a professional adventurer, scoundrel, and lover. Sinclair leaves briefly for America in search of gold; accompanied by Tom Berne, over whom he exercises a weird magnetic power, he meets Jack in the Sacramento Valley and forces Tom to kill Jack's companion Hugh, who is, improbably enough, Tom's long-lost brother. Despite this unfortunate death, Jack and Bryan become friends, and the latter takes the young man back to England with him, impressed with his intelligence, his artistry, and his noble appearance. Predictably, Jack and Madeleine meet again, at a masquerade ball, and both recognize the keepsakes that they had exchanged; but they are still not cognizant of the fact that they are contesting heirs. Madeleine is drawn to her cousin, but knows that she is destined to love the sensual Sinclair. When her friends discover the extent of Sinclair's rascality in the past, they attempt to prevent the elopement of the couple; but Sir Stanhope, who loves Madeleine, is killed by Tom Berne. When Bryan tries to escape the country alone, he is also killed by the man he had once enslaved. Tortured beyond endurance, Madeleine, while performing Shakespeare's *Antony and Cleopatra,* carries out her role with utter verisimilitude and commits suicide in the last act. In a gesture characteristic of Hawthorne heroes, Jack then renounces his newly discovered inheritance and goes to Paris to devote himself to his sculpture, for he realizes that he cannot continue within the confines of his father's way of life.

A plot summary of *Fortune's Fool* must necessarily exaggerate somewhat its romantic and melodramatic aspects; but the total impression of the novel is of a serious investigation of the phenomena of innocence and sophistication. Hawthorne's hero is an unbearable innocent, a kind of serious Joaquin Miller, whose primitive metaphysical speculations induced by a withdrawn life close to nature recall those of Garth. Jack is not convincing because he is cast in Julian Hawthorne's "ideal" mold; in his search for the spirituality embodied in the face in Madeleine's keepsake, in his noble savagery among the Pacific Slope Indians, in his predictable reactions to English society life, he betrays an unsophistication more childish than childlike, more postured than sincere. Much more successful, because written more obviously out of Hawthorne's own real personality and view of man, is Bryan Sinclair. Although the nominal villain, Sinclair is the most attractive of Hawthorne's characters because beneath the cynicism of his talk and actions lies a basic honesty, a non-idealistic perception of the true relations between human beings. Contrasted to Jack's monosyllabic and oracular declarations are Sinclair's magnificently eloquent speeches that picture a code of conduct cutting through the cant and sham of society life. As Sinclair's protégé, Jack is thus a distinct disappointment, but Madeleine is a success. Her dark beauty, her passionate intensity in giving her love, her conflict between the roles of society belle and great actress, make her come to life vividly, like Cornelia Valeyon, Madge Danver, and Mary Dene in the earlier novels.

The events surrounding the composition of *Fortune's Fool*

explain something of the failure of its crowded concluding chapters. Like those in *Garth* and *Sebastian Strome,* they destroy the mood created by the slow, almost serene exposition of the first two-thirds of the book. Hawthorne devotes ten pages to Indian life in California early in the novel; but the murder of Sinclair by Tom occupies scarcely a page at the end. The already familiar contrast between innocence and sophistication, dramatized in Jack and Sinclair, is set carefully in the contrasting scenes of the forests of New England and California and the elegant homes of London society. In earlier stories this contrast had made use of a familiar convention, and the pattern was to be used after *Fortune's Fool;* but one suspects that Julian Hawthorne's view of the English as "detestable," mentioned by Henry James, stemmed from his growing personal aversion to the concealed viciousness of London society. Such a belief informs, for example, Hawthorne's authorial comments on society, which must, he declares,

> sail on even keel over a sea which must be smooth, though it flow above dead men's bones and all grotesque and tragic horrors. If any one casts a demure glance of curiosity into those pregnant depths, he must not allow what he sees there to disconcert the urbane composure of his visage. If he himself, whether by chance or of purpose, sink beneath the surface, no boat must be lowered, nor any rope thrown over, for his rescue. The decorous passengers must still pace the dapper decks as unconsciously as before, and the look-out must still report all well, and fair weather present and to come. There is no doubt a certain fascination in this gay and solemn humbug. It implies a kind of bastard stoicism, which, for the sake of a glossy external serenity, suppresses everything that bleeds and breathes and speaks the startling language of humanity.[75]

Despite the purplish effectiveness of such isolated passages as this, its brilliant descriptive passages of American scenes, and its creation of one of Hawthorne's finest characters in Bryan Sinclair, *Fortune's Fool* is not a successful or memorable novel.[76]

The novels and romances produced during Julian Hawthorne's residence in England mark that period of his life as his most fertile and imaginative. The artistic success of the shorter melodramatic works *Archibald Malmaison* and *Mrs. Gainsborough's Diamonds* and the dense, rich atmosphere of the serious novels indicated the presence of great powers. Hawthorne was already a master of narrative excitement, of the ability to portray the shadings of dialogue, and of the creation of characters at once vigorous and subtle. But most of his critics discerned faults in the fiction, which were especially obvious to those seeking to evaluate it in the context of the elder Hawthorne's accomplishments. The first was the absence of balance and proportion in the long works: Hawthorne would begin well, unhurriedly, lay his groundwork carefully—and then conclude with a rush of melodramatic incident. The second was the presence of the elements of fantasy and the supernatural even in serious works like *Garth* and *Fortune's Fool.* Julian Hawthorne's allegiance to the Gothic mode tended to disfigure his novels and give them a mixed tone, as fantastic as if, for example, Silas Lapham had presided at seances, or Isabel Archer had had the power of clairvoyance. Finally, the abstract philosophical speculations on the nature of man, on human destiny and free will, and on the virtues and vices of civilization not only dammed the narrative flow but appeared out of place in stories whose settings and characters were bizarre or romantic. The speculations prevented critics from seeing such deeper themes as the one I have taken to be paramount, the value of love and brotherhood as antidotes to the civilized poison of lustful selfishness; indeed, the reviews completely ignored such themes, preferring their stale disquisition on the "mantle" of Nathaniel Hawthorne and the curious supernaturalist compulsions of the narrative. In his popular romances Julian Hawthorne was primarily enjoying himself, producing fiction that he knew would sell and add the necessary pounds to his income; in his novels he was perfecting his craft. The future augured well for Julian Hawthorne the novelist. But in the 1880's he was to reap a bitter harvest of disappointments.

The prolific, sociable, impoverished English years finally came to an end in 1882. Actually, Minne and the children made the journey to America in October, 1881. Hawthorne spent the winter of 1881–82 in Italy, gathering materials for a series of articles on the scenes of his father's romances,[77] and at Kinsale, in Ireland, with his painter friend Howard Helmick.[78] The reasons for the return to America at this time are not entirely clear. Hawthorne's paternal aunt was gratified at the decision, especially for the sake of the boys, for she had been afraid they would grow up all crusted over with English prejudices; that this was her nephew's feeling also is evident from a letter of 1874 in which she declared that Julian Hawthorne "wishes his little Jack to grow up an American. That is precisely what his father wished for him."[79] Homesickness must not be discounted as well. Except for brief visits to Europe and India and a three-year idyl in the West Indies, Hawthorne after 1882 was never again to live away from his native land.

5

The Growth of a Reputation

1. "A School by Himself"

After their brief sojourn at the Lathrops' home at The Wayside upon their return to the United States, the Hawthorne family moved to Nonquitt, Massachusetts, where, unexpectedly, the baby Gladys died in September, 1882, a bereavement that deeply affected Mrs. Hawthorne for years thereafter. After a brief residence in Morrisania, near New York City, the Hawthornes settled down on a comfortable two-hundred-acre farm on Peconic Bay, three miles from the town of Sag Harbor, Long Island. This was to be Julian Hawthorne's social and literary headquarters until the departure of the family for Jamaica in 1893. Here was born Imogen, in 1884, and a ninth and last child, Perdita, who died in the year of her birth, 1890; her father memorialized her in one of his best poems. Hawthorne's oldest son, John, recalls that his father "used to take us out on long walks and also boating and entertain us with stories; we were very devoted to him, and he was a fine companion." [1] According to Julian Hawthorne's grandson Manning, none of the children went to school except for a few odd terms now and then. Hildegarde Hawthorne recaptures these years delightfully in her juvenile book *Makeshift Farm*

(1925), in which the entire family appears in fictional form. In a sequel entitled *Island Farm* (1926), she recalls how the children had loved the rambling farm on Peconic Bay, "because it was free and simple, because there was the sea to swim in, . . . [and] all the pleasant living things of farm life." [2] To be sure, she adds, there had been much hard work and a scarcity of money; but these were compensated for by the picnics, the fishing and shooting, the jolly companionship of the children, and the visits of family friends. One of these friends, the poet and journalist Eugene Field, left a charming portrait of the Hawthorne children in a long poem of that name he wrote to commemorate his happy stay at "Makeshift Farm." The poem begins:

> The Hawthorne children—seven in all—
>   Are famous friends of mine,
> And with what pleasure I recall
> How, years ago, one gloomy fall,
>   I took a tedious railway line
> And journeyed by slow stages down
> Unto that sleepy seaport town
>   (Albeit one worth seeing),
>   Where Hildegarde, John, Henry, Fred,
> And Beatrix and Gwendolen
> And she that was the baby then—
>   These famous seven, as aforesaid,
>   Lived, moved, and had their being. [3]

Field goes on to record delightfully the events of his visit: milking cows, playing pranks, sprinting on the beach with Beatrix, and his tall-tale-telling of the Wild West.

Although, as indicated later, Hawthorne was to turn to lecturing and journalism, his income for the years 1882–93 continued to be derived mainly from the serializations and sales of his novels, most of which appeared in both England and America, and some of which saw second and third editions. For example, the novel *Dust,* which had been begun in England and finished at Morrisania in December, 1882, sold out its entire first edition of 1,300 copies on the first day of publication. Immediately upon completing *Fortune's Fool* in May, 1883—a work begun three years earlier—Hawthorne began writing and serializing *Beatrix Randolph,* and finished it early in July. His contemporary journal, while recording his numerous social involvements for the period, also records the steady, page-after-page production of the fiction and miscellaneous articles that were the support of the large family; and we can well credit John Hawthorne's remark that his father "was busy writing most of the time." [4]

Typical criticisms of Julian Hawthorne in this period were written by the critics James Herbert Morse, Charles F. Richardson, and John Nichol. The first credited Hawthorne with a distinctive fancy and imagination:

> He has the creative instinct and more than the average writer's ability; but his early tendency to work in the Nathaniel Hawthorne vein seemed almost willful. It was the most difficult vein novelist ever worked; and to approach it without a tool sharpened presupposed a willingness to "square off" against the very Fates. The author puts together the elements of strong characters, invites the Destinies to take charge of them, but refuses to let go his own hold.[5]

The literary historian Charles F. Richardson, a few years later, praised Hawthorne's "higher themes," but also noted the "faulty construction and language" and blurred figures.[6] In his study titled *American Literature,* John Nichol surveyed the whole of Hawthorne's fiction written up to 1882 and compared him favorably to his major "rivals," James and Howells. "It is boldness in Julian Hawthorne," Nichol stated in a familiar argument, "to write novels at all: the height of daring, to write them . . . in the metaphysical manner: an almost incredible audacity, that he should take for his recurring text the ruining or regenerative results of sin." [7] The younger Hawthorne's works, Nichol went on, display both reckless sensationalism and passionate intensity: he shows a determination to cleave through the crusts of society to the lava reservoirs of the heart, [and] observing and reflective powers undimmed by the storms and gusts of feeling he represents and seems to share.[8]

These qualities, Nichol concluded, "indisputably stamp him as a man of genius." Hawthorne's staunchest critical support in the 1880's came, however, and surprisingly enough, from the *Atlantic Monthly*, which had abused *Idolatry* unmercifully, but which now had the greatest praise for such works as *Dust* and *Beatrix Randolph*. Chief among Hawthorne's enemies remained the *Nation*, one of whose comments displayed both its chronically bad temper and a generally prevailing puzzlement about a writer who remained deliberately unclassifiable. Hawthorne, the *Nation* declared, "has shouldered his way into notice and repute as a novelist by sheer force of persistence, and may be said to constitute almost a school by himself, unless, indeed, we give 'Ouida' a place in it." [9]

The fiction produced between the return to the United States in 1882 and Hawthorne's involvement in journalism, the locus of which may be put at 1887, does not demonstrate an advance in technique or subject matter over the work produced in the previous decade. The prose style, for example, remains uneven, rarely displaying finished craftsmanship. To those critics like Burlingame who had complained that the length of his novels outlived his inspiration, Julian Hawthorne responded by shortening them; but the proportion between length and inspiration remained curiously constant. The variations in the quality of the fiction are as astounding as they were in the 1870's and were to be later. Finally, the writer continued to be torn between the realistic and supernatural modes, as he had been in England; thus the dichotomy early established between his "novels" and his "romances" persists. Yet this dichotomy must not be pushed too far, because the hybrid product becomes more typical: thus one sees the familiar elements of the sensational and the bizarre, with an occasional Gothic flavor, set within the superficially realistic dramatic and narrative framework.[10] With the appearance of *Beatrix Randolph* (1883), many critics felt, indeed, that Hawthorne was gradually but quite definitely abandoning the Gothic preoccupations of his earliest years. The friendly *Atlantic Monthly,* for example, declared:

> There is a freshness about the atmosphere of the book, which suggests that Mr. Hawthorne's return to his native country has benefited him. He has been quick to catch some of the local traits of New York. . . . Although his unduly fantastic strain continues in the invention of this story, it is encouraging to find that he has for a time freed himself from those gratuitously wild and forced conceits which have often overlaid his natural strength with an appearance of weakness.[11]

And the *Critic* agreed:

> Each ebullition of his fiery and untamed genius is leaving a clearer and finer residue of moral conviction, of deep and tender thought, and of sympathetic insight; while he is turning his really fine imagination . . . to actual life, [rather than to] impossible conditions, unreal circumstances, and elfish souls.[12]

These apparent new directions that the critics were so happy to point out in 1884 were, unfortunately, illusory. Julian Hawthorne continued to be ruled by the false aesthetic quoted in the discussion of his Gothic background: namely, and it is worth repeating here, that the style and method of the author of romances "purify and wax artistic" under the exertion of preventing his supernatural and fantastic elements from appearing crude and ridiculous. The novels, romances, and what I have called the hybrids of the 1880's are bound together, whatever their intention, by a thread that runs through them all: narrative improbability. Thus the reader is asked to believe in *Beatrix Randolph,* for example, that an amateur soprano could successfully impersonate a famous Russian singer on the New York stage for an entire season; in *Dust* he is called upon to accept the fact that a banker who has been cheated by a gambling associate would leave the country and entrust his daughter to the gambler's care: and these examples are chosen from the more realistic of the novels! Obviously, Hawthorne could have constructed a completely probable plot; his failure to do so is deliberate. He had chosen his path, his own artistic theory; and one must admire, if not the fiction that resulted, at least the courageous single-mindedness of the attempt.

Granted the thread of narrative improbability that gives a characterizing stamp to all his works, the fiction of this period may conveniently be divided again into "novels" and "romances." The former include, in addition to the last long novel from Hawthorne's pen, *Dust,* the shorter works *Beatrix Randolph, Love—or a Name,* and *John Parmelee's Curse.* The romances are *Noble Blood* and six considerably shorter works: *Sinfire,* "Countess Almara's Murder," "Prince Saroni's Wife," "The Trial of Gideon," "Constance," and "Pauline."

In *Dust* (1883) one is confronted with the same kind of thickly plotted story as in *Fortune's Fool,* and there is the same contrast as in earlier and later novels between the sanity of country life and the fevered anxiety of high society. Marion Lockhart, the clairvoyant heroine of the novel, muses toward the end of her adventures:

> The old house at Hammersmith! . . . It was there that her first happiness had come to her; and if Heaven ever permitted her to be happy again, it ought to happen there. All this fever of wealth and fashionable society was as a dream that is past; freshness and sanity had returned.[13]

Here is seen not only the customary conflict between the good little town (Hammersmith) and the big bad town (London) but the more revealing contrast between the "freshness and sanity" of small town mores and the "fever" of society manners. To Hawthorne's middle-class reading public, this theme undoubtedly struck a welcome, homey chord. Hawthorne always used this pattern from *Bressant* onward, most notably in *Love—or a Name* (1885), which shows the New York society circle of Seth Drayton to be corrupt, and in *A Fool of Nature* (1896), which directs the sympathies of the reader to the "natural" hero, brought up by a corrupt aristocratic father. This glorification of the virtues of the middle class is, just as much as his addiction to a puerile supernaturalism, a deadening influence on Julian Hawthorne's art.

Some twenty years before the novel opens, Charles Grantley had assumed the guilt for his friend and employer, the banker and gambling proprietor Sir Francis Bendibow, had fled England, and had left his daughter's bringing-up to Sir Francis. Returning as "Mr. Grant" as the book begins, he is slain by the cowardly banker. He leaves his fortune to his daughter, Perdita, but when she declines to acknowledge him as her father, the money passes to a friend, Philip Lancaster, a poet.

Two conflicts are skillfully developed in the novel. The first arises from Perdita's designs on Philip, who had known her in France as the Marquise Desmoines. The Marquise is one of Hawthorne's wicked women of the world, a type, prepared for by the dark heroines of the early novels, that is to appear with increasing frequency in his stories. The second contrast stems from the change in Marion, Philip's wife, who emerges from her cocoon of domestic simplicity and becomes a cynical lady of the town; because Philip is dismayed at the change, and at her supposed infidelity, Perdita's intrigues almost succeed. But Philip's invincible moral rectitude saves him from this disgrace, and he returns to a reformed Marion's really chaste embrace. Hawthorne was to use this same general situation five years later in *A Dream and a Forgetting,* in which a *femme fatale* comes between a poet and his loved one.

In *Dust,* Philip, Marion, and Grantley are all uninteresting characters, but both the tormented and criminal Sir Francis and Perdita are memorable. The marquise is a vain, passionate, cunning animal; and she is also intelligent enough to realize the kind of woman she is. In Hawthorne's most dramatic scene she cries out to Sir Francis:

See what you have made of me! . . . You brought me up to think the thoughts of a woman of the world and a libertine while

I was still a child. You gave me nothing to care for but my own success—for money and power; and at last you married me to a worn-out formalist whose very virtues made sin seem delightful. I have never had help or sympathy from a human soul.[14]

The novel, whose commercial success has been noted, was uniformly well received by the critics. The *Atlantic Monthly,* though chastising Hawthorne for the historical inaccuracy of his diction and costumes (the novel is laid in 1816) and for the unbelievable self-sacrifice of Grantley, declared: "There is so much cleverness about [the novel], so much good writing, and so many skillful touches that one cannot help admiring the author's faculty." [15]

If *Dust* marks no distinct fictional advance for Julian Hawthorne, his next novel, *Beatrix Randolph* (1883), is a step backward. The reader who manages to struggle through the opening chapters of this tepid novel—chapters that constitute a veritable Slough of Despond—will find, to sustain him on his weary pilgrimage, only the fascinating, brief appearance of the diva Vera Marana, one of Hawthorne's foreign beauties. The reader revels in her naughtiness, only to look on in dismay as she falls victim to the sentimental heroine, the young and pure Beatrix. The latter poses as the Russian singer on the opera stage in order to restore the family fortune dissipated by her wastrel brother, and succeeds, improbably, in deceiving the most learned of New York critics. Several familiar Hawthorne themes enter in this novel. Beatrix's family comes from a small town in New York State, and the pristine purities of this community are contrasted with the sinfulness that confronts the heroine in New York City. We have again, as in *Garth* and *Sebastian Strome,* the disparity in aims between the son, Beatrix's brother, and the kindly father. A "vulgar Jew," General Moses Inigo, makes a convenient villain.

Such conflicts as are developed are poor. Geoffrey Bellingham, a boring architect, becomes estranged from Beatrix, for example, because he thinks old Mr. Randolph, the father whom she cannot acknowledge publicly, is her paramour. The appearance of Marana and her denunciation of Beatrix for usurping her name breathe the only semblance of life into this tale, disfigured as it is by tedious remarks about music and general comments at critical points in the action.[16] Another contrast, between the standards of Europe and America, is pointed up by Hawthorne, and deserves citation as a species of debased Jamesian style:

> [Beatrix] told herself that Geoffrey had perhaps made up his mind to condone Marana's delinquencies, taking into account her foreign training, her temptations, and the loose standard of morals that prevailed in Europe; but that he never would forgive Beatrix for having deliberately misled him,—she, an American girl, brought up amid all the enlightenment and fastidious rectitude of the great republic.[17]

This statement, it must be added, is not ironic.

Two years after the appearance of the unfortunate *Beatrix Randolph,* Hawthorne published one of his finest novels, *Love —or a Name.* The story begins inauspiciously enough with the conventional introduction of a colorless young hero, Warren Bell, and a colorless young heroine, Nell Anthony. Bell's career parallels Julian Hawthorne's: expulsion from college, followed by a term in engineering school and a position in the New York Dock Department. Ambitious Warren attends the funeral of Nell's mother, and after being refused by the girl, who is repelled by his coldness and his lust for power, returns from her country town to New York, where he falls under the influence, unwillingly at first, of Seth Drayton.

Hawthorne's interest soon shifts from Bell to Drayton, and his study of the latter, an elderly, rich New Englander bent upon absolute behind-the-scenes political mastery of the United States, not only ranks as one of his best creations but elevates this story of political intrigue and corruption almost to the rank of DeForest's *Honest John Vane.* Drayton's cynical views of politics in a democracy, and of democracy itself, are tellingly portrayed. "The characteristic of the mass of the people," he declares, "is fickleness, which justifies itself by masking its inconsistencies behind a clamor for reform, which, being interpreted, means something new. . . . Since most men are fools, a wise man must withdraw himself from visible connection with politics altogether. . . . In this school and newspaper and ballot age those who wish to act truly great parts must wear a veil." [18] His attack on democracy becomes even more violent. "This government," he states, "is the systematized robbery of the many by the few. No one is responsible, and no one cares. . . . An alderman is a person by whose means wealthy corporations rob the city treasury. A State governor is an individual who organizes the depredations of his subordinates." [19] Although it would be unwise to ascribe any of these views to Hawthorne himself, one can sense, in the vigor of the language, his concern with the evils of democracy as he had seen them manifested since his return to America; and one may perhaps see here the germ of the speculation that eventually led him to a passionate commitment to socialism.[20] In support of Drayton, Hawthorne allows himself one authorial comment: "A political party," he says, "like an algebraic formula, is a device for dispensing with thought; though, unlike the latter, it is the product of emotion instead of reason." [21] Finally, his views may be seen implicitly in the admitted probability of Drayton's success in buying off one presidential candidate, controlling another, and installing a third-party figurehead.

Bell becomes progressively more calloused by his association with Drayton and his friends, and not even Nell, who has come to New York, can sway him. He goes so far as to become engaged to Drayton's daughter Lizzie. But Drayton's schemes collapse when one of his associates, Peekskill, informs on his plans to a bitter enemy, Judge Muhlbach; and when Lizzie, shamed at her seduction by Peekskill, leaves home, Drayton is sufficiently affected to kill himself. The *Nation* found these final scenes too sordid: Hawthorne "winds up," it declared, "with a situation too brutal to be matched among savages." [22] That *Love—or a Name* was rather strong meat for the reviewers of the time is also displayed in a comment by *Lippincott's*, which asserted that if the author "wishes to show us consummate rascals we insist that he should wrap them in some veil of decency, if not of art, and not fill his pages with incidents and talk which properly belong to the police-court." [23]

Several minor characters, such as Nell's chubby friend Susan Wayne and Warren's Irish crony O'Ryan, are well drawn, and Hawthorne seems to be able in this novel to follow a thread of narrative to its logical conclusions without sentimental or moralizing digressions. His last few pages *are* disfigured by this sort of thing, but are important for two reasons. First, they state clearly the theme of such novels as this one, *Bressant, Sebastian Strome*, and even *Idolatry*: "Love of self assumes many forms, noble and ignoble; but, whether it blaze gloriously or smoulder basely, its final outcome can only be a handful of dead ashes. After so many struggles, sophistries, triumphs, and jealousies, that is the end." [24] The transmutation of this "love of self" into love for others is, unfortunately, not dramatized as successfully in Warren Bell as it is in Bressant, Strome, and Helwyse: it is only the death of Drayton that, improbably, works a change in the hero. Second, Hawthorne's concluding pages are important in showing an antiphilanthropic attitude akin to that of *The Blithedale Romance,* as he declares:

There are many so-called philanthropists,—men who will cure the world with a patent nostrum, or a political formula, or a moral apothegm. But these infallible prescriptions, when they are analyzed, invariably resolve themselves into one essential element,—self. The men who have truly beatified mankind have done so unconsciously or inevitably, by an inborn divine energy of nature. . . . The test of a man is not whether he can govern a kingdom single-handed; but whether his private life is tender and beneficent, and his wife and children happy. [25]

This realistic political novel, with its memorable portrait of Seth Drayton, remains one of Julian Hawthorne's most satisfactory productions.

John Parmelee's Curse (1886), which succeeded *Love—or a*

Name, is, in contrast, one of Julian Hawthorne's poorest works. The "curse" of the title is not ancestral, as one might expect in Hawthorne's fiction, but rather the curse of drug addiction, or, as the nineteenth century had it, "opium-eating." Parmelee is a bank cashier, a respected man in the little community of Tisdale, whose wife had slowly deteriorated under the influence of drugs and finally had run away from her husband and child. Years later, Parmelee learns that his wife's brother is planning a bank robbery in Tisdale. Now a drug addict himself, he runs off in a confused state of mind to New York, his daughter Sophie following with a black satchel containing the bank's money that the cashier has himself appropriated.

Hawthorne manages one good scene in New York. The town is at a drunken fever pitch over an approaching election. A great rally is going on in Union Square, and the haggard, opium-clouded, yet eloquent Parmelee is hoisted onto the platform through a misunderstanding:

> Parmelee stood before them and gazed out upon them, supporting himself with his hands upon the railing. He did not realize the meaning of his position; but he felt the great wave of emotion surging in upon him from that vast assemblage. . . . He figured to himself that all these hosts of eager auditors were gathered together out of interest in his private concerns; and that they awaited in breathless suspense the recital of his misfortunes and of his hopes. He resolved, therefore, to take them into his confidence.[26]

His confused ramblings are surprisingly touching. But from pathos the story degenerates into cops-and-robbers melodrama. Parmelee is captured by his brother-in-law Blackmer and his gang in the expectation that he will disclose the whereabouts of the money, but is freed by a young friend of Sophie's. In the hope of finding his wife, Parmelee goes to an opium den, and there is arrested together with Blackmer. A court trial clears up everything, and the shattered Parmelee goes back to his old position at Tisdale. There are almost no redeeming features to this poor piece of potboiling melodrama. It may be noted that Hawthorne again attacks the big city as symbol and agency of corruption and idealizes the small town.

Chief among the romantic stories of this period of Julian Hawthorne's career is *Noble Blood* (1885), whose Irish setting is drawn from Hawthorne's visit to Kinsale in 1881–82. The opening chapters of this slight work lead the reader to expect that Hawthorne intends to exploit the Gothic potentialities of an obscure Irish town. A traveling painter named Owen Ambrose happens upon an ancient tower, supposedly uninhabited, in which he sees a ghost; when he views the same apparition at night, he feels a thrill of "expectant horror." He sets up his studio in the ruined tower, where he comes in contact with "medieval sentiment and substance." We are even introduced to an ancient manuscript, with a family history in Italian that Ambrose proceeds to translate. However, these Gothic properties are not at the heart of the story.

The ghost, for example, is soon properly introduced as Miss Anastasia Cadogna, who, like Madge Danver in *Garth,* is a proud, strong-willed, and inconsistent creature bent upon marrying only someone of "noble blood." Ambrose falls in love with her, but she fastens her ingenuously cynical attention on a silly Italian duke. The painter accidentally foils the elopement of the two and finds on the following day that Anastasia is really happy at this, for she loves *him.* "There's something nobler" than noble blood, she finally admits. Then Owen is free to tell her that, according to the ancient manuscript, she is descended from an old Italian family and is thus herself of noble blood. This is a pleasant but unimportant romance.[27]

Of the shorter romances of this period, three are intriguing murder mysteries: *Sinfire,* "Countess Almara's Murder," and "Prince Saroni's Wife." The first of these is by far the best. *Sinfire* (1887), providentially free from mangling authorial intrusions, maintains a smoothly flowing narrative and consistent point of view through the device of presenting Hawthorne as the editor of a journal kept by Frank Mainwaring.

Frank, a physician, is the youngest son of the Cedarcliffe estate; he is a kind of egoist manqué, a man competent enough, but lacking the incentive that would unleash the hidden lust for power he shares with many other Hawthorne heroes. His oldest brother, John, is fashioned upon the Squire Western prototype; the middle son, Henry, is a likable rake. We are led to believe that Frank is interested not in the estate, which would pass to him only upon the death of his brothers, but in the practice of amateur snake-charming, for which he has acquired a cobra named Sâprani.

Almost coincident with the arrival of Sâprani is the appearance of another dangerous temptress, a supposed cousin of Frank named Sinfire, who is not so easily charmed. For the first time in his life, Frank finds himself incited to a pitch of positive action. Through Hawthorne's device of Frank's first-person narrative, we find our sympathies in accord with his as he holds before himself the image of the great man he might become. He concentrates "the action and passion of a lifetime" into his Sinfire-inspired plot. Frank suspects quite rightly that she is of gypsy stock, but he misunderstands her motive in seeking to visit her revenge on Henry. When the latter is murdered, suspicion eventually falls on her. The love of Sinfire and Frank, which has restrained her from violence to his brother, has had the opposite effect on him. In an exciting denouement we learn that Frank himself has murdered his brother Henry as part of his plan to acquire the family estate; but his refraining from telling Sinfire this honestly, and then lying on the witness stand to shield her, have the ironic effect of turning the passionate gypsy against him. And since his life is shattered, not even the death of John by heart failure, and the passing of the estate to him, can stay him from deciding to press Sâprani to his breast—a death recalling that of the suffering heroine of *Fortune's Fool*. "Our wills and fates do so contrary run that our devices still are overthrown" is the theme, then, reinforced by Frank's statements of his belief in Fate and predestination. The authorial trick of having the murderer conceal his crime in his private journal until the very end seems rather cheap after the effect of the tale has worn off, but raises no doubts in the course of the narrative. Sinfire's motivations are often melodramatic and insincere. Yet despite these objections, she and Frank (and the gorgeous cobra) emerge as convincing personages in this compelling story.

"Countess Almara's Murder," a long story of 1886, evidences Hawthorne's continuing Gothic interests. The opening words, "Ten years have passed since the Countess's tragic end," lead the reader to suspect that the ambiguous "murder" of the title was visited *upon* the countess; but there is a trick ending. The narrator's painter friend Raleigh had once loved an Italian girl, but had had to give her up when their elopement was thwarted by her parents. As the story opens, Raleigh is leaving New York, and the narrator has a prophetic dream of danger imminent to his friend. He visits Raleigh's darkened studio after the artist supposedly has left, and in a scene of genuine horror, one of the best Hawthorne ever contrived and comparable to the discovery scene in *Archibald Malmaison,* finds him dead. As events turn out, the narrator learns that the Countess Almara had been the sister of Raleigh's first love, had borne him an illegitimate son years later in France, and had killed him when he had refused to marry her. The various "trick" elements of the plot—the identifying birthmark on Raleigh's son, and the countess's dressing in men's clothes when she visits Raleigh to slay him—are skillfully handled. But the reader foresees the end as soon as a few obvious clues have been planted, so that little suspense is created.

The earliest of these romantic murder mysteries, "Prince Saroni's Wife" (1884), was a great popular success. A diabolical Byronic figure, the prince, marries a young girl, murders her, and sails off to America with his true love, Ethel Moore, acting the part of the new princess. When the pair return, they are found out by Ethel's old monomaniac father, who never had believed his daughter a suicide.

Like the last-named story, the last three tales in this romantic group, all of which belong to the year 1884, are of little more than passing interest. In the lengthy introduction to "The Trial of Gideon," the narrator describes his expedition to the banks of the Euphrates and his discovery of an ancient manuscript, which he proceeds to translate. The manuscript tells, in a style that Hawthorne makes drearily sententious, a story of the ancient city of Nebo and the cause of its destruction by flood waters. Another Gothic-hued tale is "Constance," which begins pleasantly with Hawthorne's autobiographical recollections of the England of his youth, and concludes, after a series of melodramatic incidents, with the Gothic spectacle of immurement in a Dresden boardinghouse. In "Pauline," Hawthorne tells an occasionally witty tale of a painter in love with a famous actress who wins her after a series of hardly memorable misunderstandings have been successfully cleared up.

2. Editor and Biographer

The temporary laying down of arms between the Hawthornes and the Lathrops came to an end in 1882, as a battle developed over *Dr. Grimshawe's Secret,* one of Nathaniel Hawthorne's extended studies for his projected English romance. As Julian Hawthorne tells the story, he had found the manuscript among his papers almost by accident:

> It came into my possession . . . about eight years ago [in 1874]. I had at that time no intention of publishing it; and when, soon after, I left England to travel on the Continent, the manuscript, together with the bulk of my library, was packed and stored at a London repository, and was not again seen by me until last summer, when I unpacked it in this city [New York]. I then finished the perusal of it, and, finding it to be practically complete, I re-resolved to print it in connection with a biography of Mr. Hawthorne which I had in preparation. But upon further consideration it was decided to publish the Romance separately.[28]

This account is at least partly untrue, for Hawthorne had not traveled on the Continent "soon after" 1874. His earlier notice in the papers that he was planning to publish a posthumous Hawthorne novel had grievously aroused Rose and George Lathrop, who were certain that they had seen everything the elder Hawthorne had written. They did not know that Mrs. Hawthorne had begun the transcription of another late work by Hawthorne that existed independently of both *The Dolliver Romance* and *Septimius Felton,* and that she must have given to her son alone. Rose went so far as to write the New York *Tribune,* August 16, 1882:

> As it has been announced that a new and complete romance by Nathaniel Hawthorne, entitled "Dr. Grimshawe's Secret" has been found and will soon be published, will you do me the favor to correct the error? No such unprinted work has been in existence. . . . It cannot be truthfully published as anything more than an experimental fragment.[29]

In a letter to Aunt Ebe, Rose wrote that "Julian's shocking notice in the papers has been a great grief to me. His dishonesty has been a heavier blow than mere cruelty would have been, especially as I could hardly expect anything but the latter after his conduct toward us."[30] A few weeks after Rose's letter appeared in the *Tribune,* Hawthorne wrote her a pained letter: "Now, my dear Sister, you know the reason why I have hitherto refrained from making any defense or answer to the direct charge of forgery which has been again and again brought against me, always on the authority of your statements. With the proof literally in my hands—ninety thousand words of this story in my father's handwriting—I sit here day after day and wait for you to speak. . . ."[31] Rose and George did not publicly disavow their implied contention that the novella was at most a fragment finished by the editor but offered by him as a work completed by his father; but at least they came to believe that the manuscript was absolutely authentic. Not, however, before Julian Hawthorne, in his "Preface" to the published manuscript, had got in a final salvo at George Lathrop:

So many inspired prophets of Hawthorne have arisen of late, that the present writer, whose relation to the great Romancer is a filial one merely, may be excused for feeling some embarrassment in submitting his own uninstructed judgments to competition with theirs.[32]

The unfortunate and sordid episodes that had characterized the relationship of Julian Hawthorne and the Lathrops had a curiously happy sequel. After 1883, through some unexplained agency, the Hawthornes and Lathrops became genuine friends. Rose's brother wrote her a letter remarking on the "great power and originality" of her literary gifts. "If you keep on writing," he declared, "you will become the most memorable of the women novelists of this country. But do not, on that account forego your lyrical poetry."[33] He adds, in another letter: "You really have in you the entrails of Hawthorne's genius, if they are anywhere."[34] Lathrop and Hawthorne were frequently seen together in the mid-1880's—reading for the benefit of the American Copyright League, attending dinners, and planning a new literary weekly.

Although the Lathrops did not know it, Hawthorne's edition of *Dr. Grimshawe's Secret* was quite vulnerable before an informed attack; but that was not possible until this century,[35] when the manuscript that Julian Hawthorne had disposed of piecemeal to various collectors was assembled by Professor Edward H. Davidson. The scholar arraigns Hawthorne for his "high-handed" and "casual" editing and for his "editorial sleight of hand." Julian Hawthorne, he states,

> allowed himself every license an editor could arrogate to himself: he ruthlessly excised large sections of the two long drafts and patched together loosely related parts which originally had no connection with each other. What has existed . . . as *Dr. Grimshawe's Secret* has had scant resemblance to the novel Hawthorne left unfinished at his death.[36]

It should be noted that Hawthorne cannot be pardoned on the basis that excuses Sophia Hawthorne's emendation of her husband's notebooks: gentility, or "correctness."[37]

In the light of Professor Davidson's criticism, one might expect that the full-scale biography of his parents, *Nathaniel Hawthorne and His Wife*, which Julian Hawthorne published in 1884 and which has always been thought his single most valuable work, may not satisfy modern standards of biographical scholarship. Certain flaws will be pointed out, but the book remains, over eighty years later, of the first importance to the scholar shaping a definitive biography of Nathaniel Hawthorne.

The book, which is dedicated to Hawthorne's wife Minne, is presented as "a simple record of lives," and does not indulge in any literary criticism. Perhaps the most unusual feature of the biography is its presentation of the full life story of Sophia Hawthorne in conjunction with that of her husband. "To attempt," says the biographer, "to explain and describe [Nathaniel Hawthorne's] career without taking [his marriage] into consideration would . . . be like trying to imagine a sun without heat, or a day without sun. Nothing seems less likely than that he would have accomplished his work in literature independently of her sympathy and companionship." [38] Once this premise is neatly stated, the biographer proceeds to demonstrate its invalidity. The story of Sophia Hawthorne's life and concerns is interesting enough, but it sheds little light on the career of her husband, who had begun writing long before he met her, and who was as independent of her in his theories of politics and human conduct as he was in his literary imagination.

The biography is useful in gathering together Hawthorne's extant letters and appraising his relationships with the chief men of letters of his time. Frequently, the biographer simply presents thirty or forty pages of letters with no comment at all, and includes trivia along with matters of importance; but the basic data are all there. Julian Hawthorne was much attacked by later Hawthorne biographers for including an undocumented account of the novelist's supposed romantic attachment to a Salem coquette in the late 1830's; however, only ten years ago Norman Holmes Pearson showed that the incident was indeed based on fact, and that its shadowy outlines are to be ascribed to Julian Hawthorne's reticence rather than to his romantic imagination.[39]

Professor Pearson's vindication was based on the investigation of a volume of Julian Hawthorne's "Literary Memoranda" preserved in the Pierpont Morgan Library, which contains many of the biographer's notes for his book, including fragments from the recollections of his aunt Elizabeth Hawthorne and letters from the latter to Una Hawthorne. While these notes confirm the authenticity of the "coquette" story, they at the same time demonstrate rather painfully that the writer was not averse to altering or omitting materials given to him. Thus Hawthorne omits the printing of several of his father's youthful poems and cancels, when it pleases him, various references to himself. One representative example of this editorial emendation will suffice. The two passages printed immediately below are transcriptions of "Ebe" Hawthorne's letters to Una:

> If Julian makes as much as George Eliot, as perhaps he may, he will redeem the family from the curse that was nearly all its inheritance from its ancestors. But I am wicked to say that, when our forefathers bequeathed us an unblemished name, and the best brains in the world.

> You may tell E. P. P. [Elizabeth Palmer Peabody], or any one else, that I never heard of insanity in the Hawthorne family; we are a remarkably "hard-headed" race, not easily excited, not apt to be carried away by any impulse; in short, we are just what E. P. P. is not, and what she cannot comprehend that any one else can be.

And here is the biographer's synoptic text as it appears in *Nathaniel Hawthorne and His Wife:*

> I never heard of any insanity in the family. We are a remarkably "hard-headed" race, not easily excited, not apt to be carried away by any impulse. The witch's curse is not our only inheritance from our ancestors; we have also an unblemished name, and the best brains in the world.[40]

Hawthorne has combined the two fragments, gratuitously adding "witch's" to "curse," omitting mention of himself, and censoring the caustic flavoring of his aunt's remarks on her sister-in-law and on the nature of the family inheritance.

Still another kind of omission is made in the book, one motivated more by pique than by gentility or modesty. Julian Hawthorne had inherited his mother's feud with the publisher James T. Fields, and there is no mention in the book of the man who helped bring Hawthorne's *Scarlet Letter* before the public. This was a slight not to be overlooked by Fields's surviving admirers, and accordingly Thomas Bailey Aldrich of the *Atlantic Monthly* wrote to Thomas Wentworth Higginson, who had been assigned the review of the biography:

> In your notice of Julian Hawthorne's book I hope that you will find it in your way, or be willing even to go out of your way, to give Julian a rap on the knuckles for his shabby treatment of Fields. It was he who discovered Nathaniel Hawthorne in his obscurity and despondency, and put hope into his heart. The literary history of Hawthorne that omits mention of J. T. Fields in connection with the publication of The Scarlet Letter & the later books, is no history at all. The whole thing is a little piece of small revenge, growing out of a needless quarrel brought about years ago by the pestiferous Gail Hamilton. It seems to me that it is only justice to Fields' memory that Julian Hawthorne's offense should not be overlooked.[41]

The rap was forthcoming in Higginson's long and generally slighting review of the book,[42] and Aldrich wrote him again approvingly, "Your Hawthorne review is cruelly good. Of course I shall make a life-long enemy of Julian Hawthorne." Despite this and other criticisms leveled at the book, it was widely accepted at the time, and still is, as a monumental achievement in biography. Its texts are not completely reliable, but this deficiency is more than compensated for by the wealth of detailed information on Nathaniel Hawthorne's life, friendships, and literary career. The two volumes of the biography were incorporated in the Riverside edition of Hawthorne's works (1884).

This major biography was only the first of Julian Hawthorne's long series of explorations of his father's life and times, and of his writings, which appeared more or less regularly in print until his death in 1934. To the years 1884 and 1886 belong four articles that indicated the range of the son's interest in the elder Hawthorne. In "The Salem of Hawthorne" and "The Scenes of Hawthorne's Romances" (1884), Julian Hawthorne evoked the physical settings of his father's life and stories with great success. "Hawthorne's Philosophy" (1886) analyzes at length his father's view of man, without, however, the graceful prose of Lathrop's *Study,* or the searching insight of James's *Hawthorne.* Specific critical analysis is also devoted to Hawthorne's major work in "The Problems of 'The Scarlet Letter' " (1886).

3. The "Clubbable" Man

Soon after his return to the United States, Julian Hawthorne was moving as easily in the public arena of literature as he had in England. Much of his fiction had been published in America as well as England during the 1870's; his new books and stories described above found a ready market; and he was to become even more widely known as lecturer and journalist. He was a literary figure without the actual power of Howells, the critical prestige of James, or the popularity of Samuel Clemens: approximately on the same level of esteem as Lathrop, Richard Watson Gilder, George William Curtis, or Charles Dudley Warner. On June 7, 1883, the year after his return to America, he was lionized in a dinner at Delmonico's by a dozen friends, "all of whom made speeches at me," he writes.[43] At the farewell banquet for Henry Irving in New York in April, 1885, he was seated among such prominent guests as Charles Dana, Henry Ward Beecher, Bram Stoker, Henry Cabot Lodge, Gilder, and Lathrop. In that same month Hawthorne participated in a two-day series of "Authors' Readings" at the Madison Square Theater for the benefit of Lathrop's pet project, the Copyright League. Julian Hawthorne shared the speaker's platform with Howells, Warner, and Joel Chandler Harris on April 28; Clemens, Lathrop, and George Cary Eggleston were among those heard the following day.[44] As an artist, Hawthorne had enrolled himself under the banner of Ideality, which he stoutly defended in print during this decade; and this fact undoubtedly caused him to be accepted by the two leaders of the literature of gentility: E. C. Stedman, "The Poet Laureate of New York" and author of a well-known poem on Nathaniel Hawthorne; and his friend of the 1870's, Richard Henry Stoddard. Stedman wrote to him warmly at a later date: "I have long suspected that the poet in you, more or less hampered the novelist. . . . Remember that the novelist who is by blood and choice a romancer is a confessed poet." [45] Hawthorne's "New York stories," *Beatrix Randolph* and *Love—or a Name,* were singled out for praise in George Lathrop's important article of 1886, "The Literary Movement in New York," which sought to document the gradual movement of leadership in literature from Boston to New York.[46]

As usual, Julian Hawthorne took his socio-literary obligations seriously. In 1883 he became a member of the Authors Club, founded the preceding year under the leadership of his friend Stedman. The Club's membership also formed the nucleus of the American Copyright League. The Authors Club—whose members included such literary men as Edward Bellamy, O. B. Bunce, H. C. Bunner, Clemens, G. W. Curtis, the brothers Eggleston, Gilder, John Hay, Lathrop, Brander Matthews, E. P. Roe, and R. H. Stoddard—met fortnightly in its own rooms and gave public receptions to such figures as Matthew Arnold and Edmund Gosse.[47] A crisis developed in the affairs of the club late in 1885 over the election of a minor Midwestern poet named Will Carleton. He had received sufficient votes to elect him, but certain members distorted the returns and also succeeded in postponing a new election. Hawthorne and Lathrop were furious, and in a long letter to Clemens, Hawthorne outlined the case and asked the humorist for his proxy. He declared candidly:

> I don't myself care for [Carleton's] poetry, but I voted for him, because he is *par excellence* an American author, a man who has done honest work and gained solid and wide recognition. And there was another reason. The Club has lately been filling up with men who, because they have passed through a street in which there was a bookstore, are called "authors." . . . I hold that we have no right to exclude men who are bona fide authors, merely because half a dozen fellows can be found to say that they are "unclubbable" men. The Authors' Club . . . is, or ought to be, a representative and (so far as possible) complete organization of genuine American men of letters. . . . The Club is valuable . . . as a means by which our men of letters can meet each other when they wish it, and act upon or discuss, with a certain completeness, questions affecting their several interests. . . . Such transactions as those of last night will ruin the Club if they are allowed to stand. I write to you, because I have every confidence in your sense and sincerity. I daresay you may hate Carleton, or that his poetry causes you to vomit: but I imagine that will not prevent your voting for him on general principles.[48]

Hawthorne's letter, which also contained further violent criticisms of the club while proclaiming its theoretical usefulness, was answered by Clemens within the week in a note that included his proxy. Where Hawthorne had been impassioned and lofty, Clemens was ruthlessly blunt. He agreed with all of Hawthorne's strictures except the statement that such maneuvers *"will* ruin the Club"; "that sort of procedure," Clemens declared, "has already ruined it." It is no more an author's club, Clemens went on pungently, "than it is a horse-doctor's club." Its name is "a sarcasm," he added, and concluded that he would like to see a new one started "on a sane plan." This last sentiment was received gleefully by Hawthorne, who declared, "I am ready to support the new Club whenever it chooses to be born." The incident—which seems to have ended in a Pyrrhic victory for the pro-Carleton wing [49]—is significant in showing how seriously Julian Hawthorne took himself as a responsible man of letters and the extent to which he was so regarded by his contemporaries.

Another club to which Hawthorne belonged was The Kinsmen, an organization of writers, painters, and actors informally designed for the promotion of good fellowship in New York during the winter and London during the summer.[50] Among its American members prior to its demise in 1887 were Aldrich, Bunner, Clemens, Gilder, Howells, Lathrop, and Warner. Bunner and Hawthorne were good friends, but the former could note with his customary sarcasm:

> The N.Y. branch of the New London Society of Psychical Research held an impromptu meeting at Hutton's. . . . I was dining there with Julian Hawthorne and Kemys, the sculptor. Hawthorne . . . is a psychic sharp, and has just been lecturing on the Philosophy of Magic. The manifestations, however, were meagre.[51]

Two other major personal and literary friendships were formed at this period, with E. P. Roe and Eugene Field. Hawthorne's acquaintanceship with Roe had begun as early as 1886. On March 15, 1888, Roe wrote Hawthorne praising one of his stories, declaring: "It is as fine a bit of work as I have ever met with in literature, and deserves to be preserved always, as one of its gems. . . . I can never do such work, but I can enjoy it!"[52] Eugene Field and Julian Hawthorne developed a close friendship based upon their "mutual taste for the genuine in literature."[53] Field admired the stalwart and athletic figure of Nathaniel Hawthorne's son, and Hawthorne was drawn to Field by the latter's comic identification of him in print as the author of his father's masterpieces. Hawthorne was one of Field's very few literary acquaintances in 1887, and when E. C. Stedman declined to write an introduction for Field's *Culture's Garland,* Hawthorne graciously assumed the task.[54] His preface showed a clear understanding of Field's character and intellectual powers: "No man born on this continent," he declared, "is a more robust American than he; no man scents a sham more unerringly, or abominates it more effectively; no man's ideal of American literature is higher or sounder." [55] When Field visited the East in 1887, he was squired in New York by Stedman and Hawthorne, who "introduced him in literary circles." [56] In later years Hawthorne contributed another introduction to a collection of Eugene Field's writings.[57]

Hawthorne was willing to exploit his considerable prominence as a man of letters for commercial rewards. For the season of 1884–85 the Redpath Lyceum Bureau announced lectures by Hawthorne on the following topics, which leaned to publicizing the novelist's prestigious years abroad: London Environs; Walks in England; English and American Society; English and American Novels; and Readings from Nathaniel Hawthorne's Works. The Redpath puff quoted the Springfield *Republican* on one of Hawthorne's lectures:

> Julian Hawthorne won golden opinions in his appearance as lecturer at the Concord School of Philosophy. . . . His manner is very modest, without the painful shyness which his father had, and in appearance he now very much resembles the elder Hawthorne. His voice is deep and pleasing, and by practice would become very agreeable to an audience; while few of the literary essayists who lecture have so keen and finished a style.

There were approving notices quoted also from the Philadelphia *Press*, the London *Globe* and *Academy*, and from Richard Henry Stoddard, who had written in the New York *Mail and Express* that "Mr. Hawthorne is clearly and easily the first of living romancers." Hawthorne was also lecturing in the late 1880's under the auspices of his close friend for the next decade, Major Pond.

The novelist's ambitions turned in a somewhat different direction in 1885. He was invited to become the literary critic of the New York *World*, then edited by Joseph Pulitzer, and to write feature articles for that newspaper. Hawthorne had been a critic for the London *Spectator* in the 1870's, and in this sense he was not taking a new step; but the involvement with the press as a gentleman-journalist (the phrase is George Knox's) was new, and was only the first of a dozen such newspaper positions he was to hold until his death. It is an open question whether such journalistic affiliations increased his literary reputation, or helped to extinguish it. Hawthorne himself felt ambivalent toward journalism: he could both proclaim the virtues of the yellow press and write an article called "Journalism the Destroyer of Literature."

Only a year after his work on the *World* began, Hawthorne became involved in a quarrel even more celebrated than his public imbroglio with George Lathrop ten years earlier. This time Hawthorne was the more or less passive party, and his old tutor James Russell Lowell was the cudgeller. Hawthorne had interviewed the ex-minister, and had published the results in the *World* on October 22, 1886. Lowell's conversation ranged from English politics and English writers to the royal family, and some of his comments were not discreet, as when, according to the reporter, he described Queen Victoria as "very tough" and Prince Albert as "immensely fat." Lowell must have read the interview with stunned surprise, for he wrote to the Boston *Advertiser:*

> Nobody could have been more surprised and grieved than I by Mr. Hawthorne's breach of confidence in his report of my conversation with him. . . . It never entered my head that the son of my old and honored friend was "interviewing" me. . . . The reporter has made me say precisely the reverse of what I must have said and of what is the truth.[58]

Julian Hawthorne promptly replied that Lowell must have known he was being interviewed; and he was backed by the *World,* which lauded Hawthorne as a man of integrity incapable of dishonest dealings and conceded to Lowell only the fact that he may have said "some things about his aristocratic friends in England that sound unpleasant to him now." The public debate elicited another round of comments by Lowell and

Hawthorne and a chorus of gleeful editorials from the press all over the country, only too eager to bait the sage of Elmwood for his conservatism, his attacks upon a brother journalist, and what one newspaper called his public exposition as a tuft-hunting toady. Hawthorne's friend Eugene Field adopted Lowell's "Biglow" diction to spoof the sage:

> One night aside the fire at hum,
>   Ez I wuz settin' nappin',
> Down from the lower hall there come
>   The sound uv some one rappin'.
> The son uv old Nat Hawthorne he—
>   Julian, I think his name wuz—
> Uv course he found a friend in me,
>   Not knowin' what his game wuz.
>
> And iz we visited a spel,
>   Our talk ranged wide an' wider,
> And ef we struck dry subjects—well,
>   We washed 'em down with cider.
> Now, with that cider coursin' thru
>   My system an' a playin'
> Upon my tongue, I hardly knew
>   Just what I wuz a sayin'.
>
> I kin remember that I spun
>   A highfalutin story
> About the Prince uv Wales, an' one
>   About old Queen Victory.
> But sakes alive! I never dreamed
>   That cuss would get it printed.
> (By that old Queen I'm much esteemed,
>   Ez she hez often hinted.)
>
> Oh, if I had that critter neow,
>   You bet your boots I'd larn him
> In mighty lively fashion heow
>   To walk the chalk, gol darn him!
> Meanwhile, between his folks an' mine
>   The breach grows wide an' wider,
> And, by the way, it's my design,
>   To give up drinkin' cider.[59]

George Knox's summary of the Hawthorne-Lowell affair is that

> in spite of [the] crescendo of polemic editorial print in Julian's defense, one comes away somewhat suspicious. . . . Universally conceded to be "unfortunate," Mr. Lowell's attack obviously disturbed journalistic prerogatives. At best they were willing to admit . . . that Mr. Lowell misunderstood Julian's visit or that he merely forgot what he had said. The late representative from the Court of St. James's came off badly and failed to maintain his awesome dignity by ignoring the whole affair.[60]

The scales in the quarrel of 1876 had tipped against Julian Hawthorne. In this battle ten years later, even though his adversary was a mightier man than Lathrop had been, the scales tipped toward him. Julian Hawthorne's reputation as a journalist and man of letters had reached its apogee.

4. The Inner Record

Amid his successes as writer of popular fiction, as clubbable man, as lecturer, and as gentleman-journalist, Julian Hawthorne, in the years 1883–87, began to feel, nevertheless, that his life in its deepest commitments was a failure. The note of frustrated literary ambitions is confided first to the journals and then to a few friends, and is transmuted finally into what is to become a characteristic tone of self-deprecation.

Gone by 1883 was the youthful self-confidence that had led Julian Hawthorne to hope for literary fame. In his diary for November of that year, he ruthlessly attacked his own fiction. He felt that he had no deep regard, only a theoretical one, for people and that he had failed to create any convincing character in his novels and romances thus far. He recognized that for his lack of emotional sympathy he had to overcompensate by coaching an indolent, cold, and indifferent imagination. "I am too certain," he declared, "too flippant, too indifferent to everything, the truth included. I have no reverence for anything, and would sacrifice anything, truth included, for the sake of a startling or picturesque effect." He went so far as to vow never to write another novel (a vow he did not keep), and seemed to consider that his failure had been due, first, to his inability to cater to popular tastes and, second, to the curious mixture of the Gothic and the realistic that disfigured his work.

The sense of isolation he felt from other human beings was psychological rather than cultural. He ascribes this isolation to a shyness "connected with vanity and with timidity," and perhaps here is close to feeling that isolation which played so prominent a part in determining the direction of his father's genius. But the elder Hawthorne could dramatize the phenomena of isolation with a sense of ironic pity, as in "Wakefield," or consummate human sympathy, as in "Ethan Brand." It is almost as if the more asocial Nathaniel Hawthorne was, the more he understood men in society. Just the reverse is true of his son: the closer he was to men in society, the less he understood them:

> I notice, in my association with men that I very seldom . . .
> show more than one facet of myself. . . . I desire to be thought
> a superior person, and I desire to be on genial terms with those I
> meet; but I'm invariably conscious of not being so much a man
> as I would fain appear. But this disingenuousness and acting in
> me, so monopolises my care and attention, that I am able to
> spare very little for my interlocutor; in preventing him from
> getting a square look at me, I prevent myself from getting a
> square look at him; and the crisp of the joke . . . is, that, after
> all, people estimate me at pretty nearly what I am worth. . . . I
> know this, and yet I keep up the masquerade. And the result is,
> that men are to me either fools or foes, according to the degree
> of their strength and penetration. I get on much better with
> women, because I can more easily and completely subdue them;
> and also for other reasons. . . . But neither do they know me.[61]

Thus the self-critique extended to his psychological deficiencies, as well as to his composition of fictions; but one feels, in reading over the journal for this year, that Hawthorne was more sincere in the latter concern than in the former. His fiction was not distinguished, and he *knew* that; but his public front was such a resounding success that he was graciously willing to accept that compensation.

Julian Hawthorne was not above this kind of self-dramatization to others as well. He must have written in about the same mood to James Russell Lowell approximately a year before their quarrel; Lowell's kind answer makes the later battle even more ironic. He counseled Hawthorne:

> Your bitterness is, I am sure, but a passing mood. You have not failed except as all men feel that they have failed when they contrast what they have done with what they dreamed of doing. You have inherited more from your father than his great name (which will always handicap you more or less)—something, namely, that seldom runs over into the second generation, & have still a growing-time & a fine career before you.[62]

In the next month (December, 1885), when Hawthorne wrote to the poet Paul Hamilton Hayne, the note of resignation in the face of failure becomes dominant. Yet Hawthorne throws off some of the blame on the current state of literary affairs:

> I see that your own generous imagination has colored and vivified the suggestions found in my writing. If you have waited long to find the touch worthy of my origin—I have waited longer still, and shall wait forever. It will never come. I do not regret it. I do not desire it. Life has been too much a matter of hard work with me to admit of my indulging any literary ambition. I have never had the opportunity to write as I would wish. I used to fancy that the time might come: but I know better now. And, were it to come, very likely I would do nothing. I am happy and content, on the other hand, in a beloved wife and eight children, one of whom is already an angel in the house of angels. I live here by the sea (after many years' exile in foreign lands) and thank God that I shall end my days in my own dear country. This is not a place, nor a time, for literary success. The energy and imagination of our country is occupied in other directions—in commerce, in the occupations by which a mighty Continent is developed. The flower of literature must

wait for appreciation until the turmoil is over. You and such as you can find little hearing now: still less can I; but if we give birth to any pure and good thing, I am confident it will not be lost.[63]

By the time of the "Preliminary Confession" in *Confessions and Criticisms* (1887), the tone of despair, which had been replaced by resignation, was metamorphosed finally into self-mockery. Thus he can say about his early novels: "I had in those days a strange delight in rewriting my productions: it was, perhaps, a more sensible practice than to print them." He speaks of "the many pages which circumstances have compelled me to inflict upon the world" and states amusingly that the publication of *Saxon Studies* in book form "was followed by the collapse of both the English and the American firm engaging in that enterprise. I draw no deductions from that fact: I simply state it." By the late 1870's, he goes on, "I had already ceased to take pleasure in writing for its own sake,—partly, no doubt, because I was obliged to write for the sake of something else. Only those who have no reverence for literature should venture to meddle with the making of it,—unless, at all events, they can supply the demands of the butcher and baker from an independent source." He concludes:

> I cannot conscientiously say that I have found the literary profession—in and for itself—entirely agreeable. Almost everything that I have written has been written from necessity; and there is very little of it that I shall not be glad to see forgotten. . . . Not that I would appear to belittle my own work: it does not need it. But the present generation (in America at least) does not strike me as containing much literary genius. The number of undersized persons is large and active, and we hardly believe in the possibility of heroic stature. . . . Form without idea is nothing, and we have no ideas. If one of us were to get an idea, it would create its own form, as easily as does a flower or a plant. . . . For my part, I do not write better than I do, because I have no ideas worth better clothes than they can pick up for themselves.[64]

5. Hawthorne As Critic

Despite the wryness of the self-reflection in the opening pages of Julian Hawthorne's *Confessions and Criticisms,* the book contains a valuable array of critical opinions. Making no pretense to be a distinguished writer of fiction, Hawthorne could nevertheless quite seriously advance his critical views on other writers and the art of writing, which are here gathered formally for the only time in his career. Certain chapters in the book, such as those dealing with Trollope, Emerson, Theodore Winthrop, and Kemys, are interesting enough; but it is in the essays "Novels and Agnosticism," "Americanism in Fiction," and "The Moral Aim in Fiction" that Hawthorne presents his heaviest battery of critical apparatus.

One may profitably begin with Julian's theory of the imagination:

Ideality and imagination are themselves merely the symptom or expression of the faculty and habit of spiritual or subjective intuition—a faculty of paramount value in life, though of late years, in the rush of rational knowledge and discovery, it is fallen into neglect. . . . It undoubtedly belongs to an abstruse region of psychology; but its meaning for our present purpose is simply the act of testing questions of the moral consciousness by an inward touchstone of truth, instead of by external experience or information.[65]

Despite his scientific training, Hawthorne emerges here as the spiritual son of Coleridge and Emerson. Art was the imaginative expression of a divine life in man, and depended for its worth not upon the touchstone of scientific truth or literal fact, for which Hawthorne had an abiding contempt, but upon its perception of "the underlying truth, of which fact is but the phenomenal and imperfect shadow." The imaginative process must begin in nature, to be sure, refuse to distort it, and proceed to a "loftier reality." "This excludes," Hawthorne stated emphatically, "the photographic method of novel-writing. . . . Spirit gives universality and meaning; but alas! for this new gospel of the auctioneer's catalogue, and the crackling of thorns under a pot." [66] More specifically, Hawthorne traces the death of the imagination to the ascendancy of science, which has "proved nature to be so orderly and self-sufficient, and inquiry as to the origin of the primordial atom so unproductive and quixotic, as to make it convenient and indeed reasonable to accept nature as a self-existing fact, and to let all the rest—if rest there be—go." [67] Along with science has come agnosticism, which informs the temper and materials of the current literary situation. Hawthorne considered doubt a disintegrating influence upon art, for it meant conceiving of the universe as one of chance occurrences; and literary methodology was reduced to "the scientific method of merely collecting and describing phenomena," which could not result in the creation or perception of beauty. The devil in Hawthorne's system—as in Henry James's—was Emile Zola, who was capable only of "a mixture of the police gazette and the medical reporter." Along with Howells and James, Hawthorne believed that the greatest writer of his age was Turgenev. Yet American writers seemed to be more susceptible to the influences of the former, who was more typical of the new "agnostic" tendencies, than of the latter.

Far from attempting to attach any dogma to the creation of works of art, Hawthorne insisted that there was a consonance between art and morality, for the imaginative writer, in seeking the reality beyond nature, found at the same time the source of true morality. Therefore, in Emersonian terms, the artist was literally the giver of the laws, the moralist; as Hawthorne put it, instead of saying that "art should be moral, we should rather say that all true morality is art—that art is the test of morality." [68] But by this he did not mean to justify the notion of art for art's sake, a theory he viewed with contempt.

Although he was fearful that American writers, lacking a

"past, in the European sense," were overly receptive to evil influences in the contemporary situation, Hawthorne devoted an entire essay to defending the hardihood of American literature. He told American writers that the use of American materials was not a useful criterion for an "American" work; if, he said, "we cannot have a national literature in the narrow, geographical sense of the phrase, it is because our inheritance transcends all geographical definitions." [69] Such books as Henry James's *French Poets and Novelists* and E. C. Stedman's *Victorian Poets* are not only American, he declares, but more essentially American than if they had been disquisitions upon American literature:

> The reason is, of course, that they subject the things of the old world to the tests of the new, and thereby vindicate and illustrate the characteristic mission of America to mankind. We are here to hold up European conventionalisms and prejudices in the light of the new day. . . . What is an American novel except a novel treating of persons, places, and ideas from an American point of view? The point of view is *the* point, not the thing seen from it.[70]

In the light of these standards, Hawthorne's view of the two most widely discussed writers of his time, James and Howells, may fairly be predicted. He found in Henry James's early work, such as *The Madonna of the Future,* an acceptable blending of reality and ideality. But the latter was unfortunately to disappear:

> [James] seemed to feel the attraction of fairyland, but to lack resolution to swallow it whole; so, instead of idealizing both persons and plot, as Hawthorne had ventured to do, he tried to persuade real persons to work out an ideal destiny. But the tact, delicacy, and reticence with which these attempts were made did not blind him to the essential incongruity; either realism or idealism had to go, and step by step he dismissed the latter, until at length Turgenev's current caught him.[71]

In James, Hawthorne believes, "the subjects that best repay attention are the minor ones of civilization, culture, behavior;

how to avoid certain vulgarities and follies, how to inculcate certain principles: and to illustrate these points heroic types are not needed." [72] The critic also berated James for the excessive "dissection" in the novels and the absence of passion: there is a misgiving in the reader, he said, that "we do not touch the writer's true quality, and that these scenes of his, so elaborately and conscientiously prepared, have cost him much thought and pains, but not one throb of the heart or throe of the spirit." [73]

Howells is dismissed more summarily, as the historian of "our domestic and social pathology"; he has produced, says Hawthorne, "a great deal of finely wrought tapestry; but does not seem, as yet, to have found a hall fit to adorn it with." [74] Hawthorne saw the future of American literature to lie not in the "critical composure" of James, or the "gentle deprecation" of Howells, but in an anti-agnostic, courageous revelation of the full range of man's moral nature. To do that, it would not "shrink from romance, nor from ideality."

As Emerson was Julian Hawthorne's inspiration for his theory of art, so Nathaniel Hawthorne was the basic source for his theory of romance. The son drew together the remarks in his father's prefaces which constituted that theory: in summary, the difficulties attendant upon the construction of a romance with common American materials are stressed, and the alternative—the supplying of an artistic "Faery Land"—defended. "The ruin of a soul, the tragedy of a heart," states the critic, "demand, as a necessity of harmony and picturesque effect, a corresponding and conspiring environment and stage." [75] Thus it was what one may call *reverberation* that Julian Hawthorne detected as the key to Hawthorne's romances; and by this standard the modern realists and naturalists fell miserably short.

The noble motives, consistent judgments, and occasionally eloquent arguments of *Confessions and Criticisms* mark the book's value as an expression of the school of Ideality. [76] The main lines of argument laid down here were to guide Hawthorne's critical work throughout his life, a fact demonstrated by the very similar opinions expressed in the Pasadena *Star-News* columns thirty years later. Hawthorne's aesthetics also formed the basis for his embracing of Utopian Socialism after the turn of the century. Unfortunately, though we have here a coherent statement of principles, we cannot use the criticism to impose a sense of order on Julian Hawthorne's own hodge-podge fictional production. As my incidental comments on, and outlines of, the stories make clear, there is no *development* in his fiction, of the kind, for example, that he saw in James's. His own novels use romantic paraphernalia, including the heavy-handed Gothic props; but they are not romances in Nathaniel Hawthorne's sense at all, for they do not use the romantic background as a method of reverberation for the actions and passions of the characters. Julian Hawthorne, one must insist, did not understand the human heart; and the romantic tricks, the vigorously heroic characters, the supernatural elements, the "imagination" all too obviously present, and the frequent authorial intrusions on behalf of "romance" and "ideality" do not succeed in evoking the "loftier reality" that his criticism advocated. Admittedly, if he had had something to say, the romantic trappings could be defended; and if his style had been distinguished, much could be forgiven. But in the absence of what his father called "the truth of the human heart," all appears as icing, with very little cake. Only when Hawthorne completely divested himself of the romantic ideals he so cherished in his criticism did he write his better works of fiction.

6

The Decline of a Reputation

1. The Temple Falls

After the appearance of *Confessions and Criticisms* in 1887, Julian Hawthorne, despite private despairs and public self-mockery, continued to write fiction at his usual prodigious rate. The only serious novel written between the inept *John Parmelee's Curse* (1886) and *A Fool of Nature* (1896), however, was the successful *A Dream and a Forgetting* (1888). Contrasted to this realistic study of New York life, and to several thoughtful short stories, is a large group of tales that, in one way or another, conjure up the spectacle of romance. These include the five short novels advertised as the "Byrnes-Hawthorne Series," and another sensational adventure work, *An American Monte Cristo;* the fanciful and grotesque stories *The Professor's Sister* and *The Golden Fleece;* and almost all of the short stories collected in the volumes *David Poindexter's Disappearance and Other Tales* and *Six-Cent Sam's.*

Like *Love—or a Name* and *Beatrix Randolph, A Dream and a Forgetting* is set mostly in the world of New York society, which Julian both admired and damned. The hero, a conceited young poet named Fairfax Boardwine, is in love with a fair country girl, Mary Gault. In a dream one night she happens upon a marvelous story, which she tells to her poet-lover, who, embroidering it with the full force of his imagination, produces his masterpiece, the narrative poem from which Hawthorne's novel derives its title. Boardwine is too much of a prig to ascribe any of the success of the poem to Mary, and she too loving to require it; but the narrator at least sees the realities of the situation.

The "pure" native-town scene now shifts to "evil" New York, whither Fairfax goes to play the social lion, and where he meets the most fascinating character of the novel, Mrs. Cartaux, the wife of his publisher, who is enmeshed in an unhappy marriage that has never aroused her passion. Her haughtiness is conquered by Boardwine's boldness, and she not only aids him in adapting his poem for the stage but plans to run away with him immediately after the first performance. The narrator, a staunch friend of Mary, suspects all this and plans to foil the seduction; but when Boardwine's play is hooted off the stage, Mrs. Cartaux, "not the sort of woman to sacrifice herself for a beaten man," dismisses him contemptuously. The penitent Fairfax returns to Mary.

Despite the mechanical conception of character contrast ("Mary was my good angel," Boardwine says, "while Mrs. Cartaux was my evil genius; it was under her influence that I tried to change the poem into a play—to degrade it from an ideal into something popular"),[1] Hawthorne does handsomely with Mrs. Cartaux. The "experience of passion" that Hawthorne had found markedly absent in the novels of Henry James informs such passages as the following:

> She longed to come in contact with some man in whom the masculine quality was present in its most virile form, who was redolent of human nature and human want and passion. Evidently, then, these elements must have been absent from her experience hitherto; and this might be the explanation of her coldness. She wanted to be grasped by a powerful hand, to be conquered by sheer strength, to be made to feel that there was a force in the world superior to the arguments of reason, the

dictates of prudence, or the rules of morality. In other words, she had not yet fully come into her birthright.[2]

Mrs. Cartaux is not so great a character as Perdita Grantley or Cornelia Valeyon, for she never attains to an understanding of her actions. Hawthorne himself is capable of creating this fascinating creature, but not of understanding her fully; for at the end he takes the dreary conventional view and condemns her for her "cynical creed of life." *A Dream and a Forgetting,* despite its realistic emphasis, contains the familiar improbabilities of narrative, and is, finally, only a pale copy of such dense, complex works as *Sebastian Strome.*

Linked with *A Dream and a Forgetting* by virtue of their serious investigation of the psychology of love are two stories in the volume *David Poindexter's Disappearance and Other Tales* (1888). In the first, " 'When Half-Gods Go, the Gods Arrive,' " Ambrose Drayton, an elderly returned American expatriate, falls in love with Mary Leithe, daughter of an old friend. Just before Ambrose can bring himself to declare his love (which Mary would have returned), a young fellow named Redmond appears, and Ambrose, doubting himself and his gray hairs, loses his chance. The subtle weavings of the old man's emotional state are well caught. Even better is the story " 'Set Not Thy Foot on Graves,' " in which the narrator, Claude Campbell, an artist, confides to his journal details of the reappearance of a woman named Ethel, now Mrs. Courtney, who had jilted him seven years before. In the absence of her husband, and conscious of their wasted lives, Claude feels his love for her returning. When Courtney dies unexpectedly in an accident, Claude is now free to court Ethel again, for she loves him. But he hesitates, and finally goes West. While she was married, Claude's imagination was happy with the idea of loving her in some dim future; but when she became accessible, he was impelled to relinquish her. "Perhaps," he muses, "by force of habit, I had grown to love better than love itself, those self-same forlorn conditions and dreary solitudes which I was continually lamenting and praying to be delivered from!" [3] This is good, and the subtle dialogue between the two old lovers over which the shadow of the past hovers is also unusually well done.

Against this slender output of serious fiction in the late 1880's and early 90's must be placed a very large body of romantic work either sensational, melodramatic, or familiarly, Gothic. In 1887–88, for example, Hawthorne produced five short novels based upon the files of Chief Inspector Byrnes of New York. The popular group of stories was launched in the same year as the first of the Sherlock Holmes tales, *A Study in Scarlet,* and Fergus Hume's *Hansom Cab,* "the best-selling detective story of all time." [4] The series belongs most closely, however, to the "realistic" tradition of detective-crime literature. Beginning in 1856 and continuing until about 1890, declares an authority on the genre, "a gout of books gushed forth from the presses, professing to be the memoirs of this police officer or that, many of which were fiction concocted by professional writers." [5] "Such narratives," wrote Hawthorne, "have the advantage over the conceptions of the imagination, that they are a record of facts, not fancies, and carry the authority and impressiveness of fact." [6] The stories are thickly plotted in the best Hawthorne manner, and abound with romantic complications, but they do not fasten strongly enough on the intellectual overtones of the tale of ratiocination. The best novel of the series is *An American Penman,* an account of whose plot will demonstrate the prevailing tone of the whole group of stories. [7]

The hero is Count Ivan Fedovsky, a Russian nobleman traveling in Europe who loses money gambling at Monte Carlo, and then learns he has lost his estates in Russia. Going to New York with his English servant Tom Bolan, he attempts to begin a new life, but fails, even though he is charmed by Sallie Vanderblick. She erases from his heart his early love for Vera, whom her father had married off to prevent his marrying her, and whom Fedovsky had seen involved in shady dealings on the Riviera. The count becomes involved in a robbery, and thus meets Inspector Byrnes, to whom he tells his story, and who decides to give him a secret mission in Europe uncovering the head of a group of international forgers (or "penmen"). This is a man named Willis, whom Fedovsky had also seen with Vera at Monte Carlo. Willis attempts to have the count murdered, but Fedovsky escapes and tracks Willis to his headquarters, Vera's house in Italy. The unfortunate Vera, who was an enslaved accomplice, poisons herself at the end, revealing before she does so that Fedovsky really retains his estates. The dark, passionate, sinful Vera appears seldom, but very effectively; beside her, Sallie is a pallid heroine. The European adventures are excellently told; much of the latter part of the novel is set in Dresden, which of course Hawthorne knew well; and the Monte Carlo scenes are vivid. There is more sheer excitement about the melodrama—as in the scene in a darkened theater in which Fedovsky is almost garroted—than in the other detective stories. Hawthorne's interest in criminal activities, manifested in this series, was to be demonstrated again a few years later in *Confessions of a Convict* (1893).

Criminals, detectives, the beauteous maiden and the *femme fatale,* cursed jewels, and just about every sensational trick that Hawthorne had learned thus far appear in another novel of these years, *An American Monte Cristo* (1888), which was especially popular in England. A painter named Keppel Darke, falsely accused of the murder of his loved one's guardian, manages to escape his captors and (through an incredible coincidence) secure an immense fortune in jewels belonging to the French crown. He returns to New York as the Count de Lisle and succeeds in solving the crime—Hawthorne here adapted the disguise motif from "Countess Almara's Murder" —and in winning the fair ward Olympia. It may be glittering rubbish, but we know that at least it paid some of Hawthorne's bills.

The old supernaturalist compulsions of Julian Hawthorne, which had been released only intermittently in the early 1880's, returned in full force in his romance *The Professor's Sister* (1888). The first chapter, titled "Metaphysics," is a pseudo-profound discussion of the certainty of the existence of the world of spirits, and of the possibility of reincarnating those spirits. No intellectual excitement is generated, and the cloudy talk about the Buddhist "astral light" is deficient in both meaning and interest.

The familiar wicked-stepmother folktale is adapted handily to Hawthorne's purposes. A young student named Ralph Merlin loves Hildegarde [8] Hertrugge, much to the chagrin of her stepmother Catalina, who loves Ralph. After her initial attempt on Hildegarde's life is foiled by the spectral appearance of the girl's brother, a professor named Conrad, Catalina manages to poison Hildegarde. At this point in the story, one is much struck with Hawthorne's depiction of Catalina, one of his fascinating and deadly women of the world, like Mrs. Cartaux: "You received from her a powerful impression of sex. . . . And she made you feel that she valued you just so far as you were man."

Professor Hertrugge takes the narrator into his magical retreat and subjects him to electromagnetic powers so that he feels at one with the universe and sees the dead body of Hildegarde come to life. The professor, who is also a clairvoyant and who carries out the doctrines preached in the first chapter, "indulges in practices which in old times would have brought him to the stake," and Hawthorne suggests that "his results were achieved by sheer witchcraft." Conrad causes the spirit of Hildegarde to appear in a terrifying manner to her murderess. Finally, two years later, he raises her in the flesh and marries her to an understandably stunned Merlin. Catalina goes mad upon seeing the reincarnated girl—this is Conrad's revenge— but when Ralph is mortally wounded in a struggle, Hildegarde chooses to die again with him, so that they may be joined in the spiritual world. Hertrugge bears an interesting resemblance to Nathaniel Hawthorne's psychopathic scientists like Aylmer and Rappaccini, abstract speculators who engage in practices beyond the sphere of human limitations. Ralph sets the moral tone to the professor at the end of the story: "It was all wrong— what you attempted and I acquiesced in." [9] These overtones are perhaps the most interesting thing in this last important neo-Gothic romance.

Four years were to pass before the appearance of Hawthorne's next work of fiction, the short romance *The Golden Fleece* (1892). Many of Hawthorne's old tricks with the supernatural are produced and made to go through their tired paces; they betray the author's weariness and lack of inspiration. In this story we find a double reincarnation (the phenomenon first used in the early tales and repeated in *The Professor's Sister* continued to interest Hawthorne) of a priest and priestess of the age of Montezuma, Kamaiakan and Semitzin. The former has called forth the princess to reveal the whereabouts of a treasure hidden from the conquistadores and has placed her in the body of Miriam, daughter of General Trednoke, on whose California ranch the main events take place. The dual personality theme of *Archibald Malmaison* is here revived and stated by Kamaiakan: "Two women, both tenants of the same body, both in love with the same man, and therefore rivals of each other, and each claiming a right to existence." [10] Harvey Freeman is the hero in love with this schizophrenic maiden. He and the general engage in a search for a spring that can irrigate the nearby desert, but it is Semitzin, clothed in the magical "Golden Fleece," a woolen garment of Montezuma's time, who sets the spring flowing. Kamaiakan dies, however, and Semitzin with him, thus leaving Miriam in possession of herself and the hero. Except for the graphic descriptions of the Southern California desert, *The Golden Fleece* is not a memorable piece of work.

Most of the short stories produced in the decade after Hawthorne's involvement with journalism show the same preoccupations manifested in *The Professor's Sister* and *The Golden Fleece*. In the collection *David Poindexter's Disappearance and Other Tales* (1888), Gothic elements such as clairvoyant heroes and heroines, secret passageways, and medieval castles appear in such tales as "My Friend Paton" and "Ken's Mystery." The title story of the volume is a reworking of familiar materials. The Reverend David Poindexter, chained to the little

English town of Witton, is liberated when he inherits his uncle's money and property. Corrupted into gambling by the young bloods of London, he soon loses his new wealth and, in the process, his betrothed. The "Wicked Parson" then finds that he has a cousin named Giovanni Lambert, his uncle's true heir, who is his double. When Giovanni is killed in an accident, David disappears and returns later as Lambert to claim the estate and live out his life as a changed man. "Thus," writes Hawthorne, "he could escape from the individuality which was his curse, and find his true self, as it were, in another person." We see several familiar patterns: the simplicity of Witton versus the fashionable corruption of London; and the description of David's Italian aunt as a "foreign woman of great beauty, but of doubtful character and antecedents." The fall-of-the-egoist theme so characteristic of Hawthorne is also present, but the change in Poindexter is as unconvincing as it is in Warren Bell. "Ken's Mystery" is the liveliest of the romantic tales in this collection of 1888. It begins at Halloween, as the narrator visits his friend Keningale, whose youth has been blasted by a strange experience in Ireland. Ken tells a weird Gothic tale set in a seacoast town like that in *Noble Blood*. It was on another All Hallow's Eve that Ken had left a soldiers' drinking party under the influence of the story of the fair Ethelind Fionguala who, two centuries before, had been carried off by vampires and perhaps had become one herself. Returning to his house, Ken passes through a graveyard and, led by an obliging wraith, returns two hundred years through time, to become the banjo-strumming lover of the thirsty Ethelind. After courting the damsel in a gloomy old house, Ken awakens to find that his banjo has aged two centuries. The tone of this quaintly Gothic piece is set by such remarks as "The medieval age was alive once more."

Similar in spirit to this undistinguished volume was *Six-Cent Sam's*, a collection of short stories that comprised the bulk of Hawthorne's fiction for the year 1893. The frame for this group of thirteen tales is "Six-Cent Sam's," a New York hideaway of the 1890's. Eight of the stories are told in a symposium at a Christmas dinner, and most of them deal in one way or another with the familiar elements of supernaturalism in the form of mesmerism, seances, and the appearance of disembodied spirits. Two of the stories are of more than passing interest. The first, "The Author's Story," has for its hero an unbalanced painter named Linden, who is engaged upon creating "the incarnation of perfect maidenhood" on canvas; his model is an exquisite creature who is perhaps growing to love him. After completing his painting, Linden murders his model and then commits suicide. The reasons are left somewhat ambiguous by the narrator. The girl as "incarnation," Linden had believed, "should remain immaculate. [She was of] the type of maidens fit for love, but innocent of love's embrace." As for himself, it was not merely his achievement of his supreme canvas that brought about his decision. "Did Linden love the girl?" Hawthorne asks. "Did she love—or was she ready to love him? If so, no common tragedy was consummated on the day they died. It was death for an ideal, and something more— an act of self-abnegation seldom paralleled." [11] Thus the murder and suicide could perhaps have been Linden's way of preventing the desecration of the love-ideality of his portrait. This short story, one of Julian Hawthorne's most successful, achieves a tone much like that of the elder Hawthorne's best tales: the overtones of the intriguing and ambiguous love story are moral. The second interesting tale in *Six-Cent Sam's* is "The Captain's Story," a powerful narrative dealing with a man named Juan Cordoba, who is brought up by his witch-mother in Mexico to believe in astrological portents, and who expects that on a certain day in his life he will find a great treasure. He becomes a prodigal, a murderer, a brigand in Panama, and then a convict. While in chains in Brazil, on the very day he is to make his fortune, he finds what he foolishly thinks is a lump of glass and gives it away before realizing that it is the great diamond fated for him. "When a man has lived wholly under the dominion of a fixed idea," the narrator says, "and something happens to deprive him of that, his life, in a sense, comes to an end." Juan is later pardoned and lives out his days as a wretched beggar.

The interest in astrology displayed in "The Captain's Story" becomes a characteristic Hawthorne theme in the 1890's. It appears not only in the novel *A Fool of Nature* (1896) but in two short tales, "The New Endymion" and "An Inter-Planetary Episode." The treatment of this "science-fiction" material does not resemble Jules Verne's: there are no exciting journeys to outer space, for example. Rather, as in the last-named story, there is a communication of so-called spiritual states between beings on different planets. Penryn's daughter Yoga falls into a trance each time Mars' orbit swings closest to earth. Harvey, a specialist in nervous and mental diseases, manages to communicate with the spirit of the girl, which has been translated to Mars. When Yoga is abandoned by her Martian lover Kanor, she suffers her earthly death. The story, which is marred by excessively trite diction, springs, like so much of Julian Hawthorne's fiction, from his abiding belief in the reality of the spiritual world.

The decline in Julian Hawthorne's art in the late 1880's and early 1890's is perhaps too obvious for extended comment. In the two earlier periods discussed, in England and America, he had produced memorable works of fiction: *Garth, Sebastian Strome,* and *Love—or a Name.* The romantic mode had been balanced by the realistic, the popular by the serious. With the growing involvement in journalism, such ethical lapses as the Lowell interview, and certainly a severely weakened imagination, Hawthorne's fiction reached its lowest ebb. Romances dominate; characters continually run to type, and the themes appear only as stale reworkings of the more thoughtful fiction; in short, craftsmanship is replaced by cunning. His name was still valuable, and he was as prolific as ever; but the work, with the few exceptions noted, is shoddy and trivial. The great career promised by even such artistically unsatisfying works as *Garth* and *Sebastian Strome* had, ten years later, come to naught. The Moorish temple envisioned in Julian Hawthorne's letter of 1874 as the "monument" to his father had already crumbled; the Parthenon still stood.

2. Hawthorne and Whitman

Julian Hawthorne's ambitions had taken several new directions in this period. First, he had adopted historical hackwork as an additional source of income. His first attempt was his supplementary chapter to Thomas Colley Grattan's standard *History of the Netherlands* (1889), and he contributed a similar chapter of recent events to John Richard Green's *England* (1898). In 1892 he wrote a two-volume *Story of Oregon,* a lively and interesting piece of work; in its preface he seems to defend his new kind of enterprise to himself:

> History is to-day at least as much a fine art as is the writing of imaginative fiction; it is no less rich in the interest arising from the manifestations of human nature; and it is fertile in the problems of social and political science.[12]

And we find in his appraisal of contemporary life something of his characteristic opinions:

> To-day . . . religion seems rich in forms but poor in spirit; . . . science is knocking at the door of the unseen, and can gain no admittance; . . . literature refines upon itself and ceases to create; . . . social life is as the glittering crust suspended over a dark abyss.[13]

For his *Story of Oregon* Hawthorne was paid one thousand dollars, which perhaps compensated for the fact that he never received the proof sheets. The publisher, The American Historical Publishing Company, seems to have then affixed the valuable Hawthorne name to another history that appeared the following year, *History of Washington, the Evergreen State,* supposedly by Hawthorne in collaboration with a Colonel G. Douglas Brewerton.[14]

Yet another nonfictional pursuit of these years was the composition, jointly with Leonard Lemmon, a Texas school administrator, of a textbook called *American Literature* (1891). It was one of Hawthorne's most popular and perhaps most influential books, which saw numerous editions and did not go out of print until the 1920's. This was one of the first texts devoted exclusively to American literature, as distinct from English, yet the student was warned unchauvinistically:

> In dealing with the subject of American Literature, optimism is not expedient only, but indispensable. Unless we can see promise in it, there is not much, as yet, that we can see. After a few great names, . . . we are at the end of our original creative geniuses. All the rest are either reflections of these, or of European models, or else are really nothing at all but print and paper.[15]

The volume reflects contemporary judgments of the leading figures of American literature. In keeping with Hawthorne's frequently expressed opinions, Emerson and Nathaniel Hawthorne emerge as the great heroes, and Lowell is identified as "the most distinguished" of living writers.[16] Other now well-regarded figures do not come off so well. Mark Twain, classified only as a "humorist," receives the same amount of space as Charles F. Browne, and *Huckleberry Finn* is not even mentioned. Herman Melville is barely noticed except to compare him favorably to Cooper as a writer of the sea; *Pierre* is dismissed as "repulsive, insane, and impossible."

The most vicious attack in the book, one which was to have significant repercussions, is levelled at Walt Whitman:

> It is a question whether, when the shock of his grotesque style and still more grotesque "claims" is over, he may not turn out to be a comparatively commonplace and imitative writer. Much of his apparent originality is certainly due to his remarkable ignorance. . . . Since he could not use the instruments that had sufficed for Homer, Shakespeare, and Tennyson, he bethought himself to decry these as effete and inadequate, and to bray forth his message upon a foghorn. . . . In proclaiming a revolt against

the errors and prejudices of the past, he succeeded only in revolting against common sense, good taste and literary sanity.[17]

The specter of continuous public controversy that marked the career of Julian Hawthorne after 1876 once more was aroused by these remarks, as Whitman's outspoken admirers leaped to his defense. Horace Traubel quoted some of the anti-Whitman passages in his journal, *The Conservator,* cast doubts upon Hawthorne's authorship, and sneeringly compared the remarks to Hawthorne's earlier praise of Whitman at the poet's birthday dinner in Camden in 1889. Julian Hawthorne had warmly toasted Whitman in the following words: "Surely the man or poet whose sympathy can extend from the highest specimen of our time [Abraham Lincoln] to the lowest nameless outcast, is worthy of more than all the sympathy and honor that we contain." [18] Hawthorne quickly rushed to his own defense in the next issue of *The Conservator.* He took Traubel to task for quoting out of context and assumed complete responsibility for the text and its opinions. Instead of taking the position that he had merely changed his mind between 1889 and 1891, he chose instead—quite convincingly—to excuse his speech as "straining a point," in order to be in harmony with the occasion. As a critic, Hawthorne declared, he was bound to tell "the whole truth" as he saw it:

> I wished to do what service I might for our literature, and there could be no service in following the hackneyed lines worn by the compilers of former "Manuals," and echoing their perfunctory eulogies. I said, therefore, what I thought, with such explicitness as I could command; and I am gratified to see that this astonishing innovation has fluttered the dove-cotes of conventionalism and fatuity.[19]

Traubel, in the same issue, answered Hawthorne's criticism by printing the entire offensive section from *American Literature,* asserting its entire and obvious inconsistency with the remarks of 1889, and resting his case. Although one investigator concludes that he "exposed Hawthorne courteously but completely," [20] Hawthorne's motives appear sounder than his judgments.

Despite the genteel wrongheadedness and conventionality of many of the judgments made in *American Literature,* the major part of the book is penetrating and well written, and absolutely fair and right in its opinions of such writers as Franklin, Irving, Emerson, Hawthorne, James, and Howells. There is even mention of Julian Hawthorne himself, who is correctly classified in the modern "Imaginative" group, which included Aldrich, Gilder, Hearn, Lanier, Stedman, and Stoddard. The schoolboys were told that

> Julian Hawthorne has been a copious writer. . . . He is at his best in the imaginative vein; and such stories as *Bressant, Idolatry, Archibald Malmaison,* "The Pearl-Shell Necklace" ["The Laughing Mill"], and "Sinfire," indicate powers in the writer which, if conscientiously and carefully employed, might produce good results.[21]

It is somewhat amusing to find, in this surely ironic commentary, that Julian Hawthorne was still to be looked upon as a promising writer, twenty years after the launching of his career and after the publication of two dozen novels and romances and two volumes of short stories. One may, if one wishes, find the real analysis of Julian Hawthorne in the passage ostensibly devoted to the career of Bayard Taylor. The section, stylistically Hawthorne's, seems composed with a peculiar fervor, and is immediately applicable to the state of mind he had himself reached in the 1880's:

> [Taylor] desired to be a great poet: poetry was the end and aim of his life. . . . He bent himself to his lofty task with hopeful ardor. He wrote better than he had ever before written; he produced poems which were good, admirable—all but great. But they were not quite great: and no one recognized this truth so quickly and clearly as he. He had miscalculated his powers; they had sufficed to bring him almost within reach of his goal, and

there they failed him. It was a tragedy of the soul, to be appreciated by those only who were as finely organized as he. He had dreamed of being first; and to find himself, at the end of his career, anywhere else than first was to him no better than to have fallen at the outset. He died, while yet comparatively young, a disappointed man, though only those who knew him most intimately suspected it.[22]

This forms an accurate and poignant, if premature, epigraph to the literary career of Julian Hawthorne.

In the midst of writing the miscellaneous articles, romances, and histories of 1892, Julian Hawthorne was seized with one of his sudden enthusiasms for travel. His wife Minne wrote to Rose Lathrop that the whole Hawthorne family, to be christened the "Literary Argonauts," was to sail to the South Pacific in a yacht to settle down for the remainder of their lives. Hawthorne was to continue his newspaper and magazine writing, and to produce pirate novels with all the "local color." Minne exclaims: "Picture a whole family, all ages and both sexes, among the South Sea Isles. O Typee! O Omoo!" There was to be no definite course, but merely a pleasant sail until the ideal island was found. In a flash of business inspiration, Hawthorne publicized the venture widely, and many others volunteered to join the Argonauts, paying up to five thousand dollars for the privilege. Everything was ready by the end of 1892, and even the yacht that was to carry the adventurers was purchased. But for some unknown reason, the plan fell through as suddenly as it had come into being, and an adventure into the exotic was to be delayed for a full year.[23]

Meanwhile, in 1893, in the months before the Hawthornes set sail for Jamaica, two works of nonfiction were produced. The first of these was *Humors of the Fair,* a rambling, carelessly organized book that expanded several articles on the Chicago World's Fair of 1893 written for *Lippincott's* and *Cosmopolitan.* In Julian Hawthorne's sarcastic statement about "Machinery Hall," we get an echo of the frustration of his plan of the previous year: "Where would we be without machinery?

In Asia, or in the Fiji Islands. What would we do there? Nothing, except eat, sleep, and be happy. Whereas, we can have dyspepsia, insomnia, and nervous prostration here, and work and be miserable from morning till night." [24] There are interesting remarks here and there about the American character and the eventual, desirable, decay of "Fine Society"; but by far the best-written sections of the book are those dealing with the sculptures and paintings in the Palace of Fine Arts. One finds here none of the timid, tentative judgments of a Nathaniel Hawthorne in regard to art; the cosmopolitan Julian Hawthorne knew what he liked and why he liked it. He admired particularly Sargent's portrait of his friend Ellen Terry as Lady Macbeth and praised the works of his old London acquaintances Whistler and Alma-Tadema. He poured his scorn on a sentimental picture called "Breaking Home Ties," by an artist identified with "the class of paintings of real scenes of which the Englishman Frith . . . is the master. . . . From a purely artistic standpoint it is almost worthless; but it is . . . the most popular painting in the Exposition. It 'comes home' to the People." [25] He found the nude sculptures to have the "taint of the model" upon them, and compared them unfavorably with such classical works as the Faun of Praxiteles (a familiar reference point for a Hawthorne) and the Discobulus, which showed "the beauty of humanity, but of no specific human being." American artists, he felt, never attain the unconsciousness of the antique, and since their statues "know that they are naked," they are immodest. He theorizes:

> Our statues are too apt to be in the painter's vein: the subjects and the expressions of emotion we select are not adapted to the material employed. Emotion may, indeed, rightly be expressed in marble or bronze; but it should be emotion at a culminating point—at a point of rest. No transient action should be represented; the counteraction of opposite forces should be so complete, that the figure or group could retain its present pose forever without seeming to do violence to nature. This was the law evidently observed in the best ancient sculptures, and its

value is shown by the fact that the latter are still the best in the world.[26]

He excepts from this general condemnation of modern sculpture the work of his friend Edward Kemys, whose animal figures Hawthorne extols here, as he had in *Confessions and Criticisms*. Even though *Humors of the Fair* is scarcely a valuable book, it shows Julian Hawthorne as that rarity, the erudite journalist.

From the elevated comments on ancient and modern art, the versatile Hawthorne turned to the grim realities of prison life in *Confessions of a Convict* (1893), a book he purportedly edited from the manuscript of an inmate at the State Prison at Auburn, New York. The prisoner's account, declared Hawthorne, "contains criticisms on the management of our jails and on the dealings of the police with criminals out of prison, as well as statements reflecting on the moral integrity of persons conventionally supposed to be honorable, all of which are more or less serious and startling." [27] This was overstating the case. There are, however, vivid descriptions of the rottenness of prison food, the corruption of the officials and guards, and the problem of the insane prisoners, and a muckraking account of how prisons "recruit" many of their inmates through the collaboration of tavern owners and police. The portraits of the inmates are superficial, and the book is too frequently a muddle of incoherent materials; the problem is compounded in the final section, which is devoted to an objective account of criminal activities in America. The book shows Julian Hawthorne's continuing interest in the life of crime, an interest demonstrated in the popular "Inspector Byrnes" books of the late 1880's. And it makes a masterfully ironic forerunner to Hawthorne's poignant and powerful account of his own incarceration twenty years later in *The Subterranean Brotherhood* (1914). What Julian Hawthorne wrote or "edited" here in his customary slapdash style, concentrating on sensational elements, was to be repeated

in many details later but with an absolute sincerity and power
that came then from personal experience.

3. The Kingston Years

The Argonaut project, which had slumbered for a year, came
to life again late in 1893. In the diary he was to keep at
Kingston, Julian noted that "we mean to buy, ultimately, and
cultivate fruits and vegetables for the market—always suppos-
ing our $7000 from the Chicago land holds out." [28] Hildegarde
Hawthorne clarifies this cryptic reference in her fictional account of the West Indian years, *Island Farm,* when she declares
that one of her brothers had superintended the sale of a valuable
piece of land for $10,000, freeing the family from the necessity
of remaining at Sag Harbor. She goes on:

> It was decided that the tropics should be the next home, partly
> because the Princess [Minne Hawthorne] needed a softer climate
> and an easier life than she had known for some time, partly
> because Papa and she thought that there was a real opportunity
> to start a business in the island that would assure a future to the
> boys. [29]

With the assistance of his literary and journalistic friends,
including George P. Lathrop and John Habberton, Hawthorne
attempted to secure the post of consul at Kingston from President Cleveland; but this imitation of his father failed. Without
employment, then, Hawthorne and his family arrived in Jamaica, British West Indies, on December 9, 1893, and began a
tranquil residence that was to last almost three years.

"We found a lovely Island, and eternal summer," Hawthorne wrote in his journal soon after arriving. The Hawthornes had leased a house "at $30 a month. 1000 acres of
ground, large house, in West Indian style. . . . It has been of
course lovely summer weather since we came with a shower
about every day. Temperature average 80°. We are all well,

and Minne better than at Sag Harbor. We have big appetites. We know about a score of people, including Governor Blake." A few weeks later he wrote, "It is a lazy life. But I have some sleep to make up." The family spent the peaceful months visiting, hiking, dancing in the evening, and driving through the island in their new American carriage. Hawthorne's American agent was his friend Joseph M. Stoddart, the publisher of *Lippincott's,* who arranged for the publication of Hawthorne's miscellaneous articles—mostly descriptive pieces about Jamaica —in his own magazine, in *Cosmopolitan,* and in *Once-a-Week.* Judging from the very small number of articles published in 1894 and 1895, the Hawthornes were not hard pressed for money. But the relaxation of the Kingston years did not imply a corresponding ebbing of creativity, as the events of 1895–96 were to demonstrate.

In 1895 the New York *Herald* offered a prize of $10,000 for the best American novel submitted in competition that year. Eleven hundred novels were offered, and when the judges announced their selection, a Miss Judith Holinshed of Kingston, Jamaica, leaped into sudden literary prominence for her prize novel, *A Fool of Nature.* The only genuine thing about Judith Holinshed, however, was her initials. The writer, as the New York newspapers, including the *Herald,* soon declared to the world, was none other than that old hack Julian Hawthorne, who had not written a major work of fiction since 1892. In a letter to the *Critic* Hawthorne concocted a delightful supplititious history of Miss Holinshed; however, his barely credible account of the story's being written in three weeks is actually supported by a private letter in which he declares that he "rattled it off on this typewriter in 24 and a half days." [30] The pseudonymous authorship was probably undertaken in the same high spirits manifested in the *Critic* letter, and is reflected obliquely in the theme of the novel.

A reader obsessed with Julian Hawthorne's literary delinquencies comes to this new work prepared, perhaps, to make some opprobrious remarks about American literary taste in

1895; but he remains to be charmed. The theme and treatment show unquestioned maturity, an absence of supernatural frippery, and a first-rate sense of humor. Despite its limitations *A Fool of Nature* is a sparkling and delightful production, in the first rank of Hawthorne's fiction. The influence of Oscar Wilde in the early years of this decade has left its mark on the witty pages of this novel; it is amazing that Julian Hawthorne, whose sense of humor is the least discernible element in his fiction, should have fashioned such a wealth of witticisms and the "humor" characters to speak them—the Reverend Plukerose Agabag, General Stepyngstone, Mrs. Dorothy Tiptoft, and others. In the conversations at the St. Quentin Club in Boston (reminiscent of the Mulberry Club in *Sebastian Strome*) and at the Whiterduce dinner party, Hawthorne reaches his highest technical proficiency in dialogue; it is a far cry indeed from the muddy metaphysical exchanges of *The Professor's Sister* to the light-hearted effervescence of *A Fool of Nature*. One only hopes that the hero, Murgatroyd Whiterduce, is not expressing the author's sentiments when he says about the Club wits: "They seem always to be making fun of everything . . . so as to make you feel uncomfortable. It makes you laugh, but it doesn't make you feel good." [31]

The plot of the novel involves the coming-of-age of young Murgatroyd, who is not at home with his society friends but only with low companions. It emerges that "Murgy" was a changeling son, the offspring of a villainous Irishman, and has been the innocent cause of a twenty-year misunderstanding between his supposed parents. When Murgy's "father" is murdered and his "mother" dies, the young man, who had been a fool in society but withal warmhearted and generous, embarks on a process of education and mental growth that enables him to cut quite a decent figure in the world. "There was a terrible realism, or naturalism, about this young man," the author comments. "He did not take the conventional or sentimental view." Murgatroyd is thus allied to such "natural" heroes as Jack in *Fortune's Fool* and Garth.

Yet one of the ironies of the story is that the son is seeking to make himself worthy of the family name, when actually the elder Whiterduce had been an unscrupulous would-be dictator. Pynchepole Whiterduce had been planning, exactly like Seth Drayton in *Love—or a Name,* to build a secret dictatorship in America: "Power was his single aim; power absolute and practical, yet abstracted to the verge of spirituality." [32] His murder by Murgy's blackmailing father ends his plans. The development of Pynchepole in this story is not interesting, however, and at his death we have none of the feelings we share with Warren Bell when the latter comes upon the elderly Drayton, a suicide in his study.

The novel is rewarding for its truth-telling scenes, which may be traced in Hawthorne's fiction from Bressant's raging against Abbie, to Perdita's denunciation of her adopted father in *Dust,* to the scene in this novel in which Isabella, Murgy's betrothed, confronts her mother with the proof of her hypocrisy and cries, "It seems to me as if this smooth, tinkling, smirking, rotten-hearted respectability would drive me mad." The novel's minor characters—Dr. Maydwall, the unconventional physician; his friends, the astrologer Gabriel Negus and the voice teacher Polydore Seamell; and several "New Women"—are not carefully developed. Several features of the story, such as the ideal of unalterable heredity—Murgatroyd is a "low" person though brought up in a cultivated household from babyhood—may today appear antiquated. But the growth of the hero to manhood is convincing, and the flash of wit lights up these last important pages of Julian Hawthorne's fiction. [33]

In a burst of enthusiasm over winning the *Herald* prize, Hawthorne immediately produced a new romance, *Love Is a Spirit* (1896), which, failing to follow up the bright new directions apparent in *A Fool of Nature,* returned to those fictional preoccupations that had proved so disastrous in most of his writing in the 1870's and 80's. He repeated the sort of theme and treatment he probably thought most desirable: the false, "loftier" pitch of diction and sentiment, with constant emphasis on spiritual truth, and the reality of spiritual existence after death. The setting is a West Indian island, the two characters, the fair virgin Yolande and Strathspey, who is separated from his wife and falls victim to the heroine. The conversation between the lovers in the first half of the book is expanded to many times its appropriate length by the author's ruminations on such higher themes as truth, beauty, evil, and spirit versus flesh. The lush, tropical setting is suitable for the heavy luxuriance of the exalted reflections. The lovers are separated when Yolande dies; but she returns to life for one happy day, and the two ride about on a spiritual, not an earthly, island. This amounts to romance without a concomitant feeling of wonder. Hawthorne's specialized variety of supernaturalism is here, seeking to objectify in story the truth of the spiritual world. At one point Strathspey muses about the reincarnated Yolande:

> All day he had been led by a spirit! From the moment when his life had been saved from the falling tree until they halted on the brink of the ravine, he had dwelt as a spirit among spiritual things. For that world, though unperceived, abides always not elsewhere than where we are. To us at all times, have we but eyes to see, may be visible, as to the young man who was with Elisha, the mountain and the chariots of fire.[34]

One can only vainly wish that Julian Hawthorne had ended his career as a writer of book-length fiction on the note of high comedy and silver laughter maintained so brilliantly in the novel *A Fool of Nature,* rather than on the note of semi-erotic spirituality and false sentiment that disfigures the romance *Love Is a Spirit.* The reality of the spiritual world, in which Julian so fervently believed, as he had been taught in his youth by Emerson and Swedenborg, was never successfully objectified in his fiction; supernatural fancies refused to come to life. The important fiction is set almost exclusively in that world of society and politics that Hawthorne knew and described so well. One pities the waste of talent on unmalleable materials. Julian Hawthorne's allegiances and preoccupations unfortunately led him, as a writer of fiction, into precisely the wrong paths.

4. Journalist and Editor

The idyllic years in Jamaica, which had witnessed the production of one of Julian Hawthorne's best novels and one of his worst romances, ended in 1896, when the Hawthorne family returned to the United States.[35] Minne's health had improved, their business plans had not prospered, and an offer had come for an editorial position on a magazine.[36] Hawthorne even planned to give public readings of his own tales in the manner of Dickens and Twain, and hoped to realize $3,000 a season from the enterprise, with Major Pond's help. For the most part the next ten years were to be spent in exciting journalistic assignments for the New York *Journal, Cosmopolitan,* and other periodicals, in occasional lecture tours, and in the production of several shelves of editions. Though Hawthorne wrote an occasional story until the end of his life, few of these were ever printed, and no novels at all were written. Despite the prize awarded to *A Fool of Nature,* few journals had bothered even to review it or the succeeding romance, *Love Is a Spirit;* and this fact may have finally extinguished Hawthorne's fictional ambitions.

Unlike the parochial years of journalism in London and New York, the years around the turn of the century saw Hawthorne traveling widely. His first assignment upon his return to America was to cover the presidential trail of William Jennings Bryan as a special reporter; the newspapers puffed up the pictures of Bryan and Hawthorne sitting together in shirtsleeves on a sun-baked Kansas porch discussing some profound political matter. Hawthorne also interviewed most of the leading men at the turn of the century, including such figures as Thomas Edison, Nikola Tesla, and Robert Ingersoll; some of them, like Ingersoll, became his friends. In 1897 came one of the "keenest experiences" of Hawthorne's life. He was commissioned by

Cosmopolitan to report on the plague and famine that had struck India with devastating fury. Though he sneered at the Hindus as "the most ignorant people in the world," considering them "paralyzed by prejudices," he was horrified by conditions in Bombay, where millions of people were dying, and wrote vivid descriptions of the city and its incredible living conditions.[37] In the following year he was dispatched by the New York *Journal* to cover the Spanish-American War; in Cuba he joined a platoon of famous correspondents including Stephen Crane, Richard Harding Davis, Frank Norris, John Fox, and Stephen Bonsal. A brief tour of duty as feature writer for the Philadelphia *North American* (1900–1902), to which he contributed columns of "Kerbstone Philosophy" and excellent coverage of the McKinley assassination, was succeeded by several years in New York as sports editor of the *American*. Very different from this fugitive bread-and-butter work was a series of articles for the socialist *Wilshire's Magazine* that he began to write in 1901. During the preceding year Hawthorne had become involved in still another literary "quarrel," but in this case a comic one: the once-famous question that for a time convulsed the literary world, "Did Rudyard Kipling write *David Harum?*"

The decade following 1896 also saw Hawthorne feeding upon his considerable literary reputation to produce some of the sumptuously bound editions of literature then very much in vogue. In 1897, in association with J. P. Lamberton, he edited a ten-volume compendium called *The Literature of All Nations and All Ages*. Its success led not only to its fourfold re-issue under varying titles but to a host of similar editions, including a twenty-volume *Masterpieces of the World's Literature, Ancient and Modern* (1898) and the *World's Great Classics* (1899), in sixty-one volumes. To these massive works Hawthorne lent not only his name but his considerable erudition, in the form of introductions and brief historical sketches. These were commercial enterprises, of course, with genteel fronts like Stoddard and Timothy Dwight and related "courses of reading under the auspices of the four leading universities." More specialized work of this kind was also produced. There was, for example, *The Library of the World's Best Mystery and Detective Stories* (1908), one of the very earliest of American anthologies of crime literature. The *Library* was expanded into ten volumes the following year and retitled *The Lock and Key Library*. In this work Hawthorne created from *Bleak House*'s fourteen chapters on Inspector Bucket a new narrative, *Inspector Bucket's Job,* which Haycraft calls "an ingenious and on the whole surprisingly successful" work.[38] The historical hackwork that Hawthorne had begun in 1889 was also continued past the turn of the century. In 1898 he helped to edit a history of the United States; his own three-volume *History of the United States,* published also in that year by Collier, became extremely popular, and was brought up to date in 1902, 1910, and 1915. A well-written book called *Spanish America, from the Earliest Period to the Present Time* (1899) was also widely read. The opening chapter of the book is especially intriguing for its attack upon the tenets of the evolutionists.

Somewhat more biographically interesting than the volumes so far mentioned was Julian Hawthorne's edition *The Works of Nathaniel Hawthorne,* a collection that appeared in 1900 under the Collier imprint. It is an undistinguished gathering of tales in a cheap, "popular," three-volume format. However, it seems to be the last chapter in the Hawthorne-Lathrop relationship; for even though Julian's *Works* scarcely replaced the standard Riverside edition associated with Lathrop's name, it rather crudely satisfied Hawthorne's long-cherished dream of producing a "definitive" edition and evaluation of his father's fiction. Nathaniel Hawthorne's life and milieu were also the basis for several biographical works of this period. The first was a series of articles for the Denver *Sunday Post* in 1900, which discussed, in addition to his father, the careers of Emerson, Thoreau, and Alcott. Hawthorne had discovered the great subject of his later years. He wrote:

Men and women whose names are consecrated apart in the dearest thoughts of thousands were familiars and playmates of my childhood; they supported my youth, and bade my manhood Godspeed. But to me, for a long while, the favor of these gracious giants of mind and character seemed agreeable indeed, but nothing out of the ordinary; my tacit presumption was that other children as well as I could if they would walk hand in hand with Emerson along the village street, seek in the meadows for arrowheads with Thoreau, watch Powers thump the brown clay of the "Greek Slave," or listen to the voice of Charlotte Cushman, which could sway assembled thousands, modulate itself to tell stories to the urchin who leaned, rapt, against her knees.[39]

In *Hawthorne and His Circle* (1903), Julian Hawthorne wrote a lively account of the family's life abroad between 1853 and 1860. The objectivity of *Nathaniel Hawthorne and His Wife* is replaced by the son's own point of view, and indeed, his own adventures in England and on the Continent form the bulk of the recollections. In the following year Hawthorne published a small group of his father's letters to William D. Ticknor and wrote a brief interpretation of his father's last years in Concord.

There is very little evidence concerning Julian Hawthorne's personal and family life for the period between 1896 and 1912.[40] Among certain members of the family still living, there is considerable reticence on the subject, and speculation is not encouraged. Minne Hawthorne, so vivid a figure in her letters, disappears from both public and private view in these years, not in fact to reappear until one learns of her illness and death in 1925. Manning Hawthorne, her grandson, remembers her as a remarkable woman. "She had a wonderful way with children," he writes. "The greatest treat in my childhood was to stay with her. Her children were all devoted to her all their lives." [41] An estrangement between Julian and Minne Hawthorne took place; it was doubtless connected with Harwthorne's friendship for young Edith Garrigues, a talented painter whom he met around 1906 and who was to be his constant companion until their marriage after the death of Minne Hawthorne. Edith was born in Copenhagen, Denmark, on August 29, 1874, and was brought to the United States when a few months old. Her father was the distinguished gynecologist Dr. Henry Garrigues, and her aunt was married to Thomas Masaryk, president of Czechoslovakia. Hawthorne described her warmly in a letter to his old English friend Sir Frederic Macmillan:

> She is an artist; her paintings are in the great tradition; she is a sculptor too, and a creator of the House Beautiful,—if that happens in her way. . . . She is lovely to see and hear. . . . She is thirty years my junior, but doesn't look even half of that.[42]

Hawthorne's sons and daughters married and dispersed in the early years of the century; of them all, Hildegarde had probably the most interesting career. Julian Hawthorne had arranged for the publication of her first short story, "A Legend of Sonora," in *Harper's Magazine* in 1891, when she was barely twenty. Beginning with *A Country Interlude* (1904), Hildegarde Hawthorne produced over thirty books of adult and juvenile fiction, poetry, and biography. The latter included a work on her famous paternal grandfather, *Romantic Rebel,* and lives of Emerson, Longfellow, Holmes, Frémont, Matthew Maury, and Napoleon II. The willfulness of temperament recorded in the family journals and letters of the 1870's persisted into her maturity; her "bossiness" allegedly terrified her sisters Imogen and Beatrix, and even alienated such close family friends as the Wilshires. In 1919 she engaged in war work in France for the YMCA and the American Red Cross; after her return from abroad she married John M. Oskison in 1920. A relentless traveler, camper, and sportswoman, Mrs. Oskison, a member of the Authors' League of America, died in Berkeley, California, in 1952. She matched her father in her vigorous constitution, her prolific literary output, her socialistic proclivities, and her impassioned Swedenborgianism.[43]

Hawthorne's surviving sister, Rose Lathrop, had been formally separated from her husband George in 1895. The following year she turned to helping care for indigent victims of incurable cancer, a work to which she devoted her remaining years. In 1899 she was received into the Dominican order as a novitiate with the name Sister Alphonsa; two years later she founded a home for her patients at a town in New York State that was renamed Hawthorne, and as head of the Rosary Hill Home there became Mother Alphonsa. Until her death in 1926, she was a devoted friend to her brother.

5. The Socialist Period

One of the most important friendships of Julian Hawthorne's life was formed at the turn of the century with the millionaire socialist Henry Gaylord Wilshire, who published Hawthorne's utopian speculations in his magazine and, many years later, subsidized the writer's exile in California. Wilshire, fifteen years Hawthorne's junior, was born in Cincinnati of a prosperous family, studied briefly at Harvard, and, after a brief career as a San Francisco boulevardier, turned to socialism in the late 1880's. To Upton Sinclair, one of his disciples, he insisted that his conversion had been purely intellectual: he had become convinced that capitalism was self-eliminating, and that its breakdown was near. Wilshire founded the Los Angeles *Weekly Nationalist* in 1889, and in the next year ran unsuccessfully for Congress. Widely respected in California radical circles, he nevertheless did not neglect capitalist enterprises; he amassed a fortune in Los Angeles billboard advertising, laid out the great boulevard in that city that bears his name, and founded the city of Fullerton, where he maintained several prosperous ranches. For his flamboyant courting of jail for his beliefs, Wilshire earned the title of a "Socialist Barnum." [44]

The initial number of *The Challenge*, with the motto "Let the Nation Own the Trusts," was published by Wilshire in Los Angeles in December, 1900. In the following year he moved his magazine to New York, only to find that the United States Post Office was to deny it second-class mailing privileges. He promptly renamed the journal *Wilshire's Magazine,* moved it to Toronto, and eventually won his battle in the courts for mailing rights. *Wilshire's Magazine* gradually became "the most widely circulated socialist journal in the United States during the Progressive period," [45] and the Wilshire Book Company published pamphlets by such leading socialists and agnostics as Sinclair, Jack London, and Clarence Darrow. Wilshire himself was a handsome, well-groomed, and articulate spokesman for his causes, who later became the confidant of such English radical intellectuals as Shaw and Wells. Sinclair, who came under Wilshire's influence at about the same time that Julian Hawthorne did, describes "Comrade Wilshire" as "a small man with a black beard and mustache trimmed to sharp points, and twinkling mischievous eyes—for all the world the incarnation of Mephistopheles." [46] Perhaps like Sinclair, Hawthorne too found *Wilshire's Magazine* "like the falling down of prison walls about my mind. . . . There were actually others who understood." [47]

Hawthorne's general libertarian sympathies, which appear clearly in his *Wilshire's Magazine* articles, may be traced back at least as far as 1891, when he attacked the imprisonment of a journalist, E. H. Heywood, for publishing articles in defense of free love. Though Hawthorne felt Heywood to be merely a "harmless eccentric," he defended him as a reformer and declared that the suppression of free speech is self-defeating. In an opinion more in accord with present-day thought than with that of his contemporaries, Hawthorne argued that "obscenity and lasciviousness reside not in words, but in motives. . . . A vicious motive has never been proved in regard to the outpourings of Mr. Heywood's muse. . . . He ought not to be put in gaol any more than Robert Ingersoll or Walt Whitman. . . . It would be better to have the country flooded with genuinely vicious and obscene literature, than to establish the precedent of imprisoning men for publishing their honest opinions." [48] Hawthorne's stirring letter had an alleged biographical base: it was written, he says, in "contrition" for the acts of his forefathers who had helped to "burn" witches in New England.

The equation of personal and artistic liberty implied in Haw-thorne's defense of Heywood was to be conjoined ten years later with the socialist ideal for the restructuring of society. We can see the link in Hawthorne's statement, "Socialism is the best thing in the world. . . . Personal liberty can never be known or enjoyed by any man living under any other conditions." [49] His socialist thinking, shot through with para-doxes as it is, emphasizes the primacy of personal liberty in an artistic-oriented community. Just as his Emersonian literary aesthetic led him toward conceiving the artist as seer and prophet, his concurrent political theory led him into rebellion against Hobbesian enlightened selfishness. Though he dis-missed Marx, he believed that man would evolve toward a lawless, selfless community:

> The life of man under Socialism must not be virtuous, self-con-scious, or moral, nor immoral, of course, either, but unmoral, spontaneous, unself-conscious, selfless, realizing self only in others, and, therefore, really for the first time in history *good*.[50]

Hawthorne described the progress toward socialism only vaguely; at first he even prophesied the hanging of some great capitalists who had distorted "natural law" into their own law, maintained to support the privileged classes. But this statement brought forth a strong rebuttal from Wilshire, and Hawthorne modified his theories. His contributions to *Wilshire's Magazine* are not concerned with the mechanics of change: although Hawthorne often expressed his admiration for such reformers as Tolstoy, Ruskin, Riis, and G. W. Curtis, he himself never *acted,* never faced political and social realities. He was con-cerned only with picturing and preaching the ideal state of things in the future.

In that future, art was to be one of the great social functions of mankind; for socialism, by relieving man of the burden of laboring for the bare means of subsistence, would free him " to study the arts which beautify and ennoble life." In Hawthorne's rather naïve aesthetics, all artists are socialists because they are in harmony with natural law:

> Art may be regarded as the good of the individual universalized for the good of the many. The artist gets his personal impression of beauty in a subject, and he plucks out its soul and represents it as a work of art, which others, seeing it, and consulting their own personal experience, recognize as beautiful and true, only elevated somewhat above what they have personally felt and seen.[51]

Appreciation of art, then, was a kind of ownership; in non-economic terms, the brotherhood of art-producers and art-viewers was the spiritual side of socialism. This sense of brotherhood was inevitable *after* socialism; it was also immensely important on the way *to* socialism. From the point of view of the individual releasing his self, identity was to be sought through the achieving of unity, of what his father had called "holy sympathy," with all men and with the continuum of art.

To Julian Hawthorne America was the ideal ground for this future utopia of the artistic intelligence and the free citizen. America, he believed, had begun with the generating motive of communal selflessness, that is, with the socialist idea of government, and to that idea it must return:

> The soul of the true America is now, as at first it was, Socialism. . . . The nation, being a soul, was bound like individual souls to pass through hell on its way to regeneration; but is even more certain than the individual soul to get there. For the individual soul is subject to free-will, but the national soul is under unconscious and therefore inevitable Divine guidance, and must come out right anyway.[52]

This deterministic socialism hewed closely to the Wilshire party line. It should be noted that Hawthorne's individual-oriented socialism was always a shade more theistic than the New England utopianism of sixty years earlier; an anarchy under divine jurisdiction may be difficult to imagine, however.

Hawthorne's "political aesthetics," then, can be shown to be closely allied to his interpretation of Emersonian transcendentalism. The emphasis on the artist as seer and leader of mankind; the fusion in socialism of the ideal and the actual; the attempt to see history as the evolution of an ideal; the faith in America; and the promulgation at the same time of individualism and "identity": all point in the same direction. But it must be remembered that Emerson stood off from the Brook Farm project, and was ambiguous on the issue of man's moral perfectibility; and Nathaniel Hawthorne, though a member of the community briefly, expressed the gravest possible doubts, in such stories as "Earth's Holocaust," of moral positivism in the light of the debased condition of man's heart.[53] To such latter-day socialists as Sinclair, who attempted to duplicate the Brook Farm experiment at Helicon Home Colony, and Julian Hawthorne, no such conservative doubts were valid. The latter embraced socialism enthusiastically as the ideal means to eradicate at one blow the trusts, on the one hand, and such deprivations of personal liberty as the incarceration of Heywood, on the other. Although we have in Hawthorne's novels such as *Bressant, Sebastian Strome,* and *Love—or a Name,* constant thematic emphasis on the evils of self-glorification and the necessity for altruistic love, the real link between his fiction and his politics of this period is his view of man solely in the framework of his social and moral *environment.* Hawthorne's utopianism is really optimistic determinism, the reverse side of Crane's and Dreiser's pessimistic determinism. It is his own rewriting of the Whitman myth into a "Spiritual Democracy," but without Whitman's understanding of the recesses, dark as well as fair, of the human temperament. This is not to argue that socialism is morally shallow; it is, in Hawthorne's thought, beyond legalistic morality. In the ideal, anarchic state, moral problems, choices, and complexities simply do not exist, for each man is a morally pure agent. Julian Hawthorne's thought had swung a full half-circle from that of his father.

7

Scandal and Exile

1. The Yellow Letters

"Socialists ought not to fool with money-making schemes in capitalist society," Upton Sinclair once declared when his publisher Gaylord Wilshire began running a gold mine in California, a project that was to be as financially disastrous as his later speculations in magnetic nostrums. Sinclair's statement applies also to Julian Hawthorne, who, in the year following his last contributions to *Wilshire's Magazine,* embarked upon a money-making scheme that was to ruin at one stroke the personal and literary reputation so sedulously cultivated for sixty years.

Julian's Harvard crony William Morton had gone on to an illustrious career as a neurologist, but there had been a falling-out between the two old friends, perhaps before the turn of the century. On July 10, 1908, the long chain of circumstances that was to lead to the disgrace and imprisonment of both men began. Morton wrote, asking Hawthorne to see him, for he wished to ask him "to take part in a business proposition which may turn out to be of considerable value to you." [1] Hawthorne went, was greeted with Morton's "bland smile and soft speech and speeches," and literature dealing with certain Canadian mines. Morton had bought over eight hundred acres supposedly rich in silver, gold, copper, and cobalt, with a yield as high as $3,000 a ton. The region was divided into claims of forty acres each, and a small part was set aside for sale of stock, to the value of $100,000. Morton hoped that these claims would be as successful as the then famous Cobalt mines in Canada. Hawthorne told these facts to his friend Edith Garrigues, and further described the interview:

> He said, "Now what I propose to you is that you become a director in the company; all that you will have to do is to accept a block of stock, and to draw your dividends as they fall due."
> I was very glad of all this because it makes the future, financially speaking, safe. The company of course is very exclusive and it was very kind of Will to ask me to join. It is evident, that though my name will be of some value the returns will far exceed any possible good I can be to the enterprise.

On September 18 of that year, Morton wrote Hawthorne from White Bear Lake in Northern Ontario, whither he had gone to inspect the property. His attitude toward the enterprise is all too clearly revealed in his letter:

> But where does the public come in—They do come in. And, now you see them—and now you don't—that is by & by. Buy some stock—and goodby John. Here is Diabase Peninsula—that bare rocky chunk of land—good for minks and chipmunks up to this time now erected into a $20000000 fairy tale. Yet who shall say there is *not* $20000000 worth of silver in it—from here down to China. I believe there is. . . . But seriously it *is* a good proposition.

Despite Morton's "come-on" in the original interview, Hawthorne's role in the enterprise was not to be merely a passive one. On light yellow stationery bearing the letterhead "Julian Hawthorne, Author, Journalist, and Historian," he wrote enticing letters to hundreds of people all over the country, many of them friends and acquaintances of half a century. Even Edith was addressed with the conventional pitch plus a personal note or two:

My beloved and revered Friend :—

Well, Edith, I just want to warn you in time against paying attention to the enclosed prospectus. . . . If you want to make money,—SAVE it; don't do any risks on chances of making six hundred percent. It is better to be a poor artist than a rich one, because the rich ones always paint portraits, which is a degradation of True Art. I myself, though a director only, have abandoned Literature, which had always treated me in a way to stimulate to the highest pitch my craving for the Ideal :—she had not only dissembled her love, but had kicked me down stairs repeatedly. . . . I hope what I have said may influence you; but if not, a check to the above address will be appreciated. No subscriptions are received for less than Three Hundred Dollars.
(August 6, 1908)

The company issued handsome prospectuses, all of them written by Julian Hawthorne. To the years 1908 and 1909 belong four little pamphlets meant to catch the eye of the general public and solicit its savings. These ephemera were rather grandiosely titled *Ishmael in Search of an Oasis; Julian Hawthorne and Company; Solomon Columbus Rhodes and Company;* and *The Secret of Solomon,* and all proclaimed that the secret of getting rich was adventurous speculation. Hawthorne wrote to one correspondent in 1908 :

I seriously object to selling any of the treasury shares through brokers. I know that I am going to make my fortune from my investment in this enterprise; I have put into it all I had. I told my associates, that I am satisfied there are enough people who know me, or know of me, who would believe in my representations, and would invest in the enterprise if they knew I was connected with it. . . . In the past forty years I established a reputation which I am anxious to maintain and I want to know therefore that the company's literature is under its own control.

The tone is disingenuous—but Hawthorne was certainly believed.

Two other men were associated prominently with Morton

and Hawthorne in the enterprise. The first (and possibly the originator of the scheme) was Josiah Quincy, a descendant of the famed Quincys of Massachusetts, assistant secretary of state under President Cleveland and mayor of Boston from 1895 to 1899. The second was certainly the most notorious of the lot, a professional promoter named Albert Freeman.

The promotion succeeded astonishingly. Three and one-half million dollars were invested by the public in shares of the Canadian stock, but not a penny in dividends was ever paid. The United States attorney general, prompted by outraged buyers, soon investigated, and in 1912 the four men were indicted for using the United States mail for fraudulent purposes. Their trial began in New York before a federal court on November 27, 1912. They were accused by the government's prosecuting attorney of being the "most notorious gang of swindlers that had ever infested New York. . . . We all know that some of these men bear honored names. Theirs is the greater crime, for they have prostituted them." The defense countered only that the defendants had believed in the gainful production of the mines. The parade of witnesses lasted until March 12, 1913, and all the defendants, except Quincy, were convicted. Albert Freeman was sentenced to imprisonment for five years, but afterward he appealed and was released on bond. Later, he received a retrial on a technicality, and his lawyers charged successfully that defense witnesses had been intimidated in the original trial by agents of the United States government. The slippery Freeman never spent a day in jail. Hawthorne and Morton, on the other hand, disdaining to appeal their convictions, were sentenced to one year, their terms to be counted as having started on the day the trial began, the preceding November twenty-seventh. On March 23, 1913, the two old Harvard men set out for Atlanta Penitentiary.

The editorial writers were generally unsympathetic. "Julian Hawthorne has exemplified," wrote one, "that no man is proof against the lure of quick wealth." Wrote another: "Nathaniel Hawthorne and his writings helped to make Salem famous, but it took Julian Hawthorne to put the easy marks of Harvard in the limelight with his classy literature on gold mines that existed only in his fertile brain." The unkindest cut, perhaps, was the comment "How much better it would have been if Julian Hawthorne had written one Scarlet Letter instead of all those yellow ones!" [2]

Some writers, however, like Arthur Brisbane of the New York *Journal,* were more charitable. It was to Brisbane—an old journalistic friend since the 1890's, whose father, like Julian's, had been at Brook Farm—that Hawthorne wrote feelingly from Atlanta:

> I understand the good motive of the pardon-petitioners and memorialists: but I would rather have stayed here another year than allow them to send their appeals to the President. I am not concerned about myself personally, nor about the present, but about my family, about the long future, and even about the disgrace—not to my name, which can only be hurt by the act of some one who bears it, but—of America itself. And for me to appear in the light of a suppliant for pardon and clemency, in such circumstances, is ridiculous, and would obstruct any explanations of statements I might have to make to the public hereafter.

Yet, in a letter from prison to his old acquaintance William Jennings Bryan, Hawthorne, while repeating the noble tone above, asks Bryan to use his good offices to secure a pardon for him from President Wilson, and goes on:

> The statements as to the mines which I made I believed at the time and I believe so still, and were the thing to do again I would act as I did then.
>
> My position therefore is that whatever disgrace attaches to this affair belongs not to me but to the government which found me guilty and sentenced me to gaol, on a charge of which I am innocent. This government being stronger than I is able to dispose as it pleases of my body. But it cannot *make* me guilty by saying that I am.[3]

Despite this letter to Bryan, the help of well-wishers, and even a frantic appeal to President Wilson by Hawthorne's sister, Mother Alphonsa, nothing was done. Hawthorne and Morton were eligible for parole on the basis of good conduct on July 25, 1913, but even though the federal prison board recommended it, Attorney General McReynolds vetoed the board's actions.

The first picture of Julian Hawthorne in Atlanta is rather pathetic. On April 1, a week after he had exchanged his jaunty cap and checked suit for the prison garb with the number 4435 on the breast, Hawthorne attended a concert given by the University of Georgia Glee Club for the inmates:

> The young singers on the platform had seen in recent weeks so many newspaper snapshots of the notorious son of the author of *The Scarlet Letter* that they spotted him without difficulty. With his drooping moustache only slightly gray and a look of alertness in his brown eyes, he appeared nearer forty than sixty-seven. The first half of the concert was devoted to comic college songs, and at the end of each Julian laughed and applauded with spirit. But in the course of the second half, which was given over to sentimental nostalgic numbers, he broke down and wept.[4]

On June 9 the friendly Washington *Post* reported that Hawthorne was the chief contributor to the prison newspaper *Good Words,*

> and is giving cheer and comfort as well as moral education to all the other prisoners. He refuses to give interviews wherein he might appear as a martyr. He devotes his days to those who are in prison with him. He says that he feels he can turn his imprisonment to good account by studying the defects in our prison system, learning the temperamental needs of the prisoners, and pointing out the way of hope in the future. In forgetting himself and aiding others, Hawthorne has given to his punishment an air of heroism.

Probably by Hawthorne were two articles in *Good Words* picturing utopian conditions in jails of the future and damning the dress and numbering of prisoners and the absence of proper names as calculated "to produce in the prisoner a feeling of radical and permanent separation from his fellow men." Of the three poems he published in this newspaper, "Punishment," "The Convict," and "Footfalls," the latter is the most poignant despite its crude diction:

> In the cell over mine at night
> A step goes to and fro
> From barred door to iron wall—
> From wall to door I hear it go,
> Four paces, heavy and slow,
> In the heart of the sleeping jail;
> And the goad that drives, I know!
>
>> I never saw his face or heard him speak;
>> He may be Dutchman, Dago, Yankee, Greek;
>> But the language of that prison step
>> Too well I know!
>> Unknown brother of the remorseless bars,
>> Pent in your cage from earth and sky and stars,
>> The hunger for lost life that goads you so,
>> I also know!

The note of sympathy here expressed did not fail to impress Hawthorne's fellow prisoners. At the conclusion of the sad year in Atlanta, the prison newspaper carried an editorial by its editor-in-chief praising the contributions of Hawthorne and Morton. "Their published articles," he wrote, "have attracted the attention of the whole country to prisons and prison conditions. . . . Their coming to this prison benefited the men here. Full of a sincere and understanding sympathy they were father confessors to their fellows; they heard our stories, and passed among us, leaving behind a trail of hope and encouragement."

Hawthorne emerged from Atlanta at the end of 1913 bursting with anger and a sense of mission astounding in a man in his late sixties. The newspapers quickly picked up and reported his blasts at the penitentiary as a "living hell" and at Warden Moyer as "unfit" for his duties. He arraigned conditions in

Atlanta as repressive, cruel, and the equal of the most lurid descriptions in fiction. The remainder of the year 1913 and part of 1914 were spent in the writing of Julian Hawthorne's most deeply felt work, *The Subterranean Brotherhood*. The "inward impulse" to write the book was irresistible, Hawthorne declared, "in spite of the other impulse to go off somewhere and rest and forget it all. . . . I had promised my mates in prison that I would do it, and I was under no less an obligation, though an unspoken one, to give the public an opportunity to learn at first hand what prison life is, and means." [5]

Hawthorne's method in the book is basically radical and prophetic rather than constructive. He argues that penal imprisonment for crime be abolished, a proposal he expects the public will greet as "preposterous and impossible." And yet, he declares,

> nothing is more certain in my opinion than that penal imprisonment for crime must cease, and if it be not abolished by statute, it will be by force. It must be abolished because, alarming or socially destructive though alternatives to it may appear, it is worse than the alternative, being not only dangerous, but wicked, and it breeds and multiplies the evils it pretends to heal or diminish. [6]

He stresses, for example, the impossibility of criminals reforming themselves because of the inimical attitude of the police toward ex-convicts; the cruelty and barrenness of life imprisonment; the psychological cruelty of pardons that hang fire; the cruelty and corruption of the guards and stool pigeons; the waste and inefficiency of the administration in using labor; the horror of the "dark holes" in which prisoners are punished; the rottenness of the food; and the hypocrisy of the wardens who bamboozle inspectors. Against the formidable array of horrors, the prisoners can place only the sense of brotherhood that makes life in prison tolerable.

That sense of brotherhood Julian Hawthorne came to know and admire. And it was not only the camaraderie among the prisoners that he idealized but also the unspoken brotherhood of all mankind, which had been a major theme in his fiction and in his politics. He asserted, in words that echo his father's belief in the "magnetic chain of humanity," that sin was universal:

> The assumption that a criminal class exists among us separate and distinct from any and the best of the rest of us is Pharisaical, false, and wicked. The "Subterranean Brotherhood" are our brothers—they are ourselves, unjustly and vainly condemned to serve as scapegoats for the rest.[7]

Vanished, in this book, are the romantic obsessions of the fiction, the adulatory tones of the biographies, the self-pity of the journals. The book is original, sincere, powerful. But it was published in 1914, when the eyes of America were turned outward to Europe rather than inward to its own evils, and it was not widely reviewed or widely sold. *The Subterranean Brotherhood* deserves to be remembered.

2. A "Charming Lovable Writer"

The last twenty years of Julian Hawthorne's long life were, essentially, years of exile from the family and the traditions that had surrounded him since his return to America in 1882. Yet these exilic years were not disfigured by self-pity or senescent decay. Hawthorne's productivity increased rather than abated, and, following the tack indicated in *Hawthorne and His Circle* (1903), he set himself to the task of re-creating the social and literary milieus he had known in the nineteenth century. Reminiscence is perhaps always unreliable, and Hawthorne's recollections are in this respect no better than most; but the warmth and vividness and undoubted accuracy of the greater part of what he wrote in California assure him a tiny niche in literary history.[8]

After the writing of *The Subterranean Brotherhood,* whose chapters had been syndicated nationally, Hawthorne's friends helped to secure other writing assignments for him. In 1914 the

Wheeler Syndicate distributed a series called "Love Romances from the Bible," by "An American author of national reputation who bears a name that is linked with all that is best in American literature." The unidentified author was Julian Hawthorne, anonymous for the first time since his earliest short story was published in 1871. But the byline returned in the columns of the Boston *American,* which published, in 1915, an extensive series of reminiscences by the writer. His Harvard classmate Sam S. Chamberlain, with whom he had worked for Hearst's *Journal* in the 1890's and who was now editor of the *American,* was one of Hawthorne's closest and most loyal friends at this time, along with Edith Garrigues, Gaylord Wilshire, and William Morton. Early in 1915, Morton wrote Hawthorne about a projected trip: "I feel the call of Florida, but it is a wild goose honk high in the air & I can only honk honk in reply for my wings are clipped. You are a base old bird of freedom." [9]

It was probably late in 1915 that Wilshire persuaded Julian Hawthorne and Edith Garrigues to settle permanently in California. He had an estate in Pasadena, and the two were invited to use a cottage on his grounds. Wilshire also attempted to use his influence to secure Hawthorne a position as feature writer on the weekly Los Angeles *Graphic,* but the editor allegedly snubbed the ex-convict, remarking to an associate that he felt Hawthorne had sullied a noble name.

Hawthorne continued to write miscellaneous fiction, very little of which was published; but the movies fascinated him, and he spent long months adapting some of his old stories for the screen, including *Archibald Malmaison* (retitled *The Black Doll*), *Fortune's Fool,* and *Beatrix Randolph.* In 1920 he concocted a new tale about two sisters of dual temperaments, the soul of one of whom enters the other. An unidentified studio correspondent wrote to him, "If it is possible for me to give you the picture angle so that you can adapt your supernatural twist to it I believe some great pictures will result. . . . As your story stands it is impossible pictures material." [10] To another filmmaker Hawthorne wrote bravely in 1920 concerning an abstract of *Fortune's Fool* he had made for the screen, "I have had movie people on my trail for the last six or seven years, but never saw my way to accepting their propositions." Perhaps when Hawthorne was finally ready to accept "propositions," the movie people were no longer willing to make them; for Hawthorne never saw his stories on the screen.

In 1923 Hawthorne began an assignment with the Pasadena *Star-News* that was to continue to his death and that, after Wilshire's death in 1927, increased his financial independence. He contributed articles and reviews to the newspaper's book page, then edited by Harold Carew. Although some of this journalistic outpouring concerned current literature, most was devoted to an attempt to recapture the life and times of the late nineteenth century. Julian Hawthorne's memory was apparently inexhaustible, and his notebooks were thick. Some of the columns were later used in *Shapes That Pass* (1928) and *Memoirs* (1938). A related project of the 1920's was the publication of a brief series of reminiscent articles in the Dearborn *Independent*. An especially pleasant publication of this period was an illustrated version of *Rumpty-Dudget's Tower: A Fairy Tale,* which had exhibited an amazing longevity in the memory of adult readers since its first appearance in a book of children's stories in 1879. Hawthorne edited the story considerably for its 1924 appearance, but fortunately did not mar its unique charm.[11]

Minne Hawthorne died on June 5, 1925, in Georgetown, Connecticut, after a long illness. On July 6 Julian Hawthorne married Edith Garrigues; "All well at last," his diary notes. During the 1920's the couple traveled up and down the California coast, living at various times in the San Francisco Bay area, and at Lake Tahoe, La Jolla, and Newport Beach, as well as Pasadena. It was for his beloved Edith that Julian wrote many of his poems in this period; indeed, his poetic output was characteristically enormous, old-fashionedly sentimental—and bad. Perhaps typical are the closing stanzas of the obviously autobiographical "Infinitude":

> In my grave maturity
> I saw my valiant projects die;
> Forty, fifty years were gone,
> Projects plenty, nothing done!
> Lonely, loveless, poor I stood
> Musing on Infinitude!
>
> Is the Word a flaunting lie?
> In my crippled Age, quoth I.
> Then a woman answered low,
> Naught know I, yet this I know,—
> Wasting Time cannot intrude
> On holy Love's Infinitude!
>
> Love?—long since he passed me by,
> In my weary heart, said I.
> But she pressed her heart to mine,
> New Life glowed in my veins like wine,
> And in her eyes I understood
> The secret of Infinitude!

Julian Hawthorne's last public appearance was on the occasion of his eighty-fifth birthday on June 22, 1931. Harold Carew was toastmaster for the event, held in Pasadena, and over 125 prominent literary figures attended. The major address was delivered by Helen Haines, Hawthorne's associate on the book page of the *Star-News,* who asserted—extravagantly, to be sure—that many of Julian Hawthorne's writings ranked "on an equal plane with his father's." His best work, she said, would be "read and re-read; it will be cherished as a thing beautiful, undimmed by time." [12] Upton Sinclair, his old socialist friend, who was present, called him a "charming lovable writer." Messages of good will were received from eminent men of letters all over the country and abroad. Robinson Jeffers, for example, praised his "distinguished work," and Bliss Perry recalled "when a word of praise from him meant much to me."

Sinclair Lewis declared: "Just the other day . . . I was reading his recollections [*Shapes That Pass*] and wishing that I possessed that grace and charm which enabled him to come so close to the great of literary and political England." H. L. Mencken confessed to a "great liking" for Hawthorne: "No one, indeed, could fail to admire both his professional work and his extreme enthusiasm. He will go on, I believe, to a round century." Other words of praise and fond reminiscence came from Hamlin Garland, Ellen Glasgow, William Allen White, S. S. McClure, Lincoln Steffens, William Lyon Phelps, and, most amusingly, from George Bernard Shaw, who cabled: "What—Julian still alive! And I had mourned him for years! Are you sure he is not an imposter? . . . However, if you are convinced of his genuineness, give him my best regards." The sentimental evening closed appropriately with the presentation to Hawthorne of a portrait of his father executed by a niece of Mrs. James T. Fields, whose husband, all chose to forget, had been so carefully neglected in the writer's most important biographical work.

During the winter of 1933–34, Hawthorne suffered an attack of influenza, and was critically ill for several weeks. He kept up his writing into the spring; but a heart attack came in June of 1934, and on Saturday morning, July 14, he died in his apartment in San Francisco. He was eighty-eight years old. Gaylord Wilshire's son Logan recalls him, in a remark that makes a suitable epitaph, as "a Jovian character, remote and unapproachable, and somewhat shabby in the genteel tradition. There was a sadness at the back of his eyes and little was left of the Harvard oar and blood. Yet, he remained a noble ruin." [13]

3. Recollections in Tranquillity

One of the most sincere tributes to Julian Hawthorne had been delivered at his birthday dinner by his distinguished friend Hamlin Garland, himself past seventy. Garland had tried to help Hawthorne find publishers and speaking engagements and had urged him to set down his Concord recollections at the greatest possible length. After Hawthorne's death he was to volunteer his help to the widow in preserving the writer's manuscripts. At the celebration he declared:

> As I think of your span of life I am stirred by the events it covers. Reaching from your illustrious father in his Concord home to Pasadena with its new school of physics and astronomy, it covers more of change, of scientific discovery than any other age in history. Some call this change advance and I am willing to grant that claim but I am not so sure that we who write have gone very far beyond that group of men in Concord who from their cottages under the elms sent out great books to a smaller world. Of all men living you are best fitted to speak of them and for them. The long list of your own books is evidence of a brave and busy life, and among them none are more lasting than those which record your own experiences in Concord and your associations with the men of that group.[14]

Although an occasional friend of Hawthorne like Helen Haines could allude to the power of his twenty-odd works of major fiction, these were generally neglected; the volumes of biography and reminiscence, as Garland suggested, were considered Hawthorne's most lasting contribution to the literature of his time. The biography of his parents published in 1884 had been only the first in a long series of biographical books and articles dealing primarily with his father and the men he called, in a tentative title for one of his volumes, "Giants of Old Concord." As he grew older, he fashioned various newspaper series, first for the Denver *Sunday Post* (1900), then for the Boston *American* (1915), and finally for the Pasadena *Star-News* and Dearborn *Independent*. Gradually, the biographies began to include autobiographical elements, especially, for example, in *Hawthorne and His Circle* (1903); and the solipsistic ring is completed with the late works of autobiography and reminiscence: *Shapes That Pass,* the reconstruction of England in the 1870's, and the posthumously published *Memoirs.* Even though his later literary career depended on the public taste for this sort of thing, Hawthorne invariably became crotchety when pressed unreasonably for additional biographical information; after one newspaper interview in 1933, he wrote sarcastically:

> Intensive study reveals that this Hawthorne wrote a novel called "The Scarlet Letter," and likewise begot a son after the flesh, who, improbable though it may seem, is still living. Obviously, then, the first step of a would-be biographer is to locate his son and put him to the question. Let this person then disclose whatever biographical details he may possess, and our enterprise is well under way. This is better or at least easier than to consult libraries for such data, if any exist; and the son should be eager to gratify a curiosity all the more complimentary because so belated.[15]

Hawthorne satisfied some of this curiosity himself in the articles he published in national magazines in the late 1920's and early 30's. In "Such Is Paradise: The Story of Sophie and Nathaniel Hawthorne" (1927), he lovingly retraced the same ground covered in his biography of 1884. The reverential mood also inspired the critical article "The Making of *The Scarlet Letter*" (1931) and the sentimental "Nathaniel Hawthorne's Blue Cloak" (1932). In these three short pieces Julian Hawthorne added very little new or worthwhile concerning his father's life or works; they are essentially rewritings, for a new generation, of ideas and themes he had treated before. A different chord is struck in "A Daughter of Hawthorne" (1928), which presents for the first time Hawthorne's impressions of his sister Rose. All old enmities are stilled as he praises her literary gifts and her selfless devotion to the victims of incurable cancer. He appears saddened, however, that her life had taken its final turn toward the church, feeling that her contributions to literature were thereby thwarted. Theodore Maynard, Mother Alphonsa's chief biographer, is more convincing when he declares that Rose Hawthorne's early career, her gifts, and even her unhappy marriage pointed unmistakably to the saintly life that was her real fulfillment. Two other brief articles of this period deserve notice as indicating both the survival of Julian Hawthorne's quarrelsome disposition and his intense devotion to the family name. The first of these was an attack upon Lloyd Morris's biography of his father, *The Rebellious Puritan* (1927), which, like Newton Arvin's more famous work the following year, sought to picture Nathaniel Hawthorne as a withdrawn, isolated artist weighed down by the burden of man's sinfulness and his own gloomy heritage. Julian Hawthorne countered that his father was essentially a "man of action," a healthy, outgoing person whose concerns in his fiction were not mirror images of a twisted psyche. These statements of course foreshadowed and perhaps influenced such later interpretations of the father as Randall Stewart's. Hawthorne also opened fire on Stewart, however, in 1932, when the scholar's edition of Hawthorne's *American Notebooks* severely arraigned Sophia Hawthorne for her excisions and emendations of her husband's text prior to her own publication of it. Sophia Hawthorne's son castigated Professor Stewart on somewhat shaky grounds: primarily, that the deletions were of little importance or even improved the text. Already in his late eighties when this last article appeared, Julian Hawthorne displayed the same devotion to the family name and honor, and to his own interpretation of the Hawthorne heritage, that had characterized his entire public career.

In 1928 Julian published *Shapes That Pass,* a nostalgic book of recollections about the life he had led in London society in the 1870's. "Memory and love," he wrote, "are parents of art. So, my picture of England is not less true for being eulogistic." [16] If he had simply quoted from his contemporary journals, he tells us, *Shapes That Pass* would have been a fault-finding book; he used the journals, finally, merely to orient himself, "and no longer allowed my view of the forest to be obscured by the trees." The book does not mention Julian Hawthorne's prolific literary and journalistic output in this period, discuss his problems and anguishes, or even touch on

his domestic life. It is instead a testimonial of love and memory
to a culture that Hawthorne deeply cherished, and not any the
less accurate for that. Indeed, in its recollection of strong emotions in tranquillity, it would be a sort of poetry if we could
make allowances for the sometimes incoherent, sometimes
bloated style. Hawthorne's words do, however, conjure up the
decade glowingly:

> There were good men and fair women in that epoch, and nobody
> thought of apologizing for being Victorian. . . . Society inno-
> cently welcomed its handsome and courtly scientists; art, long
> since untied from the apron-strings of the Church, saw nothing
> hostile in *pithecanthropus;* the clergy dined and wined and
> administered the Sacraments as usual; and if any of us felt
> restive under the orthodox Church of England service, we could
> be entertained with Oriental dance-interludes—the "Pas Theos-
> ophique," the Buddhist waltz, the Confucian polka—danced in
> costume, and to appropriate jingles. The bishops would look on,
> rosy-gilled and tolerant, and Monsignor Capel was also present,
> wearing the unfathomable smile of his Order; he might even
> beckon a pretty dancer to his knee for a kind word and a caress;
> he understood it all, and he feared nothing.

After depicting the "rich and glowing tapestry" of political life,
Hawthorne goes on:

> The Queen was in her pantry, eating bread and honey in
> preparation for her jubilee: Gilbert and Sullivan were lulling us
> with playful satires; Tennyson and Irving were aiding and
> abetting each other in that weird succession of dramas; George
> Eliot, George Meredith, and Swinburne were fearlessly expa-
> tiating, confident that the old literature was approaching its
> apogee, instead of facing its funeral; Huxley was lecturing;
> Tyndall was writing in *The Contemporary;* Millais was painting
> "The Pears' Soap Boy"; and "Alice Through the Looking-
> Glass" was the most popular romance in England. Our founda-
> tions were firm; radium was no more anticipated than was the
> war or bolshevism; if there were murmurs of approaching
> earthquake they were inaudible in the music of our purring. It
> was a golden age.[17]

Julian makes much, too, of his spiritual identity with the English, failing to mention the hostility he had displayed in his youth. "My blood," he says, "was English from as long ago as any Englishman's, and becoming a New Englander didn't change it. I see John Bull as my kin, and as the incarnation of a great human spirit on earth." [18]

The richness and charm of Hawthorne's recapture of a bygone age in *Shapes That Pass,* which was the last book published in his lifetime, led his widow, four years after his death, to bring together for the first time in book form his boyhood and childhood recollections of life in Concord. She drew upon the *Star-News* columns and much material previously unpublished.[19] Hawthorne's method is explained at the outset:

> [I] have felt the importance of the unimportant: not analysis of Emerson's "Sphinx," but the squeaking of his boots during one of his lectures; . . . not that Thoreau built a hut beside Walden, but that he lost his temper when the Selectmen put him into Concord jail. And because I was an unconsidered urchin instead of a Peer of the Realm, I was admitted to sights and contacts withheld from the elect.
>
> But the urchin remembered what he saw, and lived long enough to understand its value for the succeeding era, which had been fed up and to spare with the heroic sort of thing. So, although academic historians may find small value in my reminiscences, archeologists will grin over the mouldering pages: "So, the Concord Group were human after all!" [20]

Despite these sly comments, the book is filled with Hawthorne's mature judgments and prejudices. Thus he expresses his belief that Emerson is the greatest American poet in an anecdote that disparages Richard Watson Gilder. And alongside Thoreau's comment about Julian Hawthorne to his father—"Good boy! Sharp eyes and no tongue!"—he can state unerringly that "Nature absorbed [Thoreau's] attention, but I don't think he cared much for what is called the beauties of nature; it was her way of working, her mystery, her economy in extravagance [that attracted him]." Nathaniel and Sophia Hawthorne, the

Alcott family, Frank Sanborn, Elizabeth Peabody, Horace Mann, Lowell, and the James family all came to graceful life in the pages of the *Memoirs* through illuminating anecdotes, comparisons, and judgments. Some of the stories, however, are twice-told tales, as when Hawthorne, probably inadvertently, tells as if for the first time the intriguing story of Ada Shepard's conjuring forth of "Mary Rondel," a tale he had told before in *Nathaniel Hawthorne and His Wife*. The portrait of his father in this volume preserves the reverential tone used by Julian Hawthorne in all his published writings. He begins with recollections of his father as "playmate," the man whose large, supple hands could readily manufacture a manikin, a toy house, or a boat; the man whose painting of comic faces grinning unawares on the underside of lids and covers Julian never understood as an unconsciously symbolic and educative act. There are anecdotes about family life in Salem, the Wayside, Concord, and abroad, and some incidental comments on Hawthorne's fiction. But a reader of the *Memoirs* will discern that Ralph Waldo Emerson was almost as great a hero to him as Nathaniel Hawthorne, for during his adult life, in his role as literary critic and utopian socialist, Hawthorne had been ideologically the son of Emerson. *Memoirs* is lively reading despite the tepid quality of much of its prose. Along with *Shapes That Pass* and other biographical works, it will be valued by the literary historian who is able to discount its occasional unreliability and its often puckish tone.

Julian Hawthorne's brother-in-law, George Lathrop, at one point in his career had reason to reflect bitterly upon the old Hawthorne curse that had been, in a sense, passed on to him through his marriage to the great novelist's younger daughter. Of course, he was a genuine admirer of Nathaniel Hawthorne, but there can be little doubt that he hoped that an alliance with the great name would help his own fortunes in the literary marketplace. Like Julian Hawthorne, however, he came at last to see that the name was a two-edged sword. He confided to a friend: "I firmly believe I might be a good novelist did I not have weighing upon me the enormous Hawthorne prestige. How am I to live up to that standard? It gets me all paralyzed. Everybody says, 'George Lathrop? Ah, yes! Hawthorne's son-in-law.' I recognize that it has done me good, but it also crushes me. What could I not have been except for that?" [21]

Julian Hawthorne's dilemma was of course even more intense. He took a sincere vow in his twenties to walk in as divergent a path as possible from his father's, but ultimately this was impossible; his compulsive duplication of his father's themes and manner and his own dubious supernatural aesthetic led him unwaveringly down the great trail charted by the elder Hawthorne. Gradually the son came to realize that his destiny was to be only a reflector of Nathaniel's genius, a reverberator of the sounds of old Concord. It was thus that the biography of his parents constituted a turning point in his life, for henceforth he accepted his fate: "Ah, yes! Hawthorne's son." That he nonetheless carved out one career after another with undiminished enthusiasm and filled his mature years with achievement as a man of letters, though of a lesser order of magnitude than his father, is perhaps the most remarkable thing about Julian Hawthorne.

Footnotes

A Note on Sources

In 1949, after the death of Julian Hawthorne's second wife, Edith Garrigues Hawthorne, the numerous notebooks and unpublished manuscripts of the author passed into the hands of Mr. Albert Vallière of San Francisco. The General Library of the University of California, Berkeley, purchased a large part of this collection and has supplemented this acquisition with other purchases of manuscripts, letters, and first editions. The collection now includes eighty holograph manuscripts and typescripts, eleven journals, some three hundred letters by and to Julian Hawthorne, and memorabilia, including clippings and photographs. A small quantity of material by and about the writer's parents, Nathaniel and Sophia Peabody Hawthorne, is included. A "Register of Papers" for the Julian Hawthorne Collection (JHC) was prepared in 1958; in the footnotes following, the organization of this Register is used in identifying particular items in the collection (e.g., JHC IV).

The Berg Collection of the New York Public Library contains valuable manuscript and typescript material. There are approximately sixty letters, mostly to members of the family, a diary for 1868–69, about three hundred pages of miscellaneous fiction, half a dozen business documents, and sixty-five letters to Julian Hawthorne. Several additional Hawthorne manuscripts and letters are in the Library's Manuscript Room. A third important manuscript source is the Henry E. Huntington Library and Art Gallery, San Marino, California. There are seventeen letters by and to Julian Hawthorne, and nine manuscripts, plus much incidental information about the son in the papers of his father held by the Huntington. A fourth major repository is Yale University, which has an important notebook of 1871–72, a group of letters, and Hawthorne's India journal of 1897; this collection is summarized in the present writer's "Julian Hawthorne Papers at Yale," *Yale University Library Gazette*, XXXIX (October, 1964), 84–89.

Additional materials, of varying degrees of importance, are in the following libraries and collections: Boston Public Library; Brown University; Cleveland Public Library; Duke University; Essex Institute; Historical and Philosophical Society of Ohio; Historical Society of Pennsylvania; Johns Hopkins University; New Hampshire Historical Society; Newberry Library; Pierpont Morgan Library; Rosenberg Public Library, Galveston, Texas; St. John's Seminary, Camarillo, California; St. Lawrence University; State College of Washington; University of California, Los Angeles; University of Michigan; University of Southern California; University of Texas; and University of Virginia. Many letters and other materials remain in the hands of private collectors.

233

Abbreviations

AN	Nathaniel Hawthorne, *The American Notebooks,* ed. Randall Stewart (New Haven, Conn., 1932)
JH	Julian Hawthorne
JHC	Julian Hawthorne Collection, Rare Books Department, General Library of the University of California, Berkeley
Memoirs	Edith Garrigues Hawthorne, ed., *The Memoirs of Julian Hawthorne* (New York, 1938)
NHAHW	Julian Hawthorne, *Nathaniel Hawthorne and His Wife,* 2 vols. (Boston and New York, 1884)
Works	George Parsons Lathrop, ed., *The Works of Nathaniel Hawthorne,* 15 vols. (Boston and New York, 1883)

Preface

1. "Dean of American Letters: Julian Hawthorne," *Bookman* LXXIII (April, 1931), 166.

2. *Confessions and Criticisms* (Boston, 1887), p. 11.

3. Ibid., p. 137. In less high-flown moments Hawthorne argued the case for fiction merely as entertainment.

4. See Benjamin T. Spencer, "The New Realism and a National Literature," *PMLA* LVI (1941), 1127–28; and JH's essay, "Americanism in Fiction," in *Confessions and Criticisms.*

5. *A Dictionary of American Authors* (Boston and New York, 1901), p. 176.

6. *A History of American Literature Since 1870* (New York, 1917), p. 408.

7. "Dean of American Letters," p. 165.

8. Stevenson, now James B. Duke Professor of English at Duke University, remarked in a recent letter to the present writer that "in view of the intensive research that has been done in American literature during the past quarter-century, it is amazing that Hawthorne remains uninvestigated."

9. XXI, 387.

10. "Julian Hawthorne: Concordian in California," *Historical Society of Southern California Quarterly* XXXIX (March, 1957), 22.

11. Ibid., pp. 33–34.

12. *Works,* III, 13.

Chapter 1

1. *Memoirs,* pp. 154–55. Cf. Samuel Eliot Morison, *Three Centuries of Harvard, 1636–1936* (Cambridge, Mass., 1936), p. 424.

2. *NHAHW,* II, 347. Julian Hawthorne noted the coincidence of these events in his unpublished sketch "The Harvard of Our Forefathers" (JHC VII).

3. *Memoirs,* p. 157.

4. Ibid., p. 158.

5. Maurice Bassan, "A New Account of Hawthorne's Last Days, Death, and Funeral," *American Literature* XXVII (January, 1956), 563.

6. Horatio Bridge, *Personal Recollections of Nathaniel Hawthorne* (New York, 1893), pp. 95, 96. Una was born March 3, 1844; this letter is dated April 1, 1844.

7. Julian Hawthorne was born at one o'clock in the morning of June 22, at the home of Mrs. Hawthorne's parents, Dr. and Mrs. Peabody, 36 West Street, Boston. Cf. *Memoirs*, p. 10.

8. Bridge, *Personal Recollections*, p. 187.

9. The evils of Julian Hawthorne's Puritan heritage, which weighed upon his father so heavily, are referred to only rarely in his writings, and even then not very sincerely. An early journal notes: "No one, in the other life, is punished for hereditary evil, but for so much of hereditary evil as he has made his own by actual life" (quoted in Bassan, "Julian Hawthorne Papers at Yale"). Another reference is contained in an open letter of 1891 protesting against a violation of civil liberties. In the seventeenth century, Hawthorne wrote, "a strange disease called witchcraft, and now known as hysteria, arose in the land, and the so-called witches were by the authorities whipped, hanged, and burned [sic]; since which time their accusers, judges, and executioners have lain under the ban of history and of their fellow-men. . . . My forefathers were among those who came here two hundred and fifty years ago to enjoy the right to call their souls and bodies their own. Others of them helped to burn the witches. Out of sympathy for the first-named act, and in contrition for the other, I have written this letter, and sign my name to it" ("A Letter from Julian Hawthorne," *Twentieth Century* VI [February 5, 1891], 4–5).

10. *AN*, p. 206.

11. Julian Hawthorne, "Nathaniel Hawthorne, and Other Friends of Fifty Years," MS, Henry W. and Albert A. Berg Collection, New York Public Library, Astor, Lenox, and Tilden Foundations.

12. *NHAHW*, I, 310.

13. Bridge, *Personal Recollections*, p. 187.

14. Ibid., p. 122.

15. *AN*, pp. 194, 202.

16. Cf. Rose Hawthorne Lathrop, *Memories of Hawthorne* (Boston and New York, 1897), p. 132.

17. *AN*, p. 203.

18. *NHAHW*, I, 324.

19. Randall Stewart, *Nathaniel Hawthorne: A Biography* (New Haven, Conn., 1948), p. 81.

20. Lathrop, *Memories of Hawthorne*, p. 97.

21. *AN*, p. 196.

22. Ibid., p. 213.

23. Ibid., p. 197.

24. Ibid., p. 251.

25. Ibid., p. 234.

26. Ibid., p. 207.

27. *Works,* X, 294.

28. *AN,* pp. 213–42. Also reprinted separately (New York, 1904).

29. The original of this letter, written from West Newton, Massachusetts, on February 25, 1852, is in the Berg Collection of the New York Public Library. Several other childhood letters by Julian are there.

30. *NHAHW,* II, 12.

31. Stewart, *Nathaniel Hawthorne,* p. 158.

32. *NHAHW,* II, 22.

33. *Memoirs,* p. 15.

34. Ibid., pp. 15–16.

35. *Works,* X, 152–53. The text, presently unsatisfactory, of Nathaniel Hawthorne's French and Italian Notebooks will eventually be superseded by a scholarly edition by Professor Norman Holmes Pearson.

36. *Works,* X, 247.

37. *Memoirs,* p. 16.

38. Bridge, *Personal Recollections,* p. 152.

39. Quoted in Stewart, *Nathaniel Hawthorne,* p. 157.

40. Randall Stewart, ed., *The English Notebooks by Nathaniel Hawthorne* (New York, 1941), p. 265.

41. These letters from Nathaniel Hawthorne to Sophia are reproduced by permission of the Henry E. Huntington Library, San Marino, California. Words in brackets are my textual guesses for the occasionally indecipherable script.

42. This and the following journal entry are in the Julian Hawthorne collection of the Pierpont Morgan Library and are reproduced here by permission. Cf. Nathaniel Hawthorne's account of Lincoln in *Our Old Home* (*Works,* VII, "Pilgrimage to Old Boston").

43. Cf. *Works,* VII, 242–43.

44. JHC I:10. The letter is dated August 24, 1857.

45. *NHAHW,* II, 172.

46. Cf. *Memoirs,* p. 202.

47. There are "a great many references to Julian in the letters from Ada Shepard to her fiancé," according to Professor Pearson, who possesses copies of these letters. They may appear in the projected biography of Miss Shepard by her granddaughter.

48. *Works,* X, 69.

49. Ibid., pp. 131–32.

50. JHC V:1. The following note appears on the first page of the book: "A study in concology [sic], in line with my doings in natural history about my 10th to 14th year. JH Calif 1933."

51. *NHAHW,* II, 227.

52. Bridge, *Personal Recollections,* p. 136.

53. Ibid., p. 152. These feelings were to be almost precisely duplicated in Julian after his own lengthy encampment abroad with his family; see below, p. 142.

54. Ibid., p. 146.

55. Caroline Ticknor, *Hawthorne and His Publisher* (Boston and New York, 1913), p. 221.

56. There are glimpses of JH's Concord boyhood in the letters and journals of Emerson; see, for example, Ralph L. Rusk, ed., *The Letters of Ralph Waldo Emerson*, 6 vols. (New York, 1939), V, 250, 284. See also Bradford Torrey, ed., *The Writings of Henry David Thoreau*, 20 vols. (Boston and New York, 1906), VI, 60.

57. *Memoirs*, p. 81.

58. Ibid., p. 47.

59. *Works*, X, 537.

60. Ibid., p. 543; cf. also pp. 518, 528, 548.

61. *Memoirs*, pp. 180–81.

62. Ibid., p. 181. Julian also made an illumination of Tennyson's creed of the Knights of the Round Table on a sheet of vellum and presented it to his mother (*Memoirs*, p. 18). For the Concord fair in 1863 he executed an illumination of "Ring Out, Wild Bells" (Stewart, *Nathaniel Hawthorne*, p. 217). The boy also had received the benefit of training in drawing from an eminent artist in Liverpool (*NHAHW*, II, 266, and cf. above, p. 16).

63. *NHAHW*, II, 266.

64. *Memoirs*, p. 53.

65. JHC V:2, p. 22.

66. *NHAHW*, II, 8–9.

67. The children were deliberately used to test the effectiveness of these volumes; cf. *NHAHW*, I, 407.

68. *AN*, p. 139 and n. 319; and p. 235 and n. 588. Cf. also Lathrop, *Memories of Hawthorne*, p. 126.

69. " 'Where's the Man Mountain of these Lilliputs?' cried Julian, as he looked at a small engraving of the Greeks getting into the wooden horse.— Decr 4th—1849" (*AN*, p. 130).

70. *Memoirs*, p. 17.

71. Cf. Ticknor, *Hawthorne and His Publisher*, pp. 112, 137, 144, 161, and 184.

72. *NHAHW*, II, 9.

73. *Memoirs*, p. 50. For further details see JH's little volume, *Hawthorne Reading: An Essay* (Cleveland, 1902).

74. *Memoirs*, p. 46.

75. Ibid., p. 45.

76. *NHAHW*, II, 266.

77. *Memoirs*, p. 80.

78. *NHAHW*, II, 264–65.

79. JHC III.

80. Sophia Hawthorne wrote Sanborn, "We entirely disapprove of this commingling of youths and maidens at the electric age in school. I find no end of ill effect from it, and this is why I do not send Una and Rose to your school" (quoted in F. B. Sanborn, *Hawthorne and His Friends* [Cedar Rapids, Iowa, 1908], p. 15).

81. *Memoirs*, p. 77. See also *Dictionary of American Biography*, XVI, 326–27.

82. *Memoirs*, pp. 78, 84.

83. Quoted in Sanborn, *Hawthorne and His Friends*, pp. 13–14, 16.

84. Bridge, *Personal Recollections*, pp. 191–92.

85. Sanborn, *Hawthorne and His Friends*, p. 18.

86. M. A. De Wolfe Howe, ed., *New Letters of James Russell Lowell* (New York and London, 1932), p. 103.

87. *Memoirs*, p. 143. Ephraim Whitman Gurney (1829–86), a man who was to play an important role in Julian's formative years, began his career at Harvard in 1857 as tutor in Greek and Latin, and was later professor of philosophy and of history, and first dean of the faculty under President Eliot. He was primarily a scholar, "grounded in the traditional classical training and prepared to give instruction in any subject within the range of humane learning—classics, philosophy, history, or law." In 1868–70 he was associated anonymously with Lowell as editor of the *North American Review*, and he later contributed to the *Nation*. See *Dictionary of American Biography*, VIII, 57.

88. *Memoirs*, p. 143.

89. Ibid., p. 146.

90. Stewart, *Nathaniel Hawthorne*, pp. 217–18.

91. Bridge, *Personal Recollections*, p. 191.

92. *Memoirs*, pp. 148–49.

93. On March 24, 1862, for example, Hawthorne wrote to his son from Washington: "I remember [your letter] had a great deal to say about 'sparking' the girls, together with a hint or two about your being destitute of 'tin.' I hope you will not get blown up in this sparking process, for one spark may kindle a great deal of gunpowder; as for tin, your mother may give you any old coffee pot she can spare." Reproduced by permission of The Huntington Library, San Marino, California.

94. *NHAHW*, II, 285–86. The only definite advice Nathaniel Hawthorne gave his son was to avoid the curse of authorship: see below, pp. 59, 91, and Chapter 3, Note 1.

95. "Hawthorne in Concord" (JHC VII).

96. *NHAHW*, II, 269–70.

97. *Memoirs*, pp. 83–84. Cf. Ernest Earnest, *Expatriates and Patriots* (Durham, N.C., 1968), p. 161.

98. Bridge, *Personal Recollections*, p. 169.

99. *Works*, X, 561–62.

100. *NHAHW*, II, 335.

101. Ibid., p. 346.

Chapter 2

1. An incomplete version of this letter appears in *NHAHW*, II, 348–49. The quoted portion is taken from an omitted fragment of the original letter, a photostat of which, dated May 20, 1864, is in JHC.

2. Pierce had called on the Hawthornes in Rome in March, 1859, and the author had commented: "There was something melancholy in his tone, when

he remarked what a stout boy Julian had grown. Poor fellow! he has neither son nor daughter to keep his heart warm" (*Works*, X, 492). Pierce had lost his beloved son in a railway accident shortly before his inauguration as president.

3. *Memoirs*, pp. 191–92; cf. p. 158.

4. Pierce told Julian: "In a talk with [Hillard] after your father's death, I got the impression that both your parents were looking forward to your finishing your time at college, and that funds were available assuming that your habits were not extravagant" (*Memoirs*, p. 192).

5. *Memoirs*, p. 195.

6. See Stewart, *Nathaniel Hawthorne*, p. 239; and Roy Franklin Nichols, *Franklin Pierce* (Philadelphia, 1931), p. 530.

7. The originals of this and the following letters to Pierce cited here are in the collection of the New Hampshire Historical Society; they are reprinted here by permission.

8. Because of his father's death the preceding May, Hawthorne did not complete his freshman year at Harvard College. Although he complains of his failure at mathematics in this letter and elsewhere, he recalled later that Professor James Mills Pierce was unusually indulgent and willing to pass him for merely attending class and "studying the problems" (*Memoirs*, pp. 178–79).

9. Hawthorne visited the old and sick former president near his death; see Bridge, *Personal Recollections*, p. 195, and *Memoirs*, p. 190. In his Dresden journal (November 11, 1869) Hawthorne notes that General Pierce had died and left him five hundred dollars (MS in Henry W. and Albert A. Berg Collection, New York Public Library, Astor, Lenox, and Tilden Foundations).

10. Bridge, *Personal Recollections*, p. 192.

11. Quoted in Theodore Maynard, *A Fire Was Lighted: The Life of Rose Hawthorne Lathrop* (Milwaukee, 1948), p. 151.

12. Ibid., p. 146. Rose is also quoted by her mother as saying, "If Julian went on so fast in the heavenly way, we should see an actual halo around his brows like that of the saints" (ibid., p. 137).

13. A full picture of Rose's Concord years is presented in Maynard, *A Fire Was Lighted*, Chapter XII. Other, less valuable studies of Rose are Katherine Burton, *Sorrow Built a Bridge* (New York, 1930), and James J. Walsh, *Mother Alphonsa: Rose Hawthorne Lathrop* (New York, 1930).

14. See, for example, Randall Stewart, "Mrs. Hawthorne's Financial Difficulties: Selections from Her Letters to James T. Fields 1865–1868," *More Books* XXII (1946), 45–53.

15. Maynard, *A Fire Was Lighted*, p. 137; similar sentiments are expressed in another letter of 1864 to Elizabeth (ibid., p. 138).

16. Bridge, *Personal Recollections*, p. 199.

17. Maynard, *A Fire Was Lighted*, p. 137.

18. Vernon Loggins, *The Hawthornes: The Story of Seven Generations of an American Family* (New York, 1951), p. 302.

19. The original of this letter is in the Henry W. and Albert A. Berg

Collection, New York Public Library, Astor, Lenox, and Tilden Foundations.

20. This and the following extract are from a letter dated February 9, 1866, the original of which is in the Henry W. and Albert A. Berg Collection, New York Public Library, Astor, Lenox, and Tilden Foundations.

21. Louise Hall Tharp, *The Peabody Sisters of Salem* (Boston, 1950), p. 305.

22. Ibid., pp. 305–6.

23. Ibid., p. 306.

24. The original of this undated letter, which I have here assigned to the first few months of 1867, is in the Henry W. and Albert A. Berg Collection, New York Public Library, Astor, Lenox, and Tilden Foundations.

25. Maynard, *A Fire Was Lighted,* p. 152.

26. Ibid.

27. Morison, *Three Centuries of Harvard,* p. 306.

28. Ibid., p. 324.

29. Ibid., p. 280.

30. Maynard, *A Fire Was Lighted,* p. 151.

31. Loggins, *The Hawthornes,* p. 303.

32. Maynard, *A Fire Was Lighted,* pp. 151–52.

33. Tharp, *Peabody Sisters of Salem,* p. 315.

34. *Memoirs,* pp. 181–82.

35. Ibid., p. 182.

36. Ibid., p. 180.

37. Just prior to Julian's expulsion from Harvard, Sophia had written to Lowell asking him to prepare a biography of her husband in conjunction with her editing of his notebooks. She went on: "If you consent . . . you will also help Julian in his career—: for if these journals be published now, with a biography by you, there is no doubt that when Julian graduates, there will be means to educate him for his profession, and he will owe to his father and to you a position in the world. As you are interested in Julian and know him, I speak of this. He deserves to have every legitimate facility, for he is most gifted and noble—I venture to say to so kind a friend, for I think you will not judge that I doat. Silent as Julian is, he has a gift with his pen (inherited, no doubt—) which is remarkable" (Richard Croom Beatty, *James Russell Lowell* [Nashville, 1942], p. 198; the letter is dated September 7, 1866).

38. *Memoirs,* p. 182.

39. Ibid., p. 187.

40. This entry, and the succeeding quotations from the journal of 1868–69, are drawn from the manuscript in the Henry W. and Albert A. Berg Collection, New York Public Library, Astor, Lenox, and Tilden Foundations. In *NHAHW,* II, 315 ff., Hawthorne quotes from an ostensible "journal" of his of 1862, but he is actually quoting from his own letters home at this time, which are preserved in the same collection.

41. *Memoirs,* p. 180.

42. Information concerning the family history of the Amelungs was made available by Mr. Manning Hawthorne, Julian's grandson. Discussions of Amelung glass may be found in Helen and George S. McKearin, *Two Hundred Years of American Blown Glass* (Garden City, N.Y., 1950), p. 39; the same authors' *American Glass* (New York, 1941), pp. 100–114; and Rhea M. Knittle, *Early American Glass* (New York and London, 1927), pp. 172 ff.

43. *Putnam's Magazine* IV (August, 1869), 168.

44. Hawthorne wrote Charles Honce: "My very first explosions were in verse; a sonnet while I was at Harvard, in 1864 or 5, in a local newspaper-ette, anonymous and unpaid for; and two others in Putnam's Magazine . . . signed but insignificant" (Charles Honce, *A Julian Hawthorne Collection* [New York, 1939], p. 17). This first poem has not been identified.

45. "We remained in Dresden," Hawthorne writes in *NHAHW*, II, 353, "until the summer of 1869, when I went back to America for a visit, leaving my mother and sisters in Dresden, whither I purposed to return again before winter. Circumstances, however, prevented this. . . ." Yet Hawthorne's Dresden journal does not break off until mid-November of that year; and since he had just begun his studies at the Realschule, it seems unlikely that he left Dresden until the following year.

46. Manning Hawthorne believes that Minne returned on a concert tour and sang before the emperor of Germany. In none of the contemporary journals and letters, however, are there any references to Minne's musical career, either before or after her marriage.

47. JHC I:10. Lathrop added to his letter a sketch of the ceremony that showed the bride's parents in attendance. In the same letter he speaks frankly of his disappointment at returning to America, a feeling that it is possible his friend shared. He writes: "This insucculent American life keeps one perpetually hungry after Europe. . . . New York is to London as a packing box to a Gothic cathedral. Here everything is surface, no depths to dive into; there one can seclude oneself, vegetate, study, dream, do anything to any extent. . . . But I hope to keep somewhat aloof from this rush, with the aid of George and Julian and a few other choice spirits." These were probably standard sentiments of genteel young Americans who had seen Europe—witness Henry James's letters.

48. *NHAHW*, II, 358.

49. Tharp, *Peabody Sisters of Salem*, p. 317.

50. Ibid., pp. 315–16.

51. Maynard, *A Fire Was Lighted*, pp. 153–54.

52. Ibid., pp. 155–56.

53. For a discussion of the careers of the Lathrop brothers, see *Dictionary of American Biography*, XI, 14–16.

54. Cf. Maynard, *A Fire Was Lighted*, pp. 161 ff.

55. *NHAHW*, II, 358.

56. Ibid., p. 367.

57. Ibid., pp. 370–71.

58. This letter, and the following one quoted, are in the Henry W. and Albert A. Berg Collection, New York Public Library, Astor, Lenox, and Tilden Foundations.

59. See below, p. 115.

60. Maynard, *A Fire Was Lighted,* p. 183.

Chapter 3

1. *Confessions and Criticisms,* pp. 9–10. "Parental warnings" had also been issued to his sister Rose, who recalled, "I tried to bring the stimulus of great events into the Concord life by writing stories. . . . My father hung over me, dark as a prophetic flight of birds. 'Never let me hear of your writing stories!' he exclaimed, with as near an approach to anger as I had ever seen in him. 'I forbid you to write them!'" (*Memories of Hawthorne,* pp. 422–23).

2. *NHAHW,* I, 470.

3. Cf. Frank Luther Mott, *A History of American Magazines 1741–1850* (Cambridge, Mass., 1938), p. 737.

4. *NHAHW,* I, pp. 471–74.

5. Mott, *History of American Magazines,* p. 420. Certain American writers appeared regularly in *Appleton's,* however, notably Junius Henri Browne, Edgar Fawcett, and Constance Fenimore Woolson.

6. That the story was written *before* January 11, 1871, however, is proved by a letter from H. M. Alden of *Harper's* of that date, suggesting that "Love and Counter-Love" was too long.

7. JHC III.

8. Because of the adverse publicity attendant upon his imprisonment in 1912–13, for example, Hawthorne wrote anonymously for about two years following his release from Atlanta Penitentiary; see below, pp. 220–21.

9. JHC III; dated September 4, 1871.

10. Fourteen English novelists, including Bulwer, Dickens, and Thackeray, were represented in *Harper's* before 1885, but only four Americans: Hawthorne (*Garth*), Henry James, E. P. Roe, and Miss Woolson. See Mott, *History of American Magazines,* p. 224.

11. JHC III.

12. Though the relations between Alden and Hawthorne were always to remain cordial, Hawthorne's rejection slips from *Harper's* began to mount rapidly after the 1880's. Alden rejected various stories and poems in 1894, 1910, 1912, 1916, and 1918 (and perhaps in other years as well). In turning down Hawthorne's "God and Man at the Front" in 1918, Alden comments interestingly that the writer was "guilty" of "putting both parties to this war on the same level as to justification of motive." This correspondence is in JHC III.

13. *Atlantic Monthly* XXX (October, 1872), 487.

14. Cf. Edith Birkhead, *The Tale of Terror* (London, 1921), and Eino Railo, *The Haunted Castle* (London, 1927). For the persistence of the Gothic influence in nineteenth-century literature, including American, see *The Tale of Terror,* pp. 157–96, 224–27; and Carey McWilliams, *Ambrose Bierce: A Biography* (New York, 1929), pp. 222–35.

15. Cf. René Wellek and Austin Warren, *Theory of Literature* (New York, 1942), p. 243.

16. Stevenson, "Dean of American Letters," p. 169.

17. (London, 1879), p. iii.

18. Ibid., pp. iii-iv.

19. The remark is allied, also, to Hawthorne's theories about the origin of artistic inspiration; cf. below, pp. 175–76.

20. *Ellice Quentin and Other Stories* (London, 1880), pp. 6–7.

21. JHC V:14. Swedenborg was a direct influence on the composition of *Bressant* and *Idolatry*, as revealed in Hawthorne's letter of January, 1876, to Carter—himself an avid New Churchman and possibly Julian's earliest preceptor in the mysteries. See Bassan, "JH Papers at Yale," pp. 87–88. Nathaniel Hawthorne knew such confirmed Swedenborgians as William Pike, the sculptor Hiram Powers, and Dr. J. J. Garth Wilkinson (*Memoirs*, p. 15).

22. Hawthorne's notebook bears witness to his immersion in the works of such spectacularly varied authors as Dumas *fils*, Macaulay, Heine, Lowell, Swedenborg, Carlyle, DeQuincey, Emerson, Hume, Rabelais, Pythagoras, and Plato.

23. *Saturday Review* XXXVIII (October 24, 1874), 540–41.

24. Stevenson, "Dean of American Letters," p. 171. Cf. Railo, *Haunted Castle,* pp. 309–11.

25. Julian's youthful rambles with his parents in England, in the course of which he visited ruined castles, forts, and churches, may have had a permanent effect on his imagination: see above, pp. 17–18, and cf. Stewart, ed., *The English Notebooks by Nathaniel Hawthorne,* pp. 84–86, 104–5, 118, 125–26, 157–59, and *passim.*

26. Stevenson, "Dean of American Letters," p. 169. My rejection is made even considering Professor Stevenson's own definition of Gothic romanticism cited at the beginning of this discussion.

27. *Confessions and Criticisms,* p. 18.

28. *Appleton's Journal* IX:189 (January 4, 1873), p. 49.

29. Hawthorne seems to have confused Indian and West Indies customs. In later pages of the notebook there are extensive "Notes for a Romance," drawn largely from Longworth's *A Year Among the Circassians* (1840); in these notes, as well as in several pages of speculation (planned for inclusion in a novel) about the fascinations of Salome, we may detect Hawthorne's interest—continued to the end of his life—in the exotic and the sensual.

30. Unusual, even ludicrous proper names were utilized by Hawthorne for those of his early short narratives that are deliberately fantastic. However, in such serious stories as "The Minister's Oath" and "Star and Candle," the names are quite ordinary. After 1874, this habit disappears. So far as I have discovered, Hawthorne's names carry no thematic overtones. The name "Helwyse" in one early story and in *Idolatry* appears to be filched from the elder Hawthorne's "Lady Eleanore's Mantle"; "Sophie" in *Bressant,* and other names, will be commented on below. The peculiar names in *A Fool of Nature* (1896) are chosen deliberately for the "humor" characters of that story.

31. The theme of "reenactment," which is obviously borrowed from *The House of the Seven Gables,* appears again in "The Oak-Tree's Christmas Gift" (1872), a precursor of *Kildhurm's Oak.* It is one of a limited number

of supernatural conceits in *Garth* (1877), and dominates the romance *The Golden Fleece* (1892).

32. The phenomenon of clairvoyance appears regularly in such novels as *Bressant, Dust,* and *The Professor's Sister.*

33. The story contains a scene recalling the death of Judge Pyncheon in *The House of the Seven Gables;* a similar scene was to be used in the romance *Idolatry.*

34. *Appleton's Journal* VII:170 (June 29, 1872), 707.

35. Julian Hawthorne and Leonard Lemmon, *American Literature* (Boston, 1891), p. 281.

36. *Confessions and Criticisms,* p. 10. Another obvious motive was that writing novels promised a much larger income than printing occasional short stories.

37. These comments appear even earlier. In a letter to a Mr. B. written on June 15, 1892, Hawthorne writes that he is contemplating a trip from New York to Mexico to look over some mining properties. "My original profession was Engineering," he says, "and it is a pity I didn't stick to it." The original of this letter is in the Rosenberg Public Library, Galveston, Texas.

38. *Confessions and Criticisms,* p. 10. Hawthorne's first outline of characters for *Bressant* is contained in the notebook of 1871–72 at Yale University.

39. Julian Hawthorne, *Bressant: A Novel* (New York, 1873), p. 44.

40. Ibid., p. 190.

41. The contrast here between "dark" and "fair" women, which Hawthorne was occasionally to use, is a conventional fictional device even among major nineteenth-century writers like Nathaniel Hawthorne and Melville: see, for example, Frederick I. Carpenter, "Puritans Preferred Blondes: The Heroines of Melville and Hawthorne," *New England Quarterly* IX (June, 1936), 253–72.

42. *Works,* I, 206–7. The theme of "cold observation" vs. "holy sympathy" persisted to the end of Nathaniel Hawthorne's life in such tales as "Ethan Brand" and the major novels; cf. *Works,* III, 494–95.

43. This artistic result is a function of his personal feelings, as his contrasting reactions to Miss Sherman and Minne Amelung in Dresden had indicated.

44. "I uniformly prefer my heroines to my heroes," Hawthorne once declared, "perhaps because I invent the former out of whole cloth, whereas the latter are often formed of shreds and patches of men I have met." Of his heroes he added: "I never raised a character to the position of hero, without recognizing in him, before I had done with him, an egregious ass." *Confessions and Criticisms,* p. 14. Hawthorne always, however, makes a man his central figure. Cf. above, p. 70.

45. See Herbert R. Brown, *The Sentimental Novel in America, 1789–1860* (Durham, N.C., 1940), pp. 312–14.

46. The same general "changeling" situation occurs again in four other novels: *Idolatry, Fortune's Fool, Dust,* and *A Fool of Nature.*

47. *Bressant,* p. 349.

48. Peckham, born in 1849, entered Harvard at fourteen, and was in

Julian's class of 1867. He founded the first of college newspapers. After graduation he studied law in Heidelberg and was admitted to the bar in 1870. See *National Cyclopedia of American Biography,* I, 477–78.

49. Julian Hawthorne, *Shapes That Pass* (Boston and New York, 1928), p. 61.

50. Ibid., p. 62.

51. Ibid., p. 65.

52. This letter and all the subsequent correspondence of 1872–74 between Carter and Hawthorne quoted below are in JHC III.

53. The reference to Lathrop suggests either that Julian and George were again on speaking terms by this date, or else, more likely, that Carter did not know of the bad blood between them.

54. JHC IV.

55. There were no difficulties with King, who, on September 17, 1873, offered to print Hawthorne's new romance.

56. Entry for May 19, 1873, in JHC V:12, p. 46.

57. The original of this letter describing the children (addressed to Aunt Ebe on June 29, 1873) is in the Henry W. and Albert A. Berg Collection, New York Public Library, Astor, Lenox, and Tilden Foundations.

58. The original of this letter is in the Henry W. and Albert A. Berg Collection, New York Public Library, Astor, Lenox, and Tilden Foundations.

59. The original of this letter, dated February 25, 1873, is in the Henry W. and Albert A. Berg Collection, New York Public Library, Astor, Lenox, and Tilden Foundations. The "notes and reservoirs" consisted of a 200-page notebook containing plot outlines, character analyses, and the like. When Julian dabbled with the idea of suppressing his first novel, he was perhaps moved by his father's example in suppressing *Fanshawe.*

60. The original of this letter, dated June 29, 1873, is in the Berg Collection. Ironically enough, Julian *did* wear "his father's mantle"—the dark blue talma, which his mother made over into a Prince Albert coat that he wore for ten years after his father's death (*Memoirs,* p. 20).

61. Entry for June 22, 1873, in JHC V:2, p. 49.

62. The original of this letter, dated June 2, 1873, is in the Henry W. and Albert A. Berg Collection, New York Public Library, Astor, Lenox, and Tilden Foundations.

63. Entry for June 22, 1873, in JHC V:2, pp. 47–48.

64. Letter to Una dated March 19, 1873, the original of which is in the Henry W. and Albert A. Berg Collection, New York Public Library, Astor, Lenox, and Tilden Foundations.

65. Ibid. The "consideration of lucre," mentioned in a letter to Una quoted above, was already considerable to Hawthorne; compare his journal entry (June 22, 1873): "I am as comfortable at this moment in body and mind, as though I had a million. . . . And yet my whole endeavor as long as I live will be to get rich."

66. William James Morton (1845–1920) was graduated from Harvard in 1867, and from Harvard Medical School in 1872. He became an outstanding neurologist and pioneer in the use of x-rays in the treatment of skin disorders

and cancer. His father was William T. G. Morton, discoverer of sulphuric ether as an anesthetic in dental surgery. See *Dictionary of American Biography,* XIII, 267–68, and below, pp. 212–18.

67. Hawthorne's list of his library in 1875 (JHC V:14) shows the presence of the complete works of Goethe, Lessing, Schiller, and Zschokke.

68. Source of the "Damon" material is an undated clipping in JHC headed: "Springfield Republican's Dresden Letter. The Younger Hawthorne: Reminiscences of His College Days—His Later Life."

69. So Hawthorne records in his notebook. However, in *Confessions and Criticisms* (pp. 11–12), he declares: "This unknown book was actually rewritten, in whole or in part, no less than seven times. *Non sum qualis eram.* For seven or eight years past I have seldom rewritten [a page]. . . . But the discipline of 'Idolatry' probably taught me how to clothe an idea in words."

70. *Idolatry: A Romance* (Boston, 1874), p. 6.

71. This weird name is compounded by spelling Hawthorne's wife's maiden name, Amelung, backward, and adding the romancer's last initial. This fanciful name-play is not so ludicrous as the pathetic attempt at humor in "Dr. Hiero Glyphic."

72. *Idolatry,* p. 211.

73. Ibid., p. 358.

74. Ibid.

75. Ibid., p. 139.

76. Ibid., p. 97.

77. Ibid., p. 6.

78. *Atlantic Monthly* XXXIV (December, 1874), 747.

79. This and other reviews quoted in this paragraph are preserved in JHC V:15, pp. 2–35.

80. This letter, dated October, 1874, and the undated letter from Bright quoted immediately below, are in JHC III.

81. Entry dated June 6, 1874, in JHC V:2, p. 106.

82. This letter, dated January, 1876, is quoted in Bassan, "JH Papers at Yale," p. 88.

83. The original of this letter, dated July 30, 1874, is in the Henry W. and Albert A. Berg Collection, New York Public Library, Astor, Lenox, and Tilden Foundations.

84. *Saxon Studies* (Boston, 1876), p. iii.

85. Ibid., p. v.

86. Ibid., p. 116.

87. Ibid., p. 131.

88. Ibid., pp. 317–18.

89. Ibid., pp. 451–52.

90. George Knox, "Dissonance Abroad: Julian Hawthorne's *Saxon Studies," Essex Institute Historical Collections* XCVI (April, 1960), 131. Professor Knox was unable to verify this fact on a recent visit to Dresden.

91. "Recalling Heinrich Heine," *Pasadena Star-News,* October 22, 1932, p. 24.

92. *Nation* XVII (July 10, 1873), 27.

93. *Nation* XXII (March 30, 1876), 214–15.

Chapter 4

1. *Confessions and Criticisms*, p. 16.

2. Pp. 225–26. Hawthorne did not pass the "better part" of his "third and fourth decades" in England; he was twenty-eight when he arrived, thirty-five when he left.

3. Hawthorne's Aunt Elizabeth wrote in 1874 that "Julian means to come [to America] in the course of a few years, when he has made a little money, which he thinks he can do more easily, at present in London" (Manning Hawthorne, "Aunt Ebe: Some Letters of Elizabeth M. Hawthorne," *New England Quarterly* XX [June, 1947], p. 227).

4. Clarence Gohdes, *American Literature in Nineteenth-Century England* (New York, 1944), pp. 17–18.

5. Ibid., p. 33.

6. In the fall of 1874 Una had left London to visit the Lathrops in New York.

7. JHC II:10.

8. *Shapes That Pass*, pp. 80–81.

9. Ibid., p. 82.

10. JHC V:3.

11. JHC V:7. Cf. above, Chapter III, n. 22. The discovery of Smollett's *Adventures of Peregrine Pickle* had been one of the delights of Julian's boyhood: cf. *Memoirs*, pp. 200–201. His praise in this passage for the picaresque as the "true, right form of fiction" was theoretical, merely, and was not translated into his own practice.

12. JHC II:10. These notebook entries are a perhaps unimportant duplication by the son of the father's practice (examples of which have been given in Chapter I).

13. An obituary of Lord was contributed by Hawthorne to the *Critic* XVIII (December 10, 1892), 331–32. Dixon was memorialized in an essay in *Belgravia* XL (December, 1879), 193–97.

14. *Shapes That Pass*, p. 184.

15. Ibid., p. 76.

16. Ibid., p. 199.

17. Ibid., p. 211.

18. Ibid., p. 71.

19. Henry Murray, Christopher's brother, describes "The Cousinhood of the Oasis," which included Hawthorne, in *A Stepson of Fortune* (London, 1909), pp. 48–49.

20. *Shapes That Pass*, p. 168.

21. JHC III.

22. *Shapes That Pass*, pp. 140–41.

23. The original of this letter is in the Yale University Library.

24. An exception was the American merchant and diplomat John Welsh, who preceded Lowell at the Court of St. James's. Hawthorne had applied to

him for a recommendation to the Russell Club, and was deeply chagrined when Welsh refused to acknowledge even his acquaintance. He wrote Welsh on April 18, 1878: "I conceived that your public position as American Minister entitled me to claim from you a certain degree of social countenance, especially in view of the fact that my father enjoyed a high reputation not only in the literary world, but as incumbent of the Diplomatic post which he held during 1854–7 at Liverpool: and that I, his son, have never been known to so far outrage the laws of good breeding as to justify my being ranked below him in the social scale." This letter is in JHC III.

25. *Shapes That Pass,* p. 78.

26. There is a letter from White to Hawthorne, discussing Henry James (April 22, 1878), in JHC IV.

27. *Memoirs,* pp. 126–27.

28. Cf. below, pp. 134 and 177–78.

29. Copy of a letter dated January 15, 1879, in JHC IV. In the light of Hawthorne's own pretensions, the letter seems lacking in tact, and one wonders if Hawthorne was chagrined at the third of James's reasons for undertaking the work.

30. *Memoirs,* p. 127.

31. The amity would seem to have ended, at least on James's side, by 1887, when he commented on what he considered Hawthorne's "beastly and blackguardly betrayal" the previous winter of James Russell Lowell: see F. O. Matthiessen and Kenneth B. Murdock, eds., *The Notebooks of Henry James* (New York, 1955), p. 83. However, the two men met briefly in California in 1904, while James was visiting America and Hawthorne was writing a series of articles for a Los Angeles newspaper: *Memoirs,* pp. 125–26. See also George Knox, "Reverberations and *The Reverberator,*" *Essex Institute Historical Collections* XCV (October, 1959), 348–54, which further documents James's disgust at Hawthorne's "damnable doings" in the Lowell affair and suggests Julian as the model for the unprincipled George Flack in James's *The Reverberator.*

32. Loggins, *The Hawthornes,* p. 310.

33. Cf. Loggins, p. 310, and Maynard, *A Fire Was Lighted,* p. 179.

34. *NHAHW,* II, 373.

35. JHC I:10.

36. *NHAHW,* II, 373–74.

37. Manning Hawthorne, "Aunt Ebe," p. 228.

38. JHC V:5 (Journal for 1877).

39. *NHAHW,* II, 372–73.

40. Maynard, *A Fire Was Lighted,* p. 180.

41. Clippings of the following letters and newspaper comments are in JHC V:15, pp. 182–85.

42. Maynard, *A Fire Was Lighted,* p. 194.

43. Ibid., p. 190.

44. *Confessions and Criticisms,* p. 29.

45. JHC V:2 (January 1, 1875).

46. Quoted in Bassan, "JH Papers at Yale," p. 87. The letter is dated January, 1876.

47. JHC V :5.

48. Letter to Charles E. Honce, dated January 17, 1939, in JHC III.

49. Clippings of this and the succeeding articles quoted on the "Rose of Death" controversy are in JHC V :15, pp. 81–82.

50. Such incidents as these led Hawthorne to become a strong partisan of international copyright laws upon his return to the United States. Still another quarrel of these years was caused by a timid publisher changing one of his stories before publication in order to supply a marriage: see Stevenson, "Dean of American Letters," p. 167.

51. The original of this letter, dated June 30, 187[8?], is in the Henry W. and Albert A. Berg Collection, New York Public Library, Astor, Lenox, and Tilden Foundations.

52. The fiction was occasionally published with a subtitle that identified its mode, e.g., *Garth: A Novel; Miss Cadogna: A Romance;* but this is not a reliable index. *Bressant,* for example, was published as a "Novel" in America but as a "Romance" in England; and some of the fiction has either no subtitle or the general "A Story." Hawthorne produced no true "novel-romances" of the characteristic American type identified by Richard Chase in *The American Novel and Its Tradition* (Garden City, N.Y., 1957). At least one novel of this period, *Two Old Boys,* appeared only in serial form in the *World;* Hawthorne attempted unsuccessfully to have it published by Kegan Paul (JHC, uncatalogued letter). Perhaps a dozen longer tales remain to be recovered from the files of literary journals of the 1870's.

53. *Confessions and Criticisms,* p. 15.

54. *Archibald Malmaison* (New York, 1884), p. 5. First published, London, 1879. Reprinted New York and London, 1899.

55. Ibid., p. 13. The pun implicit in the family name conveys the same idea. A hint for this device of alternating life and "death" may have been taken from the elder Hawthorne's *American Notebooks* for 1835: "Follow out the fantasy of a man taking his life by instalments, instead of at one payment,—say ten years of life alternately with ten years of suspended animation" (*Works,* IX, p. 27).

56. Ibid., p. 125.

57. Ibid., p. 37.

58. Ibid., p. 41.

59. *Ellice Quentin and Other Stories,* pp. 83–84. The story was reprinted in *Kildhurm's Oak* (New York, 1888) and *A Strange Friend* (New York, 1890), and separately (New York, 1889).

60. *Kildhurm's Oak* bears a very close resemblance to the imaginary novel *Quercus* satirized by Vladimir Nabokov in *Invitation to a Beheading* (New York, 1960), pp. 120–22.

61. Also published as "The Pearl-Shell Necklace" (with "Prince Saroni's Wife") (New York, 1884).

62. The story was reprinted in 1924 as *Rumpty-Dudget's Tower: A Fairy Tale,* with an autobiographical preface by Hawthorne discussing the writing and publication of the stories of 1879; see below, p. 222.

63. Certain elements of plot and characterization in *Garth* suggest that Hawthorne may have been dabbling with the idea of constructing a fictional

biography of his father. The Bowdoin scenes, for example, deliberately recall to the reader his father's experiences there.

64. Hawthorne himself admitted that when the novel had run serially for a year or more, with no signs of abatement, "the publishers felt obliged to intimate that unless I put an end to their misery they would. Accordingly, I promptly gave Garth his quietus. The truth is, I was tired of him myself. With all his qualities and virtues, he could not help being a prig" (*Confessions and Criticisms*, pp. 12–13).

65. Julian Hawthorne, *Garth: A Novel* (New York, 1877), p. 201.

66. *Confessions and Criticisms*, p. 90.

67. This repeats a comment found in the elder Hawthorne's "The Prophetic Pictures": "Some [of the colonials] deemed it an offence against the Mosaic law, and even a presumptuous mockery of the Creator, to bring into existence such lively images of his creatures" (*Works*, I, 195).

68. *Garth*, p. 160.

69. *North American Review* CXXV (September, 1877), 315.

70. Julian Hawthorne, *Sebastian Strome: A Novel* (London, 1879), p. 60. For this novel Hawthorne retained the skeletal plot and characters of the story "Star and Candle" (1872).

71. One of Hawthorne's reviewers speculated whether the writer had imbibed his anti-Semitism during his sojourn in Dresden. Other Jewish villains in the longer tales are General Inigo in *Beatrix Randolph* and the Bendibow clan in *Dust*. But such characters are almost stock types; compare Sim Rosedale in Edith Wharton's *The House of Mirth*.

72. *Scribner's Monthly* XIX (April, 1880), 945.

73. *Confessions and Criticisms*, p. 28.

74. The novel was dedicated to Edward Kemys, the animal sculptor, by whom Hawthorne was undoubtedly influenced in his descriptions of Jack's artistry.

75. *Fortune's Fool* (Boston, 1884), p. 193.

76. The ever-critical *Nation* found the novel "improbable, fantastic, queer, and disagreeable" (*Nation* XXXVII [November 15, 1883], 421). Hawthorne's success with Madeleine and the stage scenes is testimony to his continual fascination with the theater. He was a friend of Charlotte Cushman, Claire Kellogg, Edwin Booth, and many other late nineteenth-century actors and actresses in both London and New York.

77. Aunt Ebe declared in a letter of October, 1881, that "Julian . . . was obliged to go to Italy on business, so could not come with [the rest of the family]" (Manning Hawthorne, "Aunt Ebe," p. 229). See also the *Critic* I (November 5, 1881), 309.

78. The Kinsale experiences later found expression in the romance *Noble Blood* and the short story "Ken's Mystery."

79. Manning Hawthorne, "Aunt Ebe," p. 227.

Chapter 5

1. Undated letter to the present writer, c. July, 1958.

2. Hildegarde Hawthorne, *Island Farm* (New York, 1926), p. 18. Other

recollections of the Sag Harbor home appear in Julian Hawthorne's "The First American Submarine" (JHC VII).

3. *The Poems of Eugene Field* (New York, 1910), p. 223.

4. The publishing history of Hawthorne's novels, stated in terms of number of copies sold, date published, extent of second and later editions, and final disappearance from publishers' lists, is meager, to say the least. The information about *Dust* in this paragraph, for example, is a lucky find from the journal of 1883; one finds scattered bits of evidence also about *Bressant* (see Chapter 3), *American Literature* (see Chapter 6), and a few other works. Most of the surviving publishers of Hawthorne's books assert that their old records have disappeared: this is the case with Chatto and Windus, J. B. Lippincott, Scribner's, Harper, Funk and Wagnalls, Cassell, and Houghton Mifflin. The only firm able to supply sales figures (for *American Literature*) was D. C. Heath.

5. "The Native Element in American Fiction," *Century* XXVI (1883), 366.

6. *American Literature 1607–1885,* 2 vols. (New York and London, 1887–89), II, 446.

7. *American Literature* (Edinburgh, 1882), p. 380.

8. Ibid., p. 387.

9. *Nation* XXXVII (November 15, 1883), 420. The reviewer found Hawthorne and De la Ramée linked by their contempt for realism and their enthusiasm for old-fashioned romance: a passion-flower, the English romancer was quoted as saying, is just as real as a potato.

10. This tendency was remarked upon by the *Nation,* which declared: "Realism depends for its success upon the accuracy and force of the details and upon the skill with which they are grouped. Romance depends upon the subtlety of the suggestion. If Mr. Hawthorne means to be realistic, the work is too hap-hazard; if romantic, it is too crude and bald" (*Nation* XL [March 26, 1885], 266).

11. *Atlantic Monthly* LIII (May, 1884), 712.

12. *Critic* IV (February 9, 1884), 64.

13. Julian Hawthorne, *Dust: A Novel* (New York, 1883), p. 378.

14. Ibid., p. 231.

15. *Atlantic Monthly* LI (May, 1883), 706.

16. Curiously enough, the style of *Beatrix Randolph* was much praised: the *Dial* thought it "excellent," and the *Atlantic* found the book carefully written, with "brilliant ease" in narration. See *Dial* IV (March, 1884), 286; and *Atlantic Monthly* LIII (May, 1884), 711.

17. Julian Hawthorne, *Beatrix Randolph: A Story* (Boston, 1884), pp. 169–70. The novel was first published in London in 1883.

18. Julian Hawthorne, *Love—or a Name: A Story* (Boston, 1885), pp. 194–95.

19. Ibid., p. 200.

20. One must immediately contrast, however, the anti-philanthropic statements quoted at the end of this discussion of the novel.

21. *Love—or a Name,* p. 202.

22. *Nation* XLI (November 19, 1885), 428.

23. *Lippincott's* XXXVI (November, 1885), 532.

24. *Love—or a Name,* p. 300.

25. Ibid., pp. 300-301.

26. Julian Hawthorne, *John Parmelee's Curse* (New York, 1886), p. 120.

27. The story was also published as *Miss Cadogna: A Romance* (London, 1885). When English and American titles differ, my text employs the latter.

28. *Works,* XIII, xiii.

29. Maynard, *A Fire Was Lighted,* pp. 192-93.

30. Ibid., p. 193.

31. Ibid., p. 194.

32. *Works,* XIII, vii.

33. Maynard, *A Fire Was Lighted,* p. 198; the letter is dated October 16, 1883.

34. Ibid.; the letter is dated December 12, 1883.

35. See, however, an intelligent criticism of Julian's editorship of *Dr. Grimshawe's Secret* in *Nation* XXXVI (January 18, 1883), 66.

36. Edward H. Davidson, ed., *Dr. Grimshawe's Secret* (Cambridge, Mass., 1954), p. vi. Cf. p. 15.

37. Another edited romance by Nathaniel Hawthorne was published by his son in 1890 as "Nathaniel Hawthorne's 'Elixir of Life'" (*Lippincott's,* January-April). A spirited defense of his mother's edition of Hawthorne's notebooks—and by implication, his own editing—was contained in his review, in 1932, of Randall Stewart's edition of the *AN.*

38. *NHAHW,* I, 38.

39. "Hawthorne's Duel," *Essex Institute Historical Collections* XCIV (July, 1958), 229-42. Randall Stewart justly complains about Julian Hawthorne's faulty transcription of certain letters of Nathaniel Hawthorne in "Letters to Sophia," *Huntington Library Quarterly* VII (August, 1944), 389. The "gross emendations and grosser inaccuracies" occur in letters printed in *NHAHW,* I, 202-8, 210-26, 236-42, 293-94, 295-96, 325-28; and II, 51-52.

40. *NHAHW,* I, 9. That it was the unfortunate Una who had broached the topic of insanity is of course also obscured by Hawthorne's revision. For a full acount of Hawthorne's revisions, see Maurice Bassan, "Julian Hawthorne Edits Aunt Ebe," *Essex Institute Historical Collections* C (October, 1964), 274-78.

41. The originals of this letter, dated November 24, 1884, and the following one quoted, dated December 13, 1884, are in the Huntington Library, San Marino, California, and are reproduced here with its permission. The background of the quarrel is discussed in Randall Stewart, "'Pestiferous Gail Hamilton,' James T. Fields, and the Hawthornes," *New England Quarterly* XVII (September, 1944), 418-23.

42. *Atlantic Monthly* LV (February, 1885), 259-65.

43. JHC V:7. One of the friends was Kemys the sculptor, whose genius was to be analyzed in *Confessions and Criticisms.* Another was Hubert Thompson, whom Hawthorne had not seen since his boyhood in Rome.

44. Information concerning the "Authors' Readings" of 1885 was secured from papers in the Mark Twain Collection, General Library, Berkeley.

45. Laura Stedman and George M. Gould, eds., *Life and Letters of Edmund Clarence Stedman*, 2 vols. (New York, 1910), II, 264. The letter was written August 5, 1899, partly to solicit Hawthorne's permission to reprint his poem "Were-Wolf" in Stedman's *An American Anthology*. In the JH Papers at Yale University are two letters (of 1878 and 1892) from Hawthorne to Stedman; in the latter he declares, "You and Stoddard are the best poets now living."

46. *Harper's* LXXIII (November, 1886), 813–33.

47. Lathrop, "The Literary Movement in NY," pp. 830–31.

48. The original of this letter, dated December 11, 1885, is in the Mark Twain Collection; the excerpt is reproduced here by permission of the Estate of Clara Clemens Samossoud (Mark Twain's daughter). The relationship between Clemens and Hawthorne is discussed in the latter's article "Mark Twain As I Knew Him," *Overland Monthly* n.s. LXXXVII (April, 1929), 111, 128.

49. For a full discussion of the Carleton incident see my article, "The Poetaster and the Horse-Doctors," *Midcontinent American Studies Journal* V (Spring, 1964), 56–59.

50. Still other club memberships of this period were in the Nineteenth-Century Club and the Twilight Club. In 1893 Hawthorne joined with twenty other writers (including Lathrop and Thomas Nelson Page) to form the "Syndicate of Associated Authors." Hawthorne was also a Mason.

51. Gerard E. Jensen, *The Life and Letters of Henry Cuyler Bunner* (Durham, N.C., 1939), p. 95; Bunner's letter is dated March 16, 1884. Hawthorne's interest in the supernatural was not manifested only in his fiction and in entertainments for the delectation of his friends. His journal for October, 1885, for example (in JHC), records with considerable interest Hildegarde's experiments with automatic writing and the whole family's engaging in "table-tipping" adventures on an amateur basis, that is, without the use of professional mediums. Hawthorne was also fascinated by palmistry. In his London days, he wrote a letter to the *Daily News* (in a humorous vein, probably) outlining graphically his own experiences with the phenomenon of levitation, a letter that drew forth a rash of inquiries. Finally, the Swedenborgianism that both he and Hildegarde embraced attracted him primarily, it seems, because of its occult doctrines.

52. JHC V:16, p. 336. Hawthorne wrote a warm obituary letter about Roe to the *Critic* XIII (n.s. X) (July 28, 1888), 43–44.

53. Slason Thompson, *Life of Eugene Field* (New York, 1927), p. 133.

54. The introduction may also be viewed as a kind repayment for Field's support in the Hawthorne-Lowell quarrel of 1886, treated below. A full discussion of the events surrounding the writing of the preface may be found in Caroline Ticknor, *Glimpses of Authors* (Boston and New York, 1922), pp. 229–31.

55. Eugene Field, *Culture's Garland* (Boston, 1887), p. viii. In a letter of June 22, 1887, the original of which is in the Huntington Library, Field thanks Hawthorne for his criticism.

56. Charles H. Dennis, *Eugene Field's Creative Years* (New York, 1924), p. 158.

57. Eugene Field, *The Writings in Prose and Verse of Eugene Field* (New York, 1911).

58. George Knox, "The Hawthorne-Lowell Affair," *New England Quarterly* XXIX (December, 1956). My account of the quarrel is based on this lively article. Previously, Carl J. Weber had written two accounts of the affair: "Lowell's 'Dead Rat in the Wall,'" *New England Quarterly* IX (September, 1936), 468–72; and "More about Lowell's 'Dead Rat,'" *New England Quarterly* IX (December, 1936), 686–88.

59. "The Official Explanation," Chicago *Daily News*, October 31, 1886.

60. Knox, "The Hawthorne-Lowell Affair," p. 502. Cf. chap. iv, n. 31.

61. JHC V:16, p. 14 (entry for November 9, 1883).

62. The original of this letter, dated November 28, 1885, is in the Huntington Library, San Marino, California, and is reproduced here with its permission.

63. The original of this letter, dated December 24, 1885, is in the Duke University Library. The literary judgments of this letter are howlers; in the mid-1880's James, Clemens, and Howells were doing some of their finest work.

64. *Confessions and Criticisms*, pp. 15–16.

65. Ibid., pp. 111–12.

66. Ibid., pp. 37–38.

67. Ibid., p. 42.

68. Ibid., p. 137.

69. Ibid., p. 99.

70. Ibid., pp. 77–78.

71. Ibid., pp. 61–62.

72. Ibid., p. 63.

73. Ibid., p. 65.

74. Ibid., p. 68.

75. Ibid., p. 89.

76. Hawthorne's statements in this work were considered significant enough to be recalled seventy-five years later in an anthology of criticism of the American novel: see Louis D. Rubin, Jr., and John Rees Moore, eds., *The Idea of an American Novel* (New York, 1961), pp. 38–39, 66–68.

Chapter 6

1. Julian Hawthorne, *A Dream and a Forgetting* (Chicago and New York, 1888), p. 200.

2. Ibid., pp. 102–3. Hawthorne introduced carnal passion as an important element in all his novels; his romances, except for *Love Is a Spirit* (1896), stress instead the spirituality of love.

3. Julian Hawthorne, *David Poindexter's Disappearance and Other Tales* (London, 1888), p. 174.

4. Howard Haycraft, *Murder for Pleasure: The Life and Times of the Detective Story* (New York and London, 1941), p. 93. Conan Doyle's first story was not, however, immediately popular, and probably did not influence the composition of the Hawthorne tales.

5. Ellery Queen, "The Detective Short Story: The First Hundred Years," in *The Art of the Mystery Story*, ed. Howard Haycraft (New York, 1946), pp. 486–87. In addition to the undoubtedly legitimate memoirs such as Allan Pinkerton's *Thirty Years a Detective* (1884), the genre included such

works as Charles Martel's *The Detective's Note-Book* (1860), Alfred Hughes's *Leaves from the Note-Book of a Chief of Police* (1864), and James McGovan's *Brought to Bay* (1878).

6. Julian Hawthorne, *Another's Crime* (New York and London, 1888), p. 3. Despite the authenticity of the skeletal plots of these stories, they can scarcely be viewed as realistic novels like *Garth* or *Dust*. The quotation cited uses the familiar technique of an avouched verisimilitude, like that in *Archibald Malmaison, Sinfire,* and other romances.

7. The stories were published by Cassell in the following order: *An American Penman, A Tragic Mystery,* and *The Great Bank Robbery* in 1887; and *Section 558; or The Fatal Letter* and *Another's Crime* in 1888.

8. Hawthorne had utilized this name of his eldest daughter before, in the early story "A Picturesque Transformation" (1872); and "Hildegarde" appears again as his companion in *Humors of the Fair* (1893). Of the writer's other children, only Beatrix was also so honored, in *Beatrix Randolph* (1883).

9. Julian Hawthorne, *The Professor's Sister: A Romance* (Chicago, 1888), p. 179; published in London, 1888, as *The Spectre of the Camera.*

10. Julian Hawthorne, *The Golden Fleece: A Romance* (Philadelphia, 1896), p. 155; first published in *Lippincott's Monthly Magazine,* XLIX (May, 1892), 513–72.

11. Julian Hawthorne, *Six-Cent Sam's* (St. Paul, Minn., 1893), pp. 145–46; also published in New York, 1896 as *Mr. Dunton's Invention and Other Stories.*

12. Julian Hawthorne, *The Story of Oregon,* 2 vols. (New York, 1892), I, p. vii.

13. Ibid., p. 19.

14. In 1926 Hawthorne wrote to a Spokane correspondent about this history. "I did not write a line of it," he declares, "or was aware that it existed. Neither did I ever before hear of my alleged collaborator, the poetical colonel. I was not consulted in its making, or knew that it was projected." The original of this letter, dated November 14, 1926, is in the Washington State University Library, Pullman.

15. Julian Hawthorne and Leonard Lemmon, *American Literature,* p. ix.

16. However, in a letter of January 15, 1892, addressed to E. C. Stedman, Hawthorne writes, "The Boston people (thank God!) are much incensed because I did not deify and canonize every one who bore the Beacon-street brand, and countersign them all 'Best.' The West and South are much more affable." Quoted in Bassan, "JH Papers at Yale," pp. 88–89. Cf. n. 20, below.

17. *American Literature,* pp. 261–62.

18. Quoted in Traubel's article, "JH's Several Opinions of Walt Whitman," *Conservator* VII, no. 9 (November, 1896), 136. The complete speech appears in *Camden's Compliment to Walt Whitman,* ed. Horace L. Traubel (Philadelphia, 1889).

19. "Hawthorne-Lemmon on 'American Literature,'" *Conservator* VII, No. 10 (December, 1896), 152.

20. Charles B. Willard, *Whitman's American Fame* (Providence, R.I., 1950), p. 131. The antipathy toward Whitman in the textbook, coupled with remarks allegedly "grossly prejudiced and unfair" in regard to the abolitionists, led some critics to accuse it of a southern bias, and to attempt to remove

the text from the public school system of Flushing, New York, in 1896. See the New York *Herald* and the New York *Sun* of October 7, 1896, and the New York *Times* of October 17, 1896.

21. *American Literature,* p. 281.

22. Ibid., pp. 217–18.

23. This paragraph is based upon an account in Maynard, *A Fire Was Lighted,* pp. 227–28.

24. Julian Hawthorne, *Humors of the Fair* (Chicago, 1893), p. 74.

25. Ibid., p. 129.

26. Ibid., pp. 102–3.

27. Julian Hawthorne, ed., *The Confessions of a Convict* (Philadelphia, 1893), p. 7.

28. JHC V :8.

29. P. 19.

30. "Hawthorne-Holinshed," *Critic* XXV (February 1, 1896), p. 83. The published letter is dated from Jamaica, December 22, 1895; the "private letter," dated December 14, is in the Stauffer Collection, New York Public Library. According to *Island Farm* (p. 165), which is not a reliable source, her father completed the story in two months. Working titles for the novel were *Between Two Fires* and *Against Himself.*

31. Julian Hawthorne, *A Fool of Nature* (New York, 1896), p. 123.

32. Ibid., p. 221.

33. The novel was not, unfortunately, widely noticed in the press. One distinctly uncomplimentary review appeared in the *Dial* XXI (August 16, 1896), 95.

34. Julian Hawthorne, *Love Is a Spirit* (New York, 1896), p. 196. Hawthorne wrote a melodramatic romance, *The Jewels of Nobleman Jack,* which also utilized the Jamaican scene as backdrop.

35. Hildegarde went abroad for a year to visit friends. Meanwhile, John, the oldest son, had been named vice and deputy consul at Kingston in November, 1895, a post he held until June, 1897 (information supplied by the National Archives and Records Service). After serving in the Spanish-American War as a soldier—while his father wrote dispatches for the New York *Journal*—John F. B. Hawthorne entered upon a long career in journalism. His longest connection was with the New York *Evening Post* as reporter and editor from 1920 to 1933. He died on April 28, 1960, at Pound Ridge, N.Y., aged eighty-six.

36. Hildegarde Hawthorne, *Island Farm,* p. 165; and letter to Pond, January, 1896, in JHC (uncatalogued).

37. See *Memoirs,* pp. 291–96. At Yale University there is a forty-page diary of 1897 on which the India articles are based.

38. The first such anthology, published in 1895, was English; the first American anthology was compiled by William Patten in 1906. Other pioneer anthologists in addition to Hawthorne were J. L. French, J. W. McSpadden, and Carolyn Wells. See Haycraft, *Murder for Pleasure,* p. 307; and Queen, "The Detective Short Story," p. 489.

39. Julian Hawthorne, "Nathaniel Hawthorne, and Other Friends of Fifty Years," a manuscript in the Berg Collection that is the basis for Julian Hawthorne's *Hawthorne and His Circle.*

40. A journal for the year 1899 survives in JHC (V:10), but it records primarily business transactions for that year. There are also a number of business letters for this period in the Huntington Library and elsewhere in JHC.

41. Letter to the present writer, dated May 26, 1958.

42. JHC IV; dated February 9, 1932. Information about Edith Garrigues may also be found in JHC II:8 and V:18.

43. Brief biographical treatments of Hildegarde Hawthorne may be located in *Who's Who in America*, XX, 1159; and in the unreliable *Who's Who among North American Authors*, VIII, 455–56. Many references to her life and career appear in the letters, journals, and clippings of JHC.

44. Ralph Hancock, *Fabulous Boulevard* (New York, 1949), p. 95.

45. Howard H. Quint, "Gaylord Wilshire and Socialism's First Congressional Campaign," *Pacific Historical Review* XXVI (November, 1957), 340.

46. Upton Sinclair, *American Outpost* (Pasadena, Calif., 1932), p. 1.

47. Ibid., p. 143. I have been unable to identify the first encounter between Wilshire and Hawthorne; presumably this occurred in New York in 1901. Hawthorne's romance *The Golden Fleece* (1892) shows, however, a firsthand acquaintance with southern California also documented elsewhere, and it is thus possible that the two men met in California some time before 1892. Wilshire's published work includes a collection of editorials, *Socialism Inevitable* (New York, 1907). In addition to the materials relating to Wilshire in Quint, Hancock, and Sinclair, further information may be found in Stewart H. Holbrook's *The Golden Age of Quackery* (New York, 1959), which deals with Wilshire's fraudulent exploitation of a "magnetic belt," the I-ON-A-CO, in 1926, the year before his death; in *Who's Who in America*, VII, 943; and in the Gaylord Wilshire papers at the Library of the University of California at Los Angeles.

48. Julian Hawthorne, "A Letter from Julian Hawthorne," p. 5. Reprinted separately as *In Defense of Personal Liberty* (New York, 1891). See above, Chapter 1, note 9.

49. "The Soul of America," *Wilshire's Magazine*, No. 45 (April, 1902), p. 14.

50. "Personal Liberty in Socialism," *Wilshire's Magazine* X (December, 1906), 7.

51. "The Individual Universalized," *Wilshire's Magazine* X (January, 1906), 12.

52. "The Soul of America," p. 14.

53. That Julian, even late in life, seems to have missed the point of "Earth's Holocaust" is evident from his comment about it that Nathaniel Hawthorne "turns almost playfully, the seamy side of civilization to the light, but leaves no defect or absurdity untouched" (*Memoirs*, pp. 214–15).

Chapter 7

1. The letters, articles, poems, and factual information in this section have been gathered from the following sources: JHC II:2, II:8, and V:18; and Loggins, *The Hawthornes*, pp. 328–33.

2. These newspaper comments are quoted in *The Hawthornes*, pp. 331–32.

3. Hawthorne ironically repeats here the substance of a passage in Wilde's *De Profundis,* which he had called "degenerate" in 1905: "[Reason] tells me that the laws under which I am convicted are wrong and unjust laws. . . . I feel that not to be ashamed of having been punished is one of the first points I must attain to." By 1907, however, covering the Harry Thaw trial for the press, Hawthorne had grown more charitable. When crime is revealed, he wrote, we come to see that this universe in which we live is really a universe, and not a poliverse, and "we know that other men and women are but our own selves subjected to accidents and conditions only a little different from those which have occurred to us. By what fortuitous chance was it that you or I are not sitting in yonder prisoner's dock: that your wife or mother, or mine, is not telling her tale of grief and despair in that witness chair?" This theme recurs in *The Subterranean Brotherhood,* discussed below. Meanwhile, the Thoreauvian echoes in the letter to Bryan are also worth noting.

4. Loggins, *The Hawthornes,* p. 330.

5. Julian Hawthorne, *The Subterranean Brotherhood* (New York, 1914), p. vii.

6. Ibid., p. xiii.

7. Ibid., p. xvii.

8. Hawthorne is accorded brief mention in Franklin Walker's *A Literary History of Southern California* (Berkeley and Los Angeles, 1950), pp. 257–58.

9. JHC IV. The later history of Morton is pathetic. Although he had been reinstated as a doctor, he became involved again with Albert Freeman, who, according to Morton's wife Ellen, took every penny from him. Morton even wrote Hawthorne in 1917: "As to the copper mine I believe it is really a big thing and the sooner he [Freeman] sends you your stock the better." Morton died in 1920.

10. This letter, and the following one quoted, are in JHC III.

11. Hawthorne had attempted to publish another volume of juvenile stories, including "Rumpty-Dudget," as early as 1902: see the letters from him to Albert B. Paine, the originals of which are in the Huntington Library.

12. The quotations in this paragraph are drawn from the memorabilia of the celebration preserved in JHC II:4.

13. Quoted in Knox, "JH: Concordian in California," p. 34.

14. The original of this letter, which was read at the celebration, is in the University of Southern California's Hamlin Garland Collection.

15. Pasadena *Star-News,* March 18, 1933.

16. *Shapes That Pass,* p. 341.

17. Ibid., pp. 340, 347–48.

18. Ibid., p. 358.

19. The recollections also extend into Hawthorne's mature years as far as 1900, but these occupy only a small number of pages. In 1932 Hawthorne had put together a book titled *Giants of Old Concord,* which had been rejected by at least one publisher, Stokes.

20. *Memoirs,* p. 3. Julian was of course only a year old when Thoreau went to jail.

21. Loggins, *The Hawthornes,* pp. 315–16.

Bibliography*

PART I. WORKS BY JULIAN HAWTHORNE

(*Arranged chronologically.*)

A. IMAGINATIVE WORKS: FICTION AND POETRY

1. Longer Fiction: Novels and Short Novels

Bressant: A Romance. 2 vols. London: King, 1873; New York: Appleton, 1873, under title of *Bressant: A Novel.*

Idolatry: A Romance. 2 vols. London: King, 1874; Boston: Osgood, 1874.

Garth: A Novel. 3 vols. London: Guildford, 1877; London: Bentley, 1877; New York: Appleton, 1877; London: Chatto & Windus, 1880, 1881.

Sebastian Strome: A Novel. 3 vols. London: Bentley, 1879; New York: Appleton, 1880; London: Chatto & Windus, 1881, 1883.

Archibald Malmaison. London: Bentley, 1879; New York: Funk & Wagnalls, 1884, 1899.

Dust: A Novel. 3 vols. London: Chatto & Windus, 1883, 1884; New York: Fords, Howard & Hulbert, 1883.

Fortune's Fool. 3 vols. London: Chatto & Windus, 1883, 1885; Boston: Osgood, 1883, 1884.

Beatrix Randolph. 3 vols. London: Trübner, 1883; 2 vols. London: Chatto & Windus, 1884; Boston: Osgood, 1884.

* The reader should note the following omissions in this bibliography. Part I: Newspaper stories, columns, reviews; serial publication of novels; translations and adaptations; unpublished manuscript fiction, poetry, articles, letters. Part II: Reviews (with several exceptions); works by members of the Hawthorne family; works on the family (with one exception); incidental allusions to Hawthorne's life and writings in books of literary criticism, history, or biography; summaries of his life and work in all standard works of reference (except the *Dictionary of American Biography*).

Love—or a Name: A Story. London: Chatto & Windus, 1885, 1888, 1906; Boston: Ticknor, 1885.

Noble Blood: A Novel. New York: Appleton, 1885; London: Chatto & Windus, 1885, 1888, under title of *Miss Cadogna: A Romance.*

John Parmelee's Curse. New York: Cassell, 1886, 1888.

"Sinfire." *Lippincott's* XXXIX (January, 1887), 1–83; Philadelphia: Lippincott, 1888 [with Fawcett's *Douglas Duane*].

[The five novels following are subtitled "From the Diary of Inspector Byrnes."]

An American Penman. New York; Cassell, 1887.

A Tragic Mystery. New York; Cassell, 1887, 1888.

The Great Bank Robbery. New York: Cassell, 1887, 1888.

Section 558; or, The Fatal Letter. New York: Cassell, 1888.

Another's Crime. New York: Cassell, 1888.

A Dream and a Forgetting. London: Chatto & Windus, 1888; Chicago: Belford, Clarke, 1888.

The Professor's Sister: A Romance. Chicago: Belford, Clarke, 1888; London: Chatto & Windus, 1888, 1890, 1915, under title of *The Spectre of the Camera; or, The Professor's Sister: A Romance.*

A Miser of Second Avenue. New York: Cassell, 1888.

An American Monte Cristo. London: Butterworth, 1888; 2 vols. London: Allen, 1892, 1893, 1894, 1898.

"Millicent and Rosalind." *Lippincott's* XLV (January, 1890), 1–65.

A Messenger from the Unknown. New York: Collier, 1892.

"The Golden Fleece." *Lippincott's* XLIX (May, 1892), 513–72; Philadelphia: Lippincott, 1896, under title of *The Golden Fleece: A Romance.*

A Fool of Nature. New York: Scribner's, 1896; London: Downey, 1896, 1898.

Love Is a Spirit: A Novel. New York: Harper, 1896.

2. Volumes of short stories

The Laughing Mill and Other Stories ["Calbot's Rival," "Mrs. Gainsborough's Diamonds," "The Christmas Guest, A Myth"]. London: Macmillan, 1879.

Ellice Quentin and Other Stories ["The Countess's Ruby," "A

Lover in Spite of Himself," "Kildhurm's Oak," "The New Endymion"]. 2 vols. London: Chatto & Windus, 1880, 1881, 1882, 1885.

Yellow-Cap, and Other Fairy Stories for Children ["Calladon," "Rumpty-Dudget," "Theeda"]. London: Longmans, Green, 1880.

Prince Saroni's Wife and Other Stories ["Constance," "The Countess Felicita's Discovery," "Pauline"]. 2 vols. London: Chapman, 1882; London: Chatto & Windus, 1882, 1884.

David Poindexter's Disappearance and Other Tales ["Ken's Mystery," " 'When Half-Gods Go, The Gods Arrive,' " " 'Set Not Thy Foot on Graves,' " "My Friend Paton," "Dr. Carajo's Patient," "A Strange Friend"]. London: Chatto & Windus, 1888; New York: Appleton, 1888, with omission of last two stories.

Six-Cent Sam's ["Mr. Dunton's Invention," "Greaves' Disappearance," "Raxworthy's Treasure," "The John North Mystery," "A Model Murder", "The Symposium" (six stories)]. St. Paul, Minn.: Price-McGill, 1893; New York: Merriam, 1896, under title of *Mr. Dunton's Invention and Other Stories*.

3. Short Stories

"Love and Counter-Love, or Masquerading." *Harper's Weekly* XV (March 11, 1871), 218–19.

"Doctor Pechal's Theory." *Appleton's Journal* VI (August 19, 1871), 206–9.

"Otto of Roses." *Harper's Bazar* IV (October 21, 1871), 662–63.

"Why Muggins Was Kept." *Harper's Magazine* XLIII (November, 1871), 856–62.

"The Strange Friend." *Appleton's* VI (December 9, 1871), 651–54; "A Strange Friend, a Story." *Belgravia* LIII (May, 1884), 326–43, and (June, 1884), 418–41.

"The Mysterious Case of My Friend Browne." *Harper's* XLIV (January, 1872), 214–21.

"The Oak-Tree's Christmas Gift." *Scribner's* III (January, 1872), 320–25.

"The Real Romance." *Aldine* V (January, 1872), 10–11.

"The Bronze Paper-Knife." *Appleton's* VII (February 3, 1872), 121–27.

"Star and Candle." *Harper's* XLIV (March, 1872), 600–605.

"Mr. Maximilian Morningdew's Advice." *Aldine* V (April, 1872), 74–75.

"The Mullenville Mystery." *Scribner's* III (April, 1872), 687–93.

"Mrs. Suffrin's Smelling-Bottle." *Appleton's* VII (April 27, 1872), 449–56.

"The Minister's Oath." *Appleton's* VII (June 29, 1872), 701–8.

"A Picturesque Transformation." *Harper's* XLVI (December, 1872), 126–32; *Dublin University Magazine,* n.s.I (January, 1878), 49–63.

"The Rose of Death: a Fantasy." *Cornhill* XXXIV (September, 1876), 358–78.

Mrs. Gainsborough's Diamonds: A Story. New York: Appleton, 1878, 1885, 1886; London: Chatto & Windus, 1879.

"An Automatic Enigma." *Belgravia* XXXV (May, 1878), 294–306.

"Why Jack Went to Europe." *Harper's* LVI (May, 1878), 924–29.

"Theeda: An Allegory." *Fraser's* XXII (August, 1880), 145–63.

"Calladon." *Fraser's* XXII (September, 1880), 383–96.

"Rumpty-Dudget." *Fraser's* XXII (October, 1880), 437–61. Reprinted as *Rumpty-Dudget's Tower; A Fairy Tale.* New York: Stokes, 1924; and as "Rumpty-Dudget's Tower (A Fairy Tale)" in *The St. Nicholas Anthology.* Edited by H. S. Commager. New York: Random House, 1948. Pp. 276–90.

"The Countess Felicita's Discovery." *Belgravia* XLIV (June, 1881), 424–45; XLV (July, 1881), 64–89.

"A Rebel." *Harper's* LXV (August, 1882), 408–14.

"Dr. Carajo's Patient." *Belgravia Annual* (Christmas, 1882), 81–93.

" 'Set Not Thy Foot on Graves.' " *Manhattan* I (May, 1883), 359–69.

"My Friend Paton." *Belgravia* LI (September, 1883), 294–308.

"Ken's Mystery." *Harper's* LXVII (November, 1883), 925–35.

Prince Saroni's Wife and *The Pearl-Shell Necklace.* New York and London: Funk & Wagnalls, 1884.

"David Poindexter's Disappearance." *Harper's* LXVIII (February, 1884), 429–40.

"An Autobiographical Romance." *Manhattan* III (April, 1884), 311–22.

" 'When Half-Gods Go, the Gods Arrive.' " *Harper's* LXXI (September, 1885), 566–76.

The Trial of Gideon and *Countess Almara's Murder*. New York and London: Funk & Wagnalls, 1886.

"Colonel Spaight's Prejudices." *Century* X (August, 1886), 543–56.

Kildhurm's Oak and *A Strange Friend*. New York: Burt, 1888, 1889; New York: Street & Smith, 1890.

"Doctor Griffith Gramery." *Cosmopolitan* V (March, 1888), 25–31.

"The Third of March." *Century* XV (December, 1888), 208–17.

Constance and *Calbot's Rival: Tales*. New York: Appleton, 1889.

Pauline [also "Ellice Quentin" and "The Countess's Ruby"]. New York: U.S. Book Co., 1890.

"My Adventure with Edgar Allan Poe." *Lippincott's* XLVIII (August, 1891), 240–46.

"An Inter-Planetary Episode," in *Two Tales*. Boston: Two Tales Publishing Co., March 19, 1892. Pp. 27–34.

"Judith Armytage," in *Miss Parson's Adventure and Other Stories by Other Writers*. London: Chapman & Hall, 1893.

"June, 1993." *Cosmopolitan* XIV (February, 1893), 450–58.

"Hollow Ruby." *English Illustrated Magazine* XII (March, 1895), 3–18.

"The Billop Mystery." *English Illustrated Magazine* XIV (November, 1895), 97–114.

"Miss Peekskill's Spirometer." *English Illustrated Magazine* XVI (December, 1896), 344–50.

"Old and New Music." *Cosmopolitan* XXV (July, 1898), 303–12.

"Odin Moore's Confession: A Christmas Story," in *Best Things from American Literature*. Edited by Irving Bacheller. New York: Christian Herald, 1899.

One of Those Coincidences [by Julian Hawthorne] *and Ten Other Stories*. New York and London: Funk & Wagnalls, 1899.

"The Singing of a Bird." *Harper's* CI (June, 1900), 125–34.

"Eight Years in a Rock." *Cosmopolitan* XXXI (May, 1901), 33–45.

"Hearne's Romance." *Cosmopolitan* XXXIV (December, 1902), 191–98.

"A Secret of the North." *Metropolitan* XX (June, 1904), 358–78.

"Lovers in Heaven." *Century* XLIX (December, 1905), 232–38. Reprinted as *Lovers in Heaven*. New York: New Church Board of Publication, 1905; and in *Representative American Short Stories*. Edited by A. Jessup. New York: Allyn, 1923.

"The Men of the Dark." *Metropolitan* XXIV (August, 1906), 533–51.

"The Spirit of the Dance." *Cosmopolitan* XLII (April, 1907), 611–16.

"The Delusion of Ralph Penwyn." *Cosmopolitan* XLVI (February, 1909), 264–70.

"The Amazon." *Lippincott's* LXXXVIII (November, 1911), 701–16.

4. Poems

"The Usurper." *Putnam's* IV (August, 1869), 168.

"Yes." *Putnam's* IV (August, 1869), 165.

"Found." *Appleton's* VI (November 25, 1871), 599.

"Within and Without." *Appleton's* VII (June 22, 1872), 692.

"Lottery." *Harper's* XLVII (October, 1873), 719.

"Too Late!" *Harper's* LXXXI (November, 1890), 830.

"Atonement." *Harper's* LXXXII (January, 1891), 300.

"Song from Ayuna." *Scribner's* X (November, 1891), 644.

"Altar and Idol." *Century* XXII (May, 1892), 103.

"The Mystery." *Harper's* LXXXVI (December, 1892), 119.

"The Trilogy." *Harper's* XCI (September, 1895), 489.

"A Secret." *Lippincott's* LIX (February, 1897), 256.

"Were-Wolf," in *An American Anthology, 1787–1900*. Edited by E. C. Stedman. Boston and New York: Houghton Mifflin, 1900. P. 585.

"Adam's Prayer." *Current Literature* XLV (July, 1908), 108.

"Love Against the World." *Ladies' Home Journal* XXIX (June, 1912), 3.

B. OTHER WORKS

1. Books of biography, autobiography, travel, and criticism, and miscellaneous works

Saxon Studies. London: Strahan, 1876; Boston: Osgood, 1876.

Nathaniel Hawthorne and His Wife: A Biography. 2 vols. Cambridge, Mass.: Osgood, 1884, 1885; Boston and New York:

Houghton Mifflin, 1884, 1897; Vols. XIV and XV in *The Works of Nathaniel Hawthorne*. Edited by G. P. Lathrop. 15 vols. Boston and New York: Houghton Mifflin, 1884; London: Chatto & Windus, 1884, 1885; Grosse Pointe, Mich.: Scholarly Press, 1968.

Confessions and Criticisms. Boston: Ticknor, 1887.

Humors of the Fair. Chicago: Weeks, 1893.

Hawthorne Reading: an Essay. Cleveland: Rowfant, 1902.

Hawthorne and His Circle. New York and London: Harper, 1903; Hamden, Conn.: Archon, 1968.

[The four entries following are mining-stock promotion pamphlets.]

Ishmael in Search of an Oasis. New York: Jamaica Estates, 1908.

Julian Hawthorne and Company. New York: n. p., 1909.

The Secret of Solomon. New York: n. p., 1909.

Solomon Columbus Rhodes and Company. New York: n. p., 1909.

The Subterranean Brotherhood. New York: McBride, Nast, 1914.

Shapes That Pass: Memories of Old Days. London: Murray, 1928; Boston and New York: Houghton Mifflin, 1928.

Bliss Carman: 1861–1929. Palo Alto, California: Van Patten, 1929.

The Memoirs of Julian Hawthorne. Edited by Edith G. Hawthorne. New York: Macmillan, 1938.

2. Editions and histories

Doctor Grimshawe's Secret: A Romance [by Nathaniel Hawthorne]. Edited by Julian Hawthorne. Boston and New York: Houghton Mifflin, 1882; Boston: Osgood, 1883; London: Longmans, Green, 1883; Vol. XIII in *The Works of Nathaniel Hawthorne*. Edited by G. P. Lathrop. 15 vols. Boston and New York: Houghton Mifflin, 1884; London: Paul, 1896.

Under Mother's Wing [by L. L. Clifford]. Edited by Julian Hawthorne. London and New York: n. p., 1885.

"Nathaniel Hawthorne's 'Elixir of Life.'" *Lippincott's* XLV (January, February, March, April, 1890), 66–76, 224–35, 412–25, 548–61.

American Literature: An Elementary Text-Book for Use in High Schools and Academies [by Julian Hawthorne and Leonard Lemmon]. Boston: Heath, 1891, 1896, 1897.

Mayflower Tales. Edited by Julian Hawthorne and others. New York: Taylor, 1892.

The Story of Oregon. A History with Portraits and Biographies. 2 vols. New York: American Historical Publishing Co., 1892.

The Confessions of a Convict. Edited by Julian Hawthorne. Philadelphia: Hartranft, 1893.

History of Washington, the Evergreen State, from Early Dawn to Daylight. Edited by Julian Hawthorne [with Col. G. D. Brewerton]. New York: American Historical Publishing Co., 1893.

The Literature of All Nations and All Ages: History, Character, and Incident. Edited by Julian Hawthorne [with J. P. Lamberton and J. R. Young]. 10 vols. Philadelphia: Finley, 1897–98; New York: Art Library Publishing Co., 1899, under title of *The Masterpieces and the History of Literature;* Chicago: DuMont, 1900, under title of *The Literature of All Nations and All Ages;* Philadelphia: Century, 1900, under title of *The World's Literature Illuminated;* New York: Hamilton, 1904, under title of *The Masterpieces and the History of Literature.*

Hawthorne's History of the United States: From the Landing of Columbus to the Signing of the Peace Protocol with Spain. 3 vols. New York: Collier, 1898, 1900, 1902, 1910, 1912, 1915 [title varies].

United States. From the Discovery of the North American Continent Up to the Present Time [by Julian Hawthorne (to 1783) and others]. 9 vols. New York and London: Cooperative Publishing Society, 1898.

Masterpieces of the World's Literature, Ancient and Modern. Edited by H. T. Peck; associate editors F. R. Stockton and Julian Hawthorne. 20 vols. New York: American Literary Society, 1898–99.

Spanish America, from the Earliest Period to the Present Time. New York: Collier, 1899, 1901.

The World's Great Classics. Edited by Julian Hawthorne. 61 vols. New York and London: Colonial, 1899–1902.

The Works of Nathaniel Hawthorne. Edited by Julian Hawthorne. 3 vols. New York: Collier, 1900.

Library of the World's Best Mystery and Detective Stories. Edited by Julian Hawthorne. 6 vols. New York: Review of Reviews Co., 1908.

The Lock and Key Library. Edited by Julian Hawthorne. 10 vols. New York: Review of Reviews Co., 1909.

3. Articles (essays, sketches, review articles, published letters, contributions to books)

"A Cold Bath." *Appleton's* VII (February 24, 1872), 208–9.

"A Warm Bath." *Appleton's* VII (March 2, 1872), 232–34.

"Sunshine." *Aldine* V (May, 1872), 92–93.

"Shadows." *Aldine* V (July, 1872), 142–43.

"Lamp-Light." *Aldine* V (August, 1872), 165.

"A Golden Wedding in the Best Society." *Appleton's* IX (January 4, 1873), 49–52.

"A Feast of Blood." *Galaxy* XVI (September, 1873), 405–9.

"Willliam Jerrold Dixon." *Belgravia* XL (December, 1879), 193–97.

"Ralph Waldo Emerson." *Harper's* LXV (July, 1882), 278–81.

"The Salem of Hawthorne." *Century* VI (May, 1884), 3–17.

"American Wild Animals in Art." *Century* VI (June, 1884), 213–19.

"Scenes of Hawthorne's Romances." *Century* VI (July, 1884), 380–97.

"Building of the Muscle." *Harper's* LXIX (August, 1884), 384–87.

"Emerson as an American," in *Genius and Character of Emerson.* Edited by F. B. Sanborn. Boston: Osgood, 1885, Pp. 68–91.

"Hawthorne's Philosophy." *Century* X (May, 1886), 83–93.

"Problems of *The Scarlet Letter.*" *Atlantic* LVII (April, 1886), 471–85.

"College Boat Racing." *Century* XII (June, 1887), 176–89.

"A Tribute from Julian Hawthorne [to E. P. Roe]." *Critic* X (July 28, 1888), 43–44.

"Deputy of Nature," in *Camden's Compliment to Walt Whitman.* Edited by H. L. Traubel. Philadelphia: D. McKay, 1889. Pp. 39–40.

"French Propriety." *Lippincott's* XLIV (August, 1889), 277–79.

"Novelistic Habits and *The Morgesons.*" *Lippincott's* XLIV (December, 1889), 868–71.

"Eugene Field's 'Little Books.'" *Lippincott's* XLV (March, 1890), 447–51.

"Some Physiological Revelations." *Lippincott's* XLV (May, 1890), 752–55.

"A Popular Topic." *Lippincott's* XLV (June, 1890), 883–88.

"Late Francis Bennoch of London." *Critic* XIV (July 19, 1890), 36.

"The New Spanish Inquisition." *Lippincott's* XLVII (January, 1891), 99–103.

"An American Kew." *Lippincott's* XLVII (February, 1891), 252–60.

"A Letter from Julian Hawthorne." *Twentieth Century* VI (February 5, 1891), 4–5. Reprinted as *In Behalf of Personal Liberty.* New York: Twentieth Century Library #34, 1891.

" 'The French Invasion of Ireland.' " *Lippincott's* XLVII (March, 1891), 400–401.

"Is Spiritualism Worth While?" *Arena* III (May, 1891), 674–79.

"The New Columbus." *Arena* IV (June, 1891), 1–9.

"The Interpreter (Sidney Woollett)." *Lippincott's* XLIX (January, 1892), 107–12.

"A Literary Conversation." *Lippincott's* XLIX (January, 1892), 125–27.

"Secretary Rusk's Crusade." *Lippincott's* XLIX (February, 1892), 211–17.

"Walking." *Lippincott's* XLIX (April, 1892), 481–86.

"Richard Halkett Lord." *Critic* XVIII (December 10, 1892), 331–32.

"Julian Hawthorne's 'Young Nebraska Friend.' " *Critic* XIX (January 14, 1893), 24.

"A Description of the Inexpressible." *Lippincott's* LI (April, 1893), 496–503.

"On the Way." *Lippincott's* LII (July, 1893), 70–77.

"The Lady of the Lake: At the Fair." *Lippincott's* LII (August, 1893), 240–47.

"Foreign Folk at the Fair." *Cosmopolitan* XV (September, 1893), 567–76.

"A Poet of Manhood [D. L. Dawson]." *Lippincott's* LIII (January, 1894), 129–31.

"The Librarian Among His Books." *Lippincott's* LIII (April, 1894), 517–22.

"Scientific Creation." *New Science Review* I (July, 1894), 50–59.

"A Magician of Line [Harley D. Nichols]." *Quarterly Illustrator* II (July–August–September, 1894), 231–36.

"Two Views of Book Canvassing." *Critic* XXII (July 21, 1894), 44.

"Salvation Via the Rack." *Cosmopolitan* XVIII (February, 1895), 482–90.

"James Fenimore Cooper," in *Library of the World's Best Literature*. Edited by C. D. Warner. 45 vols. New York: International Society, 1896–97. Vol. VII, pp. 3985–92.

"Hawthorne-Holinshed." *Critic* XXV (February 1, 1896), 83.

"Hawthorne-Lemmon on *American Literature.*" *Conservator* VII (December, 1896), 151–53.

"Summer at Christmas-Tide." *Century* XXXI (January, 1897), 428–34.

"A Tropic Climb." *Century* XXXI (February, 1897), 593–99.

"Report of The Cosmopolitan's Special Commissioner to India: [I] The Horrors of the Plague in India." *Cosmopolitan* XXIII (July, 1897), 231–46.

"[II] India Starving." *Cosmopolitan* XXIII (August, 1897), 369–84.

"[III] The Real India: What Is England Going to Do About It?" *Cosmopolitan* XXIII (September, 1897), 512–22.

"[IV] England in India." *Cosmopolitan* XXIII (October, 1897), 653–58.

"[V] Beauty and Charm in India." *Cosmopolitan* XXIV (November, 1897), 3–15.

England by J. R. Green. With a supplementary chapter of recent events by Julian Hawthorne. 4 vols. New York and London: Cooperative Publication Society, 1898.

Holland: The History of the Netherlands, by T. C. Grattan. With a supplementary chapter of recent events by Julian Hawthorne. New York: Collier, 1899, 1901.

"Public Schools and Parents' Duties." *North American Review* CLXVIII (April, 1899), 399–408.

"A Side-Issue of Expansion." *Forum* XXVII (June, 1899), 441–44.

"A Transcontinental Roadway." *Cosmopolitan* XXVIII (November, 1899), 125–28.

"Rockefeller, Morgan & Co." *Wilshire's Magazine* II (February 27, 1901), 1–2.

"Some Novelties at Buffalo Fair." *Cosmopolitan* XXXI (September, 1901), 483–92.

"The Soul of America." *Wilshire's* No. 45 (April, 1902), 14–20. Reprinted as *The Soul of America.* Haverhill, Mass.: Ariel Press, 1902.

"An Idyl of the Strike." *Wilshire's* No. 53 (December, 1902), 45–50.

"Legal Penalties and Public Opinion." *North American Review* CLXXVI (March, 1903), 391–400.

"Cosmic Consciousness." *Wilshire's* No. 60 (July, 1903), 66–70.

"Delight, the Soul of Art." *Wilshire's* No. 61 (August, 1903), 14–16.

"A Group of Hawthorne Letters." *Harper's* CVIII (March, 1904), 602–7.

"Women and Socialism." *Wilshire's* VI (May, 1904), 231–33.

"Hawthorne's Last Years." *Critic* XLV (July, 1904), 67–71.

"Society at a Pregnant Moment." *Wilshire's* VI (September, 1904), 384–85.

"Barbaric Pearl and Gold." *Cosmopolitan* XXXVIII (February, 1905), 433–40.

"The Biggest Game of All." *Cosmopolitan* XXXIX (July, 1905), 228–38.

"The Reign of Law." *Wilshire's* IX (December, 1905), 7.

"The Individual Universalized." *Wilshire's* X (January, 1906), 12.

"Journalism the Destroyer of Literature." *Critic* XLVIII (February, 1906), 166–71.

"English Lawns and Literary Folk." *Atlantic* XCVII (June, 1906), 817–24.

"Personal Liberty in Socialism." *Wilshire's* X (December, 1906), 7.

"The Rent War." *Wilshire's* XII (March, 1908), 5.

"Error Through Strong Drink." *Cosmopolitan* XLV (July, 1908), 198–200.

"A Great Criminal of the Last Generation." *Cosmopolitan* XLV (September, 1908), 431–39.

"Our Barbarous Penal System." *Hearst's Magazine* XXV (February, 1914), 205–12.

"The Woman Who Wrote *Little Women.*" *Ladies' Home Journal* XXXIX (October, 1922), 25, 120–22, 124.

"William Morris and His Great Adventure." *Literary Digest International Book Review* III (February, 1925), 177–78.

"Books of Memory." *Bookman* LXI (July, 1925), 567–71.

"A Champion of the Romantic Nineties." *Literary Digest International Book Review* IV (February, 1926), 168–69.

"New Light on Hawthorne and a Salem Pepys." *Literary Digest International Book Review* IV (June, 1926), 411–14.

"When Herman Melville Was 'Mr. Omoo'." *Literary Digest International Book Review* IV (August, 1926), 561–62, 564.

"Hawthorne, Man of Action." *Saturday Review of Literature* III (April 16, 1927), 727–28. Reprinted in *Designed for Reading.* New York: Macmillan, 1934.

"Such Is Paradise: The Story of Sophie and Nathaniel Hawthorne." *Century* XCIII (December, 1927), 157–69.

"A Daughter of Hawthorne [Rose]." *Atlantic* CXLII (September, 1928), 372–77.

"Mark Twain as I Knew Him." *Overland Monthly* LXXXVII (April, 1929), 111, 128.

"Fragrant Memory." *Overland Monthly* LXXXVIII (November, 1930), 334.

"The Making of *The Scarlet Letter.*" *Bookman* LXXIV (December, 1931), 401–11.

"The Story of Ernest Mensen," in *The Omnibus of Sport.* Edited by G. Rice and H. Powel. New York: Harper, 1932.

"Nathaniel Hawthorne's Blue Cloak." *Bookman* LXXV (September, 1932), 501–6.

"Whistler as a Friend Remembers Him." *New York Times Magazine,* July 15, 1934, pp. 7, 14.

4. Introductions and prefaces

Preface to *Culture's Garland,* by Eugene Field. Boston: Ticknor, 1887.

Introduction to *The Goddess of Atvatabar,* by William R. Bradshaw. New York: n.p., 1892.

Introduction to *The Story of Evangelina Cisneros . . . Told by Herself.* New York: Continental, 1898.

Preface to *Main Street,* by Nathaniel Hawthorne. Canton, Pa.: Kirgate Press, 1901.

Preface to *Quatrains of Christ,* by George Creel. San Francisco and New York: Paul Elder, 1907–8.

Foreword to *Roadtown,* by Edgar Chambless. New York: Roadtown Press, 1910.

Introduction to *The Writings in Prose and Verse of Eugene Field*. New York: Scribner's, 1911.

PART II. CRITICISM AND BIBLIOGRAPHY

Bassan, Maurice. "Julian Hawthorne Edits Aunt Ebe." *Essex Institute Historical Collections* C (October, 1964), 274–78.

———. "Julian Hawthorne Papers at Yale." *Yale University Library Gazette* XXXIX (October, 1964), 84–89.

———. "The Literary Career of Julian Hawthorne: A Selected Check List." *Bulletin of Bibliography* XXIV (May–August, 1965), 157–62.

———. "The Poetaster and the Horse-Doctors." *Midcontinent American Studies Journal* V (Spring, 1964), 56–59.

Collins, Mabel. "The Son of Nathaniel Hawthorne." *Dublin University Magazine* XC (August, 1877), 236–39.

Hazeltine, Mayo W. "Two American Novels," in *Chats About Books*. New York: Scribner's, 1883.

Heywood, J. C. "A Son Who Would Emulate His Father," in *How They Strike Me, These Authors*. Philadelphia: Lippincott, 1877.

Honce, Charles. *A Julian Hawthorne Collection*. New York: n.p., 1939.

———. *More Julian Hawthorne Firsts*. New York: n.p., 1941.

James, Henry [Review of *Idolatry*]. *Atlantic* XXXIV (December, 1874), 746–48.

———. [Review of *Saxon Studies*]. *Nation* XXII (March 30, 1876), 214–15.

———. [Review of *Garth*]. *Nation* XXIV (June 21, 1877), 369.

Jones, Joseph *et al.*, eds. *American Literary Manuscripts*. Austin: University of Texas Press, 1960. P. 163.

Knox, George. "Dissonance Abroad: Julian Hawthorne's *Saxon Studies.*" *Essex Institute Historical Collections* XCVI (April, 1960), 131–39.

———. "The Hawthorne-Lowell Affair." *New England Quarterly* XXIX (December, 1956), 493–502.

———. "Julian Hawthorne: Concordian in California." *Historical Society of Southern California Quarterly* XXXIX (March, 1957), 14–36.

————. "Reverberations and *The Reverberator.*" *Essex Institute Historical Collections* XCV (October, 1959), 348–54.

Loggins, Vernon. *The Hawthornes.* New York: Columbia University Press, 1951. Pp. 326–33 *et passim.*

Miller, Harold P. "Julian Hawthorne." *Dictionary of American Biography* XXI, 386–87.

Nichol, John. *American Literature.* Edinburgh: Black, 1882. Pp. 380–88.

Richardson, Charles F. *American Literature 1607–1885.* New York and London: Putnam's, 1887–89. 2 vols. II, 445–49.

Rubin, Louis D., Jr. and J. R. Moore. *The Idea of an American Novel.* New York: Crowell, 1961. Pp. 38–39, 66–68.

Stevenson, Lionel. "Dean of American Letters: Julian Hawthorne." *Bookman* LXXIII (April, 1931), 164–72.

Weber, Carl J. "Lowell's 'Dead Rat in the Wall.' " *New England Quarterly* IX (September, 1936), 468–72.

————. "More About Lowell's 'Dead Rat.' " *New England Quarterly* IX (December, 1936), 686–88.

PART III. MAJOR BIOGRAPHICAL SOURCES

Bridge, Horatio. *Personal Recollections of Nathaniel Hawthorne.* New York: Harper, 1893.

Hawthorne, Hildegarde. *Deedah's Wonderful Year.* New York and London: Appleton, 1927.

————. *Island Farm.* New York and London: Appleton, 1926.

————. *Makeshift Farm.* New York and London: Appleton, 1925.

Hawthorne, Manning. "Aunt Ebe: Some Letters of Elizabeth M. Hawthorne." *New England Quarterly* XX (June, 1947), 209–31.

Hawthorne, Nathaniel. *The American Notebooks.* Edited by Randall Stewart. New Haven: Yale University Press, 1932.

————. *The English Notebooks.* Edited by Randall Stewart. New York: Modern Language Association of America, 1941.

————. *Passages from the French and Italian Note-Books.* Edited by Sophia P. Hawthorne. 2 vols. Boston: Osgood, 1872.

Hawthorne, Sophia Peabody. *Notes in England and Italy.* New York: Putnam, 1869.

Higginson, Thomas W. "Una Hawthorne." *Outlook* LXXVII (1904), 595–606.

Lathrop, Rose Hawthorne. *Memories of Hawthorne*. Boston and New York: Houghton Mifflin, 1897.

Maynard, Theodore. *A Fire Was Lighted: The Life of Rose Hawthorne Lathrop*. Milwaukee: Bruce, 1948.

Sanborn, Frank B. *Hawthorne and His Friends*. Cedar Rapids, Iowa: Torch Press, 1908.

Stewart, Randall. *Nathaniel Hawthorne: A Biography*. New Haven: Yale University Press, 1948.

Tharp, Louise Hall. *The Peabody Sisters of Salem*. Boston: Little, Brown, 1950.

Ticknor, Caroline. *Hawthorne and His Publisher*. Boston and New York: Houghton Mifflin, 1913.

Index